SHAKESPEARE SURVEY

SHAKESPEARE SURVEY

AN ANNUAL SURVEY OF
SHAKESPEARIAN STUDY & PRODUCTION

19

EDITED BY
KENNETH MUIR

CAMBRIDGE
AT THE UNIVERSITY PRESS
1970

Published by the Syndics of the Cambridge University Press
Bentley House, 200 Euston Road, London N.W. I
American Branch: 32 East 57th Street, New York, N.Y. 10022

Library of Congress Catalogue Card Number: 49-1639

ISBN O 521 06432 5

First published 1966
Reprinted 1970

Printed in Great Britain
at the University Printing House, Cambridge
(Brooke Crutchley, University Printer)

EDITOR'S NOTE

The central theme of the present volume of *Shakespeare Survey* is *Macbeth*. The next volume, No. 20, will have no central theme, but it is hoped to include some of the papers to be delivered at the International Shakespeare Conference at Stratford-upon-Avon in 1966. No. 21 will be devoted to *Othello*, with a retrospect of criticism of the present century by Professor Helen Gardner. Contributions offered for publication in this volume should reach

The Editor, Department of English Literature, The University, Liverpool 3

by 1 September 1967.

All other communications, including books for review, should be sent to: *Shakespeare Survey*, Cambridge University Press, The Pitt Building, Trumpington Street, Cambridge.

In place of the International Notes, contributed over the years by a distinguished panel of correspondents, there will be a series of articles on Shakespearian productions and scholarship in different countries. In general, however, the policy pursued by the previous editor, Allardyce Nicoll, will be followed in the future. Shakespearian scholars all over the world have cause to be grateful to him, the 'onlie begetter' of *Shakespeare Survey*, for his work as editor during the past eighteen years.

K. M.

CONTRIBUTORS

D. S. Bland, *Department of Extra-Mural Studies, University of Liverpool*

John Russell Brown, *Lecturer in Drama and Theatre Arts, University of Birmingham*

John P. Cutts, *Professor of English, Wayne State University, Detroit*

G. I. Duthie, *Regius Professor of English, University of Aberdeen*

Inga-Stina Ewbank, *Lecturer in English, University of Liverpool*

Robert B. Heilman, *Professor of English, University of Washington, Seattle*

G. K. Hunter, *Professor of English, University of Warwick*

Arthur R. McGee, *Strathbungo Secondary School, Glasgow*

W. Moelwyn Merchant, *Professor of English, University of Exeter*

Kenneth Muir, *Professor of English Literature, University of Liverpool*

W. A. Murray, *Professor of English, University of Lancaster*

Norman Sanders, *Professor of English, University of Tennessee*

J. K. Walton, *Lecturer in English, Trinity College, Dublin*

Stanley Wells, *Lecturer in English, University of Birmingham*

Glynne Wickham, *Professor of Drama, University of Bristol*

CONTENTS

[Notes are placed at the end of each contribution, except in the Reviews section]

LIST OF PLATES

LIST OF PLATES

IX. *Timon of Athens*, Royal Shakespeare Theatre, 1965. Directed by John Schlesinger, settings by Ralph Koltai

   A. The Masque

   B. The Barber Scene (III, ii)

 X. *A.* Paul Scofield as Timon, in his cave

   B. *Hamlet*, Royal Shakespeare Theatre, 1965. Directed by Peter Hall, settings by John Bury, costumes by Ann Curtis. David Warner as Hamlet, in the 'To be or not to be' soliloquy (III, i)

XI. *Hamlet*

   A. Hamlet and Ophelia (Glenda Jackson) at the Play (III, ii)

   B. Hamlet and Gertrude (Elizabeth Spriggs) on the Queen's bed (III, iv)

XII. *A.* *Hamlet*. Gertrude, Claudius (Brewster Mason), Hamlet and Polonius (Tony Church) in I, ii

   B. *Love's Labour's Lost*, Royal Shakespeare Theatre, 1965. Directed by John Barton, settings by Sally Jacobs. Brewster Mason as Boyet reads Armado's letter to the Court (IV, i)

   (Photos: Gordon Goode)

'MACBETH' IN THE TWENTIETH CENTURY

BY

G. K. HUNTER

DISINTEGRATION

All editions of *Macbeth* derive from one single and authoritative text—that of the First Folio. The number of substantive emendations that modern editors see fit to introduce is quite small; and there are no passages so hopelessly corrupt that the sense is obscured. All this would argue an uncomplex task for the editor, and a simple and mercifully brief narrative for the historian of criticism. This turns out not to be the case. The discovery that the two songs (whose first lines are invoked in III, v and, again, in IV, i) exist in full texts in the manuscript of Middleton's *The Witch* has unloosed a flood of disintegration. I am more or less discounting, of course, the views of chronic disintegrators like J. M. Robertson who found (*Literary Detection*, 1931) that 'there is clear literary evidence of the past existence of a lost pre-Shakespearean *Macbeth* by Kyd'; Middleton he found to have written the Witch-scenes, the Porter-scene and the couplet tags throughout the play; there is a case for Heywood's authorship of the closing scene. IV, iii and I, ii are non-Shakespearian but unassigned. More impressive are the views of Clark and Wright, not given to rashness, who excised whole areas of the play from the Shakespeare canon, finding the bleeding sergeant in I, ii an 'absurdity', his metre 'slovenly' and his 'bombastic phraseology . . . not like Shakespeare's language even when he is most bombastic'.

The editions of Henry Cunningham (1912)—who seems really to have despised the play that was foisted upon him—of J. Q. Adams (1931) and J. Dover Wilson (1947) continue the tradition of disintegration, though with decreasing confidence and increasing elaboration of argument. Dover Wilson's argument that there were three distinct *Macbeth* texts 'during the first dozen years of the 17th century' has found few imitators; its assumptions are more elaborate than is required to account for the facts of the text; and at the merest flourish of Occam's razor it would seem to shrink away. William Empson (*Kenyon Review*, 1952) points out that what Dover Wilson sees as muddles or abridgements may be deliberate effects, part of the play's 'atmosphere':

So far from being a cut version of a tidy historical play now unfortunately lost, it is a rather massive effort, very consistently carried out, to convey the immense confusion in which those historical events actually occur.

The work of J. M. Nosworthy has struck a welcome note of sense in all this confusion. In a series of articles he found Shakespeare parallels to make the point that the last forty lines were 'Shakespearian', found that the Hecate scenes were unlike Middleton, and that the 'bombastic' speech of the bleeding sergeant was both Shakespearian and entirely appropriate to his role as a 'passionate and weighty Nuntius'—the latter point reinforced by Holger Nørgard's discovery (*The Review of English Studies*, 1955) that the sergeant echoes Daniel's *Cleopatra*, which Shakespeare read in preparation for *Antony and Cleopatra*. The 'low soliloquy of the Porter' (Clark and Wright) was at the same time moving back into favour, for reasons I discuss below (pp. 10–11). Writing in *The Library* (1947) Nosworthy made the important point that Shakespeare had woven 'all the tractable material' in Holinshed into his play, and made the important deduction that *Macbeth* had never been a long play.

This work, and the movement of the tidal waters of reintegration, left the Hecate scenes the only part of *Macbeth* that continued to be generally suspect, though occasional throwbacks, like G. B. Harrison (1951) and Lily B. Campbell (1930), continued to cast aspersions at whole areas of the play. Verity in his edition of 1901 had defended Hecate's iambic speeches on the ground that 'Shakespeare would not make the classical goddess speak in the same manner as the grim, barbaric witches'. This point was taken up and greatly elaborated by G. Wilson Knight (*The Shakespearian Tempest*, 1932), who here argues along the lines that elsewhere have enabled him to posit the authenticity of the Vision in *Cymbeline*, and the Diana scene in *Pericles*. In relation to *Macbeth* as a whole he further extends this to a general interpretation of Evil, seen both as discordant with good (the Witches) and as completely at harmony with itself (Hecate); common-sense clearly will have greater difficulty in accepting this part of the argument. The other most vocal defender of the Hecate scenes is Richard Flatter (*Shakespeare Jahrbuch*, 1957), who elsewhere (*Shakespeare's Producing Hand*, 1948) seeks to defend Folio lineation as deliberately contrived theatrical effect. Between 1958 and 1960 Flatter and J. P. Cutts carried on a somewhat iterative and indecisive argument about the stage-directions in the Hecate scenes, in the pages of *Shakespeare Jahrbuch*.

The defenders of Hecate are, however, the exceptions; general opinion (represented *inter alia* by the editions of Kittredge (1939), Kenneth Muir (1951) and Eugene Waith (1954)) leans against authenticity; but the shaky ground on which the whole argument is conducted may be seen from Lily B. Campbell's assumption (*Shakespeare's Tragic Heroes*, 1930) that III, v must be non-Shakespearian, for the very reason that proves its Shakespearian quality to Flatter—its preparative function, in anticipation of IV, i.

A sensible middle opinion is represented (once again) by Nosworthy, who (*The Review of English Studies*, 1948) accepts the songs as Middleton's; and thinks that the Hecate speeches were written to introduce and justify the appearance of that lady in the songs. He does not exclude the possibility that they may have been written by Shakespeare.

TOPICAL REFERENCE

The connexion of this play with King James I has long been asserted. Capell could say (in 1779) that it was 'acknowledged on all hands'. Malone suggested that *Macbeth* might have been 'first exhibited' when King Christian IV of Denmark was visiting London (17 July–11 August 1606). These points have been taken up generally (e.g. by J. Q. Adams in his edition of 1931) and vastly expanded in the most important recent study—*The Royal Play of 'Macbeth'*, by H. N. Paul (1950). Paul adds some interesting new points to the argument that the play was written for the two kings. He notes that the second battle in Holinshed was fought against 'the Danes', and that Shakespeare alters this to 'the Norweyans'—as befits a courtier addressing the Scottish and Danish monarchs. He suggests that the 'milk of concord' line (IV, iii, 98) refers to the arch of welcome which greeted James and Christian on 31 July 1606. Elsewhere he greatly amplifies existing references, as where he traces James's changing taste in demonology, or his changing attitude to 'touching' for scrofula.

It must be added, however, that Paul exhibits more industry than discrimination. His notion of the play as an aesthetic organism is less effective than his sense of it as a compliment. Many of his arguments—such as the one that Macbeth is a conjurer in IV, iii—are both curious and unproductive. His use of details of poetic or theatrical technique is nearly always distorted by his desire to multiply topical references. The Appendix to Kenneth Muir's new Arden edition (ninth edition, 1962) provides a convenient short survey of principal points from Paul's book.

The references in *Macbeth* to 'equivocation' and to the Gunpowder plot have, likewise, a long history of comment; but their interest has been strengthened by some recent investigations. In *I, William Shakespeare* (1937) Leslie Hotson traces connexions between Shakespeare's known friends and men involved in the plot. H. L. Rogers (*Double Profit in 'Macbeth'*, 1964) sees the whole play riddled with references to equivocation and duplicity. In *Publications of the Modern Language Association* (1964) Frank L. Huntley discusses '*Macbeth* and the background of Jesuitical equivocation' and shows the extent to which the mode of the witches' prophecies echoes the Jesuit doctrine, substituting Satan for God.

SOURCES

No principal source of *Macbeth* has been found to replace Holinshed's *Chronicles*. H. N. Paul has picked up many supplementary suggestions that have attached themselves to the play—that Shakespeare had read Buchanan's Latin history of Scotland, Leslie's *De...Rebus Gestis Scotorum* and Skene's *Scots Acts*. Dover Wilson (1947) has repeated Mrs Stopes's suggestion (1916) that Shakespeare drew on William Stewart's *Chronicles of Scotland*. It may well be that Shakespeare had read one or all of these, but, if so, they do not seem to have influenced him into any piece of writing that was impossible to a creative use of Holinshed. Dr Gwinn's *Tres Sybillae*, who greeted James I when he went to Oxford in 1605, are more interesting; but have been known since the eighteenth century. The debates at Oxford on the questions 'whether imagination is able to produce real effects' and 'whether the child acquires characteristics from his nurse's milk', also cited by Paul, throw interesting sidelights on the kind of thinking that the seventeenth century brought to bear on such subjects. Lily B. Campbell (*Shakespeare Quarterly*, 1951), like Paul, and like Jane H. Jack (*ELH*, 1955), thinks of James I's *Basilicon Doron* as a source-book for the play; indeed she prefers to think that James's writings are the source of that passage in IV, 3, in which Malcolm denies the princely virtues, which Paul had referred to the arch of triumph welcoming James and Christian into London. Kenneth Muir in *Shakespeare's Sources* (1957) notices, in addition to matters already discussed, an apparent echo of Daniel's *The Queen's Arcadia*. He also discusses debts to Seneca and to the Bible, some of which have been known for a long time. The Biblical echoes are, of course, discussed at large in Richmond Noble's *Shakespeare's Biblical Knowledge* (1935).

In an article (*Shakespeare Survey 4*, 1951) that is unusually thoughtful for a source-study Muriel C. Bradbrook makes the point that the political 'sources' of *Macbeth* are in the end less important than an analogue like *Lucrece* which traces the 'inner structure' of the play from violence to self-destruction.

THE WITCHES

Those who survey the history of witch-definition in *Macbeth* are liable to find the identity of these ladies as equivocal as their prophecies. The very source, indeed, supplied Shakespeare with two contradictory definitions, speaking of 'three women in strange and wild apparel, resembling creatures of elder world . . . these women were either the weird sisters, that is (as ye would say) the goddesses of destiny or else some nymphs or fairies, endued with knowledge of prophecy by their necromantical science'.

Bradley, holding that 'character in action' is the stuff of Shakespearian tragedy, was not willing to admit that the witches were more than clairvoyant: 'There is not a syllable in *Macbeth* to imply that they are anything but women.' He sees that the power of the protagonist is fatally infringed if he cannot choose his own destiny and therefore asserts that 'the prophecies of the Witches are presented simply as dangerous circumstances with which Macbeth has to deal . . . Macbeth is, in the ordinary sense, perfectly free in regard to them.' Shakespeare took over, in Bradley's view, the descriptions of witch-superstitions which he found in Reginald Scot, and used them to operate upon the minds of his audience, to provide convenient symbols for the evil tendencies in the world at large. Shakespeare took nothing from Holinshed except the name 'Weird Sisters'—'which certainly no more suggested to a London audience the Parcae of one mythology or the Norns of another than it does today'.

The Norns had been suggested by Fleay (1876) and by Miss Charlotte Carmichael (1879); later the suggestion was lent greater authority, when it was adopted by Kittredge (1939). Kittredge, without Bradley's interest in avoiding even the suggestion of fatalism, baldly supposes that Shakespeare must have meant what Holinshed meant by 'Weird Sisters': 'they not only foresaw the future, but decreed it. . . . Thus the tragedy of *Macbeth* is inevitably fatalistic, but Shakespeare attempts no solution of the problem of free-will and predestination. . . . He never gives us the impression that a man is not responsible for his own acts.'

Walter Clyde Curry, in *Shakespeare's Philosophical Patterns* (1937), investigates, with great assiduity and learning, the whole 'metaphysic of evil' that appears in *Macbeth*. Starting from the definition of 'nature's germens' (IV, i, 58)—in the scholastic thought which he supposes Shakespeare to have 'more or less unconsciously assimilated'—he finds that the witches 'are not ordinary witches . . . are demons or devils in the form of witches'. The witch-attributes he takes to be 'popular domestic symbols'; but the philosophical reality is 'the metaphysical world of evil intelligences [but] distilled by Shakespeare's imagination and concentrated in those marvellous dramatic symbols, the Weird Sisters'. Curry's demonic forces can 'animate nature and ensnare human souls by means of diabolical persuasion, by hallucination, infernal illusion and possession'. They cannot plant thoughts in the mind. But they may 'incite to thought' and kindle desires. They cannot know what *must* happen, but have a contingent knowledge of the future. And they wait everywhere to disturb and torment human weakness.

H. N. Paul, *The Royal Play of 'Macbeth'* (1950), thinks that the witches are not simply witches, but (more precisely) 'Scotch witches', i.e. witches as described in the *Demonology* of James I, and found in action in Holinshed's account of King Duff and the witches of Forres, working under the control of the devil.

Another view of Shakespeare's attitude to the double definition of the witches in Holinshed appears in Willard Farnham, *Shakespeare's Tragic Frontier* (1950). Farnham quotes very extensively from the literature of this period to show how far 'fairy', 'elf', 'hag' and 'witch' were interchangeable terms. For example Peter Heylyn's 1625 account of the Macbeth story speaks of 'Fairies, or Witches (Weirds the Scots call them)'. Farnham's final suggestion is that Shakespeare used the words of Holinshed's first definition, i.e. 'Weird Sisters', but interpreted them in the light of his alternative definition, as 'nymphs or fairies', able to see the future, but not to control it.

The difficulty of the witches for a modern audience is an old subject of discussion. A. P. Rossiter gives it a new and more authentically theatrical twist by suggesting (*Angel with Horns*, 1961) that only masks as *vile* as those of some African devils would serve today to make the point required. J. R. Brown, *Shakespeare: The Tragedy of Macbeth* (1963), quotes Ingmar Bergman on the same theatrical difficulty.

INTERPRETATION

Macbeth has long been considered one of Shakespeare's 'most sublime' plays, if only because of the obvious analogues between it and Greek tragedies—see 'Shakespeare's *Macbeth* arranged as an ancient tragedy' in R. G. Moulton's *Ancient Classical Drama* (1890). But in this century it has probably attracted fewer enthusiasts than the other 'great' tragedies in Bradley. John Bailey, *Shakespeare* (1929), finds that 'it neither interests the mind nor moves the heart, nor fills the imagination, as do *Hamlet* and *Othello* and *Lear*'; G. B. Harrison (*Shakespeare's Tragedies*, 1951) thinks that '*Macbeth* has been extravagantly over-praised. It is the weakest of Shakespeare's great tragedies, and so full of blemishes that it is hard to believe that one man wrote it.' On the other hand those who have preferred 'poetry' to 'drama' (supposing these to be separable) have continued to be attracted by its intensity. Of the Bradleian 'great' tragedies, *Macbeth* is probably the one which is least centred on reactions to quasi-real characters; Johnson's comment is worth remembering here: 'It has no nice discrimination of character; the events are too great to admit the influence of particular dispositions, and the course of the action necessarily determines the conduct of the agents.' It is no accident that F. R. Leavis's anti-Bradleian spoof question 'How many children had Lady Macbeth?' was referred to this particular play.

In fairness to Bradley it has to be pointed out, however, that some of the finest statements of the indeterminacy of 'character' in a poetic structure appear in the *Macbeth* essays in *Shakespearean Tragedy*. Macbeth and Lady Macbeth, he tells us, 'are never detached in imagination from the atmosphere which surrounds them and adds to their grandeur and terror. It is, as it were, continued into their souls. For within them is all that we felt without—the darkness of night, lit with the flame of tempest and the hues of blood, and haunted by wild and direful shapes.' Bradley's evocation of the poetic atmosphere of Macbeth is justly celebrated as a *locus classicus*:

Images like those of the babe torn smiling from the breast and dashed to death; of pouring the sweet milk of concord into hell; of the earth shaking in fever; of the frame of things disjointed; of sorrows striking heaven on the face, so that it resounds and yells out like syllables of dolour; of the mind lying in restless ecstasy on a rack; of the mind full of scorpions; of the tale told by an idiot, full of sound and fury;—all keep the imagination moving on a 'wild and violent sea' while it is scarcely for a moment permitted to dwell on thoughts of peace and beauty. In its language, as in its action, the drama is full of tumult and storm.

2

Bradley had not, of course, developed the study of themes and images in the systematic way of Miss Spurgeon and her successors; and it may be thought that it is in such works that *Macbeth* has come into its own. In *Shakespeare's Imagery* (1935) *Macbeth* occupies more space than any other single play. Miss Spurgeon sees it as 'more rich and varied, more highly imaginative, more unapproachable by any other writer than any other single play . . . the ideas in the imagery are in themselves more imaginative, more subtle and complex than in other plays'. She pays special attention to trains of images concerned with clothing, with light and dark, with reverberation, with disease and with horse-riding.

Cleanth Brooks also chooses this play, in his celebrated essay, 'The Naked Babe and the Cloak of Manliness' (*The Well Wrought Urn*, 1947), to make the general point that images that may seem pointlessly grotesque in isolation turn out to be structurally important when pursued throughout a play. Starting from the celebrated image of the chamberlains' daggers 'unmannerly breeched with gore' he shows how this may be justified in terms of the importance of disguise throughout the play. In a critical atmosphere which rated irony and paradox as the highest virtues *Macbeth* was unlikely to be an underrated play. H. L. Gardner has, however—in *The Business of Criticism* (1959)—pointed out a tendency in Cleanth Brooks's essay to substitute patterns for the genuine 'Shakespearian depth of human feeling' in the individual passage; and perhaps this is inseparable from sustained image-study.

Other themes have been pursued by other authors. Few image-hunters seem to have followed the counter-stroke of Wolfgang Clemen who, in *The Development of Shakespeare's Imagery* (1951), excluded *Macbeth* from his image-study of the tragedies. John Lawlor (*Shakespeare Quarterly*, 1957) sees the idea of Macbeth as an actor 'alone against a potentially dangerous world of observers' as central. The imagery of time in the play is eloquently explored by Stephen Spender (*Penguin New Writing*, 1941)—a point on which, however, he had been anticipated by J. M. Murry, *Shakespeare* (1936).

Another theme—that of manhood—is taken up by Eugene Waith in *ELH* (1950): Lady Macbeth's power over her husband depends on persuading him to accept a partial and improper definition of manliness. As Waith says, 'the soldier may avoid the danger of effeminacy only to incur the still greater danger of brutishness'.

Brents Stirling, on the other hand, sees the play as unified round the themes of 'raptness' ('look how our partner's rapt') and inverted nature (*Unity in Shakespearian Tragedy*, 1956). Francis Fergusson (*The Human Image in Dramatic Literature*, 1957) takes the phrase 'outrun the pauser reason' to be the key to the thematic structure.

It has indeed become something of a cliché of modern criticism to say that the essential structure of *Macbeth* is 'to be sought in the poetry' (L. C. Knights), that the characters 'are not shaped primarily to conform to a psychological verisimilitude, but to make explicit the intellectual statements with which the play is concerned' (Irving Ribner), that Lady Macbeth, Macbeth and Banquo 'are parts of a pattern, a design; are images or symbols' (A. P. Rossiter). The packed and economical structure of the play (often noticed) and the relative absence of episodes of detached realistic observation (like those of the players or the gravediggers in *Hamlet*) have made *Macbeth* seem particularly suitable for symbolic (or dogmatic) interpretations, and expositions of this kind have not been lacking. A great many of the subsequent lines of such interpretation appeared first in G. Wilson Knight's essay 'The Milk of Concord' in *The Imperial Theme*

(1931), a more complete, more coherent and (I think) a more influential treatment than that in *The Wheel of Fire* (1930). 'The Milk of Concord' presents a structure tensed between 'life-themes' and 'death-themes'; attention is directed to the failure of such 'natural' activities as sleeping and eating. The broken feasts of Act I and Act III find their answer in the witches' banquet of Act IV. Time is disordered; the future is compromised and the *natural* processes of childhood and development are cut off. The perception that the play is 'about' Nature and unnaturalness has been developed more sensitively (but also more moralistically) by L. C. Knights (*Some Shakespearean Themes*, 1959). Nature offers man a choice between creativeness and destructiveness. We respond to the choice because it is embodied in the poetic texture of the play.

Symbolic interpretation of a Shakespearian play which is full of Biblical phrases and images is bound to become explicitly Christian sooner or later, and there is quite a body of modern criticism which has explicitly Christian designs on *Macbeth*. Roy Walker, *The Time is Free* (n.d. (1949)), is less critically hamstrung by this intention than one might have supposed he would be. Excesses of interpretation, such as finding Seyton equivalent to Satan, equating Hecate with 'Lady Macbeth's guilty spirit', or treating Macbeth's pursuit of 'the son' (Malcolm, Donalbain, Fleance, young Macduff) as an analogy of anti-Christ—these are not central to the book. Acute perceptions abound (some anticipated by Wilson Knight); one may cite his antithetical placing of the two women in the play (p. 153).

The same general point may be made about J. A. Bryant, Jr (*Hippolyta's View*, 1961). Bryant's central critical point is that Macbeth's two great qualities, loyalty and bravery, are released from their double harness by the witches' prophecy, and, pulling against one another, pull Macbeth apart. This is not necessarily a Christian interpretation, though in Bryant's handling it becomes one, and one can enjoy its incidental acutenesses without accepting the whole framework in which they appear.

The other complete volume devoted to christianizing *Macbeth*—G. R. Elliott's *Dramatic Providence in Macbeth* (1958)—is, unfortunately, without acuteness. Elliott's book is much more tied to character-response than either Walker's or Bryant's; he asks us to identify with a sinful soul set in a theological framework. We are supposed always to be on the edges of our seats watching for signs of grace or repentance. Thus, speaking of 'Wake Duncan with thy knocking . . .', etc., at the end of II, ii, he says 'Will Macbeth's deepening remorse open the way for true humility and repentance? That major question overshadows the minor one: will his guilt be discovered by his peers?' (p. 90). One feels that Mr Elliott would have profited greatly by reading H. L. Gardner's 'Milton's "Satan" and the Theme of Damnation in Elizabethan Tragedy' (*Essays and Studies of the English Association*, 1948), where the dangers of simple-minded christianizing are spelled out with lucid perceptiveness.

Analogous to the Christian view of the play is that approach which looks upon it as a myth or ritual, but without specific meaning. Thus John Holloway, *The Story of the Night* (1961), finds Macbeth (like other tragic heroes) to be 'a scapegoat, a lord of misrule who has turned life into riot for his limited time, and is then driven out and destroyed by the forces which embody the fertile vitality and the communal happiness of the social group'.

H. C. Goddard, *The Meaning of Shakespeare* (1951), sees the play as a winter–spring ritual, in which the spring maiden overcomes the winter king. Both these authors make much of May-game analogies to Malcolm's army advancing on Dunsinane with green boughs held over their heads—presumably the clearest 'anthropological' moment in the play.

Yet another way of looking at the play, without putting response to individual characters at the centre, is to call it a morality play, and this has been done by several authors; but it is not clear that this nomenclature can take us very far, critically. A. E. Hunter, writing in *Shakespeare Association Bulletin* for 1937, was probably the first to devote much space to '*Macbeth* as a Morality'. The most useful element in the morality analogue would seem to be that which concerns 'flat' characterization—a feature of *Macbeth* that had drawn discriminating praise from Quiller-Couch (*Shakespeare's Workmanship*, 1918). F. P. Wilson (*Elizabethan and Jacobean*, 1945) notes that: 'In *Macbeth* many characters are brought in with no attempt to make them individual: the sergeant, the messenger, the doctor, the waiting-woman, the murderers, the "Old Man" and we may add Ross, Angus and Lennox . . . are without personality as much as the characters in a morality-play.'

IV, iii is one scene in the play which has been particularly affected by this modern tendency to take 'flatness' as description rather than evaluation. Traditionally, this has been considered the least successful scene in the play, close to Holinshed only because Shakespeare was not interested enough to create new material. Grierson in his edition of 1914 calls it 'a perfunctory paraphrase from Holinshed'. To many critics interested in theme, however, the scene appears to be brilliantly successful, a keystone of the structure. Francis Fergusson sees it as the *peripeteia*, the point at which the tide turns effectively against Macbeth, in which the isolation of his victims is overcome by Grace and by suffering. The thematic significance of *testing* our friends, of the 'good' King Edward, and of 'the Evil' that he cures, are points regularly made in this context.

The flatness of the individual characters who make up the opposition to Macbeth is sometimes thought to mark a weakness in the play. Mark Van Doren (*Shakespeare*, 1941) finds that '*Macbeth* is not in the fullest sense a tragedy' and William Rosen (*Shakespeare and the Craft of Tragedy*, 1960), taking up the same point, compares the simple optimism at the end of *Macbeth* with the intense questioning generated at the end of *Lear*, to the discredit (of course) of the former.

From another point of view, the simplicity of the end of *Macbeth* is a mark of its relation to the history plays. The relationship between the Christian view and the historical view is the subject of an article by Jane H. Jack (*ELH*, 1955). Mrs Jack shows how James I's political interests were coloured at every turn by his conviction that the Kingdom of Satan was everywhere around him. *Macbeth* echoes the obsessions of James (and the age), finding its Christian focus in the Old Testament (Saul and the Witch of Endor) and in the Apocalypse, rather than in the Gospels. Tyranny is represented as a spiritual condition rather than a political problem. The historical action of the play becomes 'an imaginative exploration of evil in Biblical terms'.

W. A. Armstrong (*The Review of English Studies*, 1946) sees the play in terms of a recurrent 'dramatic convention' which sets the lawful and hereditary king (Duncan, Edward, Malcolm) against the criminal and usurping tyrant. Hardin Craig (1948) classes *Macbeth* (along with *Antony and Cleopatra* and *Coriolanus*) as a 'Great Political Play'. The most successful treatment of *Macbeth* along these lines is probably that of E. M. W. Tillyard, *Shakespeare's History Plays* (1944). Tillyard sees *Macbeth* as the 'culminating version' of Shakespeare's concern with the man of action '. . . the finest of all mirrors for magistrates'. The relationship of 'flat' characterization to this focus is quite obvious from his comment on Malcolm: '[Malcolm] is the ideal ruler who has subordinated all his personal pleasures, and with them all personal charm, to his political obligations.'

Jan Kott (*Shakespeare, Our Contemporary*, 1964) follows in this line of describing the play as a history play, but distinguishes between the 'grand mechanism' of Shakespeare's 'histories' (which operates *upon* individuals), and the existentialist responsibility of the individual hero in *Macbeth*.

All this concern for the *pattern* of Macbeth has diverted interest from the hero as a man. None the less the reaction (even of critics) to stage-figures as if to real people is not finally repressible, and few treatments succeed in ignoring the hero altogether. But the modern treatments of Macbeth the man have responded to the general distrust of individualism and have drifted in a generally reductive and anti-heroic direction. Of course, there are exceptions. Bradley's 'He never forfeits our sympathy' has been echoed most enthusiastically by John Masefield in his Home University Library *Shakespeare* (n.d. (1911)); and H. B. Charlton (1948) and Peter Alexander (1939) are generally sympathetic. But most critics, for one reason or another, have seemed anxious to de-sentimentalize Macbeth. The prevalence of clothing imagery with its presentation of Macbeth as a dwarfish thief was thought by Miss Spurgeon to provide a counterweight to the romantic image of a heroic Macbeth. From very different premises, Schücking (*Character Problems*, 1922) saw him as a self-regarding, essentially ignoble character, more hindered by nerves than by conscience. Lily B. Campbell (1930) presents him as oscillating between fear and rashness, one who 'begins with the courage that is not real courage and ends with the courage that is not real courage'. A. P. Rossiter thinks of Macbeth's intellect as 'quite the most normal—even commonplace—among Shakespeare's gallery of minds'. Stoll (*Review of English Studies*, 1943; *From Shakespeare to Joyce*, 1944) and Schücking (*The Baroque Character of the Elizabethan Tragic Hero*, 1938) have, of course, their own drastic ways of resolving the tension between Macbeth's heroic nature and his crimes: they divide the character into two irreconcilable elements, yoked together only by theatrical legerdemain. J. I. M. Stewart (*Character and Motive in Shakespeare*, 1949) asserts, against this, the psychological plausibility of such tensions: 'Before *Macbeth* we ought not to abandon the conception of a "psychology" (as Mr Stoll would have us do) but deepen it.'

Much nineteenth-century admiration for *Macbeth* had stemmed from the quality of his imagination. Bradley summed up a great deal of this when he said that his imagination was 'the best part of him' and that 'if he had obeyed it he would have been safe'. An article by C. C. Clarke (*Durham University Journal*, 1960) attacks these assumptions and does something to restore to Macbeth his status as the actor as well as the principal witness of his crimes; Macbeth is not simply the victim of his imagination; 'he is also, and more simply, a man who fails to think clearly on a moral issue'. A useful additional caveat has also been entered by W. Rosen (1960): 'Shakespeare purposely elevates Macbeth's stature above that of Duncan and Banquo. Too often this is not stressed . . . in studies which offer patterns of order against those of disorder.' These may be signs that the individuality of Macbeth is beginning to emerge from the sea of images in which it has so long lain submerged.

The Bradleian method was, inevitably, much weaker with minor characters than with major. His treatment of Banquo is an obvious case. In Bradley's view, Banquo began as a foil to Macbeth, but soon lost this role. His soliloquy in III, i ('Thou hast it now—King, Cawdor, Glamis, all . . .') was taken to show that he had failed culpably to make his suspicions of Macbeth known abroad. When it emerges in the same scene that Banquo is now the king's chief counsellor, Bradley cannot resist the suspicion that he has been bribed into silence. It is interesting to note that George Wilson Knight, starting from a very different point, finds the same 'bond of evil between Banquo and Macbeth'. But most modern critics are anxious to keep Macbeth and Banquo as distinct as possible, taking forward to its logical conclusion Bradley's perception that the characters of the play fit into its atmosphere as parts into a structure. S. Nagarajan (*Shakespeare Quarterly*, 1956) sees the two men as 'placed' by the play in polarities of good and evil that 'characterization' cannot be allowed to infringe. Leo Kirschbaum (*Essays in Criticism*, 1957) notes that Banquo is not a whole man but 'a dramaturgic foil to Macbeth'. He points to a pattern of image contrasts between Lady Macbeth and Banquo which serve to place these characters at opposite sides of the wavering and central protagonist.

The movement that has changed Banquo from a person to a 'dramaturgic foil' has also affected Lady Macbeth. The relationship between the two criminals is very liable to sentimentalism, of the kind of Moulton's 'wife-like, she has no sphere but the career of her husband' or 'she has had the feminine lot of being shut out from active life and her genius and energy have been turned inwards'. Moulton's treatment is based (like that of many modern critics) on a perception that the Macbeths are *complementary* creations; but modern critics tend to see them as complementary in terms of pattern and idea rather than in terms of personality. Maynard Mack's 'The Jacobean Shakespeare' (*Jacobean Theatre*, 1960), for example, makes the point that the heroic tone of voice needs a foil, if it is to be acceptable. So Lady Macbeth has the same function as Horatio, urging upon the hero's metaphysical anguish the 'common-sense' of 'consider it not so curiously'. Mack again relates the sleepwalking scene to the total dramatic pattern rather than to the individual psychology of Lady Macbeth.

Macbeth is absent at this juncture . . . has not in fact been visible during two long scenes and will not be visible again till the next scene after this. In the interval, the slaying at Macduff's castle and the conversations between Malcolm and Macduff keep him before us in his capacity as tyrant, murderer, 'Hell-kite', seen from the outside. But Lady Macbeth's sleep-walking is, I think, Shakespeare's device for keeping him before us in his capacity as tragic hero and sufferer. . . . The 'slumbery agitation', the 'thick-coming fancies That keep her from her rest': these by a kind of poetical displacement, we may apply to him as well as to her. . . . We are, of course, conscious as we watch the scene, that this is Lady Macbeth suffering the metaphysical aspects of murder that she did not believe in; we may also be conscious that the remorse pictured here tends to distinguish her from her husband, who for some time has been giving his 'initiate fear' the 'hard use' he said it lacked, with dehumanizing consequences. Yet in some way the pity of this situation suffuses him as well as her, the more so because in every word she utters his presence beside her is supposed. . . . Such speeches as this . . . we might call umbrella speeches, since more than one consciousness may shelter under them.

The developing perception that *Macbeth* is not so much the story of an evil deed and its consequences, but rather an exploration of the meaning of Evil and its ramifications—this, more than any textual revolution, has freed a number of scenes from the suspicion of bastardy. A taste for irony and paradox, for the baroque clash of opposites—especially evident in what S. L.

Bethell called 'The Popular Tradition'—has been effective in making the Porter's speeches a centre for appreciative comment. Kenneth Muir devotes a substantial section of his Arden Introduction to this scene, defending it on grounds of (*a*) theatrical necessity; (*b*) intensification of horror; (*c*) thematic continuity; (*d*) stylistic continuity; (*e*) to 'cut the cable that moored his tragedy to a particular spot in space and time'.

J. Harcourt (*Shakespeare Quarterly*, 1961) concentrates on the symbolic content of the Porter's imagination and of his whole situation as 'Porter of Hell-gate'. The analogy of the Infernal Porter in the medieval 'Harrowing of Hell' plays is closer than is usually noted. Christ comes to hell in these plays and awakens hell and its porter with his thunderous command, *Attollite portas*, etc. Macduff is the Christ-figure who hammers at the door of Macbeth's hell, and he is well suited for the role. His subsequent career carries forward the analogy. As Christ enters and defeats the devil, so Macduff defeats Macbeth, emerges at the end of the play with his enemy's head on a pole and declares that 'the time is free'.

William Blissett (*Shakespeare. Quarterly*, 1959) sees an analogy between the Porter's view of drunken lechery and Macbeth's political ambition, provoked in desire by the methods he adopts, but taken down in performance.

On the other hand, Terence Hawkes, *Shakespeare and the Reason* (1964), sees the porter's remarks on lechery as paralleling those of Lady Macbeth on manliness. Murder bears the same relation to politics as lechery does to love.

An interesting historical note by J. W. Spargo in *Adams Memorial Studies* (1948) helps to integrate the knocking on the door with the other death-portents in the scene of the murder— the owl's cry and the wolf's howl. In time of plague the 'knocking at the gate' signified the search for dead bodies; and the noise on the Globe stage must have reinforced the sense of a moral plague in the castle by carrying its original audience's minds back to the terror and the horror of their own plague visitations.

THE CRIMINAL AS TRAGIC HERO:
DRAMATIC METHODS

BY

ROBERT B. HEILMAN

I

The difficulties presented by the character of Macbeth—the criminal as tragic hero—have led some critics to charge Shakespeare with inconsistency, others to seek consistency by viewing the initial Macbeth as in some way morally defective,[1] and still others to normalize the hero by viewing the final Macbeth as in some way morally triumphant. Perhaps a recollection of Lascelles Abercrombie's enthusiastic phrase, 'the zest and terrible splendour of his own unquenchable mind' (1925), and of Wilson Knight's comparable 'emerges at last victorious and fearless'[2] (1930), helped stir L. C. Knights to complain (1933) that 'the critics have not only sentimentalized Macbeth—ignoring the completeness with which Shakespeare shows his final identification with evil—but they have slurred the passages in which the positive good is presented by means of religious symbols'.[3] Even after this, so unflighty an editor as Kittredge could say that Macbeth 'is never greater than in the desperate valour that marks his end'.[4] On the other hand, the editor of a *Macbeth* meant for schools describes Macbeth as a 'bold, exacting and presumptuous criminal, ... bent on destruction for destruction's sake', 'the champion of evil', 'a monster', giving 'the impression ... of some huge beast who ... dies lashing out at everyone within range'.[5] But if intemperateness of eulogy or condemnation is exceptional, the opposing impulses are not altogether reconciled; if to many critics Macbeth is damned, there is hardly consensus about either the way down or the mitigating circumstances or how good the bad man is. 'Damned, but' might be a title for an anthology of critical essays.

The problem of character, which is no more than quickly sketched by this sampling of judgments, becomes intertwined with the problem of generic placement, a standard, though rarely decisive, evaluating procedure. If the play changes from the study of a complex soul to the history of good men's victory over a criminal and tyrant, has it not dropped from the level of high tragedy to that of political melodrama? This seems harsh, and we can evade it either by discovering unmelodramatic complications in Macbeth as king (a method approached by Neilson and Hill when they acknowledge that Macbeth 'proved a desperately wicked man' but add, with mild confidence, '... we are reassured that he was more than the mere butcher the avenging Malcolm not unnaturally calls him'),[6] or by minimizing the importance of character and insisting that the play is a great dramatic poem (as in that anti-Bradleyism which can be traced at least from Knights's 1933 essay). When we look, as many critics do, at the poetic-dramatic structure, we find, among other things, that the nadaism of Macbeth's 'Tomorrow and tomorrow and tomorrow' speech is not Shakespeare's but Macbeth's and that the play contains numerous images of good kingship and affirmative life; Macbeth is regularly in contrast with the norms of order and hope. The trouble with abstracting a meaning—'Crime doesn't pay' or 'The way of transgressors is hard'—and regarding character as principally a buttress of that meaning[7] is that it has consequences for the placement of drama. Kenneth Muir faces the consequences when he says, 'We may, indeed, call *Macbeth* the greatest of morality plays . . .'.[8] However, Muir is understandably diffident about the term 'morality play'; so he not only says 'greatest' but adds a weighty series of codicils intended to cushion to the utmost, or even counteract, the implicit demotion from 'tragedy' to 'morality play'.

The critical uneasiness with the character of Macbeth is different from the usual feelings— uncertainty, attentiveness, curiosity, passion to examine, and so on—stirred by an obscure or elusive character, because it springs from a disturbing sense of discrepancy not evoked, for instance, by Shakespeare's other tragic heroes. We expect the tragic protagonist to be an expanding character, one who grows in awareness and spiritual largeness; yet Macbeth is to all intents a contracting character, who seems to discard large areas of consciousness as he goes, to shrink from multilateral to unilateral being (we try to say it isn't so by deflating the Macbeth of Acts I and II and inflating the Macbeth of Acts IV and V). The diminishing personality is of course not an anomaly in literature, whether in him we follow a gradual decrease of moral possibility or discover an essential parvanimity, but this we expect in satire (Fielding's Blifil, Austen's Wickham, Meredith's Sir Austin Feverel, Eliot's Lydgate), not tragedy. This source of uneasiness with Macbeth, however, is secondary; the primary source is a technical matter, Shakespeare's remarkable choice of point of view—that of this ambitious man who, in Muir's words that sum up the contracting process, 'becomes a villain'. We have to see through his eyes, be in his skin; for us, this is a great breach of custom, and in the effort at accommodation we do considerable scrambling. When we share the point of view of Hamlet, we experience the fear of evil action and of evil inaction; when we share the point of view of Othello and Lear, we experience passionate, irrational action whose evil is not apprehended or foreseen; but when we share the point of view of Macbeth, we have to experience the deliberate choice of evil. Hence a disquiet altogether distinguishable from the irresoluteness of mind before, let us say, some apparent contradictions in Othello.

The problem is like that which usually comes up when readers[9] must adopt the point of view of a character in whom there are ambiguities. Unless structure is based on contrasts, point of view ordinarily confers authority; but discomforts, which invariably lead to disagreements, arise when authority apparently extends to matters which, on aesthetic, rational, psychological, or moral grounds, the reader finds it difficult to countenance.[10] 'Disagreements', of course, implies studious recollection in tranquillity, or rather, untranquillity; what we are concerned with in this discussion is the immediate, unanalysed imaginative experience which precedes the effort to clarify or define. We are assuming that the person experiencing *Macbeth* is naturally carried into an identification with Macbeth which, if incomplete, is still more far-reaching than that with anyone else in the play. This should be a safe working assumption,[11] whatever the modifications of sensibility that qualify the immediate unanalysed experience and hence lead to alternative explanations of Macbeth in retrospect. Surely Muir is right in saying of our response to Macbeth that 'we are tempted and suffer with him'.[12]

Behind our condemnation of trivial literature, whether we call it 'sentimental', 'meretricious', or something else, lies the sense that the characters whom for the moment we become give us an inadequate or false sense of reality, call into action too few of our human potentialities. Hence 'tragedy' tends not simply to designate a genre, in which there may be widely separated levels of excellence, but to become an honorific term: it names a noble enterprise, the action of a literary structure which compels us to get at human truth by knowing more fully what we are capable of—'knowing', not by formal acts of cognition but by passing imaginatively through revelatory experiences. In a morality we see a demonstration of what happens; in tragedy we act out what happens, undergoing a kind of kinaesthetic initiation into conduct we would not ordinarily acknowledge as belonging to us. The problem is how far this process of illuminating induction can go without running into resistance that impedes or derails the tragic experience, without exciting self-protective counter-measures such as retreating from tragic co-existence with the hero to censorious observation of him from a distant knoll.[13] *Macbeth* at least permits this way out by its increasingly extensive portrayal, in Acts IV and V, of the counterforces whom we see only as high-principled seekers of justice. Do we, so to speak, defect to them because Macbeth, unlike Lear and Othello, moves into a greater darkness in which we can no longer discern our own lineaments? Do we, then, turn tragedy into melodrama or morality?

II

That, of course, is a later question. The prior question is the mode of our relationship with Macbeth when he kills Duncan; here we have to consent to participation in a planned murder, or at least tacitly accept our capability of committing it. The act of moral imagination is far greater, as we have seen, than that called for by the germinal misdeeds of Lear or the murder by Othello, since these come out of emotional frenzies where our tolerance, or even forgiveness, is so spontaneous that we need not disguise our kinship with those who realize in action what we act in fantasy. Yet technically Shakespeare so manages the situation that we become Macbeth, or at least assent to complicity with him, instead of shifting to that simple hostility evoked by the melodramatic treatment of crime. We accept ourselves as murderers, so to speak, because we also feel the strength of our resistance to murder. The initial Macbeth has a fullness of human range that makes him hard to deny; though a kind of laziness makes us naturally vulnerable to the solicitation of some narrow-gauge characters, we learn by experience and discipline to reject these (heroes of cape and sword, easy masters of the world, pure devils, simple victims); and correspondingly we are the more drawn in by those with a large store of human possibilities, good and evil. Macbeth can act as courageous patriot (I, ii, 35 ff.), discover that he has dreamed of the throne ('... why do you start...?'—I,iii, 51), entertain the 'horrid image' of murdering Duncan (I, iii, 135), be publicly rewarded by the king (I, iv), be an affectionate husband (I, v), survey, with anguished clarity, the motives and consequences of the imagined deed; reject it; feel the strength of his wife's persuasion, return to 'this terrible feat' (I, vii, 80); undergo real horrors of anticipation (II, i, 31 ff.) and of realization that he has actually killed Duncan (II, ii, 14 ff.). Here is not a petty scoundrel but an extraordinary man, so capacious in feeling and motive as to have a compelling representativeness; we cannot adopt him selectively, feel a oneness with some parts of him and reject others; we become the murderer as well as the man who can hardly tolerate, in prospect or retrospect, the idea of murder. The suffering is so great that the act is hedged about with penance; unless we are neurotic, we cannot pay such a price without earning it; murder belongs, as it were, to normalcy—to us in our normalcy. Further-more, the anguish is so powerful and protracted, and the 'terrible feat' so quickly done, that it marks only a brief failure of moral governance; we seem to sacrifice only a mite of the sentience that we instinctively attribute to ourselves. That, too, after solicitations whose power we feel directly: 'Vaulting Ambition', indeed, but also challenges to our manly courage, the promise of security, and, behind these, the driving strength of another soul not easy to disappoint or even, when the other speaks for a part of ourselves, to resist. These persuasions, in turn, are a supple-ment to 'supernatural soliciting' (I, iii, 130), to 'fate and metaphysical aid' (I, v, 26). Finally, Shakespeare affords the reader one more aid in accepting his alliance with the murderer: that alteration of ordinary consciousness that enhances the persuasiveness of deviant conduct by the 'good man'. From the first prophetic phrases Macbeth has been 'rapt', a word applied to him thrice (I, iii, 57, 142; I, v, 5), and when the knocking is heard Lady Macbeth adjures him,

> Be not lost
> So poorly in your thoughts;   (II, ii, 71–2)

there are also his dagger-vision speech before the murder (II, i, 33 ff.), and after it the hallucina-tory impressions that make Lady Macbeth use the word 'brainsickly' (II, ii, 46). The note of 'unsound mind' helps make the murderer 'one of us', to use Conrad's term, rather than a criminal-outsider.

If it be a function of tragedy, as we have suggested, to amplify man's knowledge of himself by making him discover, through imaginative action, the moral capabilities to which he may ordinarily be blind, then Shakespeare, in the first two acts of *Macbeth*, has so managed his tools that the function is carried out superlatively well. He leads the reader on to accept himself in a role that he would hardly dream of as his. If it be too blunt to say that he becomes a murderer, at least he feels murderousness to be as powerful as a host of motives more familiar to conscious-ness. Whether he knows it or not, he knows something more about himself. It may be that 'knows' takes us too far into the realm of the impalpable, but to use it is at least to say meta-phorically that the reader remains 'with' Macbeth instead of drifting away into non-participa-tion and censure. Shakespeare's dramaturgic feat should not be unappreciated.

III

That behind him, Shakespeare moves ahead and takes on a still greater difficulty: the maintaining of identity, his and ours, with a character who, after a savage initial act, goes on into other monstrosities, gradually loses more of his human range, contracts, goes down hill.[14] Surely this is the most demanding technical task among the tragedies. Othello and Lear both grow in knowledge; however reluctantly and incompletely, they come into a sense of what they have done, and advance in powers of self-placement. With them we have a sense of recovery, which paradoxically accompanies the making of even destructive discoveries. Renouncing blindness is growth. Macbeth does not attract us into kinship in this way; his own powers of self-recognition seem to have been squandered on the night of the first murder and indirectly in the dread before Banquo's ghost. Nevertheless there are passages in which he has been felt to be placing and judging himself. There may indeed be something of tragic self-knowledge in the man who says that he has 'the gracious Duncan . . . murder'd' and

> mine eternal jewel
> Given to the common enemy of man; (III, i, 65, 67–8)

yet he is not saying 'I have acted evilly', much less 'I repent of my evil conduct', but rather, 'I have paid a high price—and for what? To make Banquo the father of kings.' Macbeth is not so simple and crude as not to know that the price is high, but his point is that for a high price he ought to be guaranteed the best goods; and in prompt search of the best goods he elaborates the remorselessly calculating rhetoric by which he inspirits the murderers to ambush Banquo and Fleance. Again, he can acknowledge his and Lady Macbeth's nightmares and declare buried Duncan better off than they, but have no thought at all of the available means of mitigating this wretchedness; the much stronger motives appear in his preceding statement 'We have scorch'd the snake, not kill'd it' and his following one, 'O, full of scorpions is my mind . . . that Banquo, and his Fleance, lives' (III, ii, 13, 36–7). The serpents of enmity and envy clearly have much more bite than the worm of conscience.

> I am in blood
> Stepp'd in so far (III, iv, 136–7)

encourages some students to speak as if Macbeth were actuated by a sense of guilt, but since no expectable response to felt guilt inhibits his arranging, very shortly, the Macduff murders, it seems more prudent to see in these words only a technical summary of his political method. In 'the sere, the yellow leaf' lines Macbeth's index of the deprivations likely to afflict him in later years (v, iii, 23 ff.) suggests to some readers an acute moral awareness; it seems rather a regretful notice of social behaviour, such as would little trouble the consciousness of a man profoundly concerned about the quality of his deeds and the state of his soul. Finally, in Macbeth's battlefield words to Macduff—

> my soul is too much charg'd
> With blood of thine already— (v, viii, 5–6)

some critics have detected remorse. It may be so, but in the general context of actions of a man increasingly apt in the sanguinary and freed from refinement of scruple, there is much to be said for the suggestion that he is 'rationalizing his fear';[15] possibly, too, he is unconsciously placating the man who has most to avenge and of whom the First Apparition has specifically warned him (IV, i, 71).

Since different Shakespearians have been able to find in such passages a continuance of genuine moral sensitivity in Macbeth, it is possible that for the non-professional reader they do indeed belong to the means by which a oneness with Macbeth is maintained. If so, then we have that irony by which neutral details in an ugly man's portrait have enough ambiguity to help win a difficult assent to him. However, a true change of heart is incompatible with a retention of the profits secured by even the temporarily hardened heart, and the fact is that once Macbeth has become king, all of his efforts are directed to hanging on to the spoils of a peculiarly obnoxious murder. Shakespeare has chosen to deal not only with an impenitent, though in many ways regretful, man, but with one whose crime has been committed only to secure substantial wordly advantages (in contrast with the wrongs done by Lear and Othello). Perhaps what the play 'says' is that such a crime has inevitable consequences, that worldly profit—goods, honour, power—is so corrupting that, once committed to it, the hero can never really abjure it, can never really repent and seeks ways of spiritual alteration, though he may cry out against the thorns and ugliness of the road he cannot leave.[16] However far such a theory can be carried, it is plain that Macbeth, once he has taken the excruciatingly difficult first step on the new route, discovers in himself the talents for an unsurrenderable athleticism in evil.

The artist's problem is that for a reader to accompany such a character and to share in his intensifying depravity might become intolerable; the reader might simply flee to the salvation of condemning the character. This does not happen. For, having chosen a very difficult man to establish our position—to give us shoes and skin and eyes and feeling—Shakespeare so manages the perspective that we do not escape into another position. As with all his tragic heroes, Shakespeare explores the point of view of self, the self-defending and self-justifying motions of mind and heart; alert as we are to self-protectiveness in others, we still do not overtly repudiate that of Macbeth. That is, Macbeth finds ways of thinking about himself and his dilemmas that we find congenial, and, even more than that, ways of feeling which we easily share. The dramatist can rely somewhat, of course, on that ambiguous sympathy with the criminal that human beings express in various ways; even an artist who is not romanticizing a criminal can count on it up to a point if he protects it against counter feelings. Suppose, for instance, that we had seen a great deal of Duncan at Macbeth's castle or that the murder were done on the stage or that Macbeth did not undergo the agonies depicted in II, ii; he would already have lost his role as erring humanity, and we ours as secret sharer. Suppose, also, that he then took the throne by blunt force, or were grossly shameless, or rapped out lies which everyone knew to be lies. But he does not drive us away by such methods; instead, our murderer is a man who suffers too much, as it were, really to be a murderer; he agonizes more than he antagonizes. After the murder, we next see him in a painfully taxing and challenging position—the utter necessity of so acting in public, at a moment of frightful public calamity, that neither his guilt will be revealed nor his ambition threatened. The pressure on him shifts to us, who ought to want him caught right there. Can he bring it off? Can we bring it off? In some way we become the terribly threatened individual, the outnumbered solitary antagonist; further, our own secret self is at stake, all our evil, long so precariously covered over, in danger of being exposed, and we of ruin. But we miraculously come through, our terrible anxiety somehow transmuted to strength under fire; we say the right things ('Had I but died an hour before this chance', II, iii, 89), have the presence of mind to be carried away by 'fury' and kill the chamberlains and turn suspicion on them, and still to 'repent' the fury (105). Relief, perhaps triumph. This statement may require more delicacy and precision, but it should indicate the way in which Shakespeare instinctively approaches the task of enticing us into collusion. We remain the murderer in part because the pressure of other motives makes us forget that we are. What we forget we do not deny.

Macbeth is in danger of degenerating from Everyman into monster, that is, of pushing us from unspoken collusion to spoken judgment, when he coolly plots against Banquo. But Shakespeare moves Macbeth quickly into a recital of motives and distresses that invite an assent of feeling. Macbeth's important 25-line soliloquy (III, i, 47–71) is in no sense a formal apologia, but it has the effect of case-making by the revelation of emotional urgencies whose force easily comes home to us. There are three of these urgencies. The first is fear, that especial kind of fear that derives from insecurity: '... to be safely thus' (48) is a cry so close to human needs that it can make us forget that the threat to safety is made by justice. The fear is of Banquo, a man of 'dauntless temper', of 'wisdom' (51, 52); we can credit ourselves with Macbeth's ability and willingness to discriminate at the same time that, unless we make an improbable identification with Banquo, we can enter into the lesser man's sense of injury and his inclination to purge himself of second-class moral citizenship. The second great appeal is that to the horror of being in a cul de sac, of feeling no continuity into something beyond the present: all that we have earned will be nothing if we have but a 'fruitless crown', 'a barren sceptre', 'No son' (60–3). It is the Sisters that did this; 'they' are treating us unfairly, inflicting a causeless deprivation. Our Everyman's share of paranoia is at work. Yet the price has been a high one ('vessel of my peace', loss of 'mine eternal jewel'); it is as if a bargain had been unfulfilled, and we find ourselves sharing the third emotional pressure—resentment at a chicanery of events which need not be borne.

The anxiety in the face of constant threats, the pain at being cut off from the future, the bitterness of the wretched bargain—these emotions, since they may belong to the most upright life, tend to inhibit our making a conscious estimate of the uprightness of the man who experiences them. This may be a sufficient hedge against our splitting away from Macbeth when he is whipping up the Murderers against Banquo. But since Macbeth can trick us into the desire to 'get away with it', or into discovering that we can have this desire, it may be that even the subornation of murder evokes a distant, unidentified, and unacknowledgeable compliance. Here the appeal would be that of executive dispatch and rhetorical skill in a difficult cause; it is satisfying to use against another the method before which one has been defenceless earlier, the appeal to manliness (91 ff.), to hint the grave danger to oneself (115–17), to claim a meritorious abstention from 'bare-fac'd power' (118), though the power is legitimate. Then quickly, before we have time to cast off the spell, to catch ourselves tricked into a silent partnership in crime and to start backing away from it, we are enthralled in another way: again, this time with both Macbeth and Lady Macbeth, the terrible fear, the sense of constant menace, the 'affliction of these terrible dreams', the 'torture of the mind' (III, ii, 18, 21). Afflictions and tortures: we have our own, and we do not stop, step to one side, and think that ours are more just and noble than those of the wretched royal pair. Macbeth's language, in a brilliant touch, even makes the usurpers weak victims, such as we sometimes like to be: threatening them is a 'snake', cut in two, but reuniting to extend the 'danger', against which we offer but 'poor malice', that is, feeble opposition (14–15). Here is one of the subtler of the series of verbal and dramatic means by which we are held 'with' Macbeth and the queen; we are with them as long as we do not turn and say, 'But what do you expect?' And as long as we do not say that, we have not shifted to the posture invited by melodrama and morality play.

At the banquet scene the courtesy and breeding of the host and hostess hardly seem that of vulgar criminals, from whom we would quickly spring away into our better selves. But before the Ghost appears, Macbeth learns of the escape of Fleance, and he speaks words that appeal secretly to two modes of responsiveness. He introduces the snake image from III, ii, 14: as for Banquo, 'There the grown serpent lies', but then there's Fleance:

> the worm that's fled
> Hath nature that in time will venom breed. (III, iv, 29–30)

It is not that we rationally accept Macbeth's definition of father and son, but that we share his desperateness as destined victim; and his image for the victimizing forces, as long as it is not opposed openly in the context, is one to evoke the fellowship of an immemorial human fear. This, however, tops off a subtler evocation of sympathy, Macbeth's

> I am cabin'd, cribb'd, confin'd, bound in
> To saucy doubts and fears. (24–5)

The new image for fear, which we have already been compelled to feel, is peculiarly apt and constraining: it brings into play the claustrophobic distress that can even become panic. We do not pause for analysis, stand off, and say, 'It is the claustrophobia of crime'; rather the known phobia maintains our link with the criminal. Then, of course, the moral responsiveness implied by the appearance of the Ghost and by Macbeth's terror make a more obvious appeal, for here the traditional 'good man' is evident. Not only does he again become something of a victim, but the royal pair draw us into their efforts to save a situation as dangerous as it is embarrassing and humiliating. They are in such straits that we cannot now accuse them, much less triumph over them. Macbeth's demoralizing fear, finally, works in a paradoxical way: fear humanizes the warrior and thus brings us closer to him, while his inevitable reaction from it into almost hyperbolic courage, with its conscious virility ('Russian bear', 'Hyrcan tiger', etc., 99 ff.), strikes a different chord of consent. From now on until the end, indeed, Macbeth is committed to a bravery, not unspontaneous but at once compensating and desperate—a bravura of bravery— that it is natural for us to be allied with.

The danger point is that at which the admired bravery and its admired accompaniment, resolution (such as appears in the visit to the Witches, IV, i), are distorted into the ruthlessness of the Macduff murders. Here we are most likely to be divorced from Macbeth, to cease being actors of a role and become critics of it. At any rate, Shakespeare takes clear steps to 'protect' Macbeth's position. That 'make assurance double sure' (IV, i, 83) has become a cliché is con- firmatory evidence that the motive is well-nigh universal; getting rid of Macduff becomes almost an impersonal safety measure, additionally understandable because of the natural wish to 'sleep in spite of thunder' (86). We come close to pitying his failure to grasp the ambiguity of the oracles, for we can sense our own naiveté and wishful thinking at work; and his dis- illusionment and emptiness on learning that Banquo's line will inherit the throne, are not so alien to us that Macbeth's retaliatory passion is unthinkable. Shakespeare goes ahead with the risk: we see one of the cruel murders, and the next time Macbeth appears, he is hardly attractive either in his almost obsessive denying of fear (v, iii, 1–10) or in his letting his tension explode in pointless abuse of his servant, partly for fearfulness (11–18). Still, the impulses are ones we can feel. Now, after Macbeth has been on the verge of breaking out into the savage whom we could only repudiate, things take a different turn, and Macbeth comes back toward us as more than a loathsome criminal. He is 'sick at heart' (19)—words that both speak to a kindred feeling and deny that the speaker is a brute. He meditates on approaching age (22 ff.), with universality of theme and dignity of style teasing us into a fellowship perhaps strengthened by respect for the intellectual candour with which he lists the blessings he has forfeited. Above all he has a desperately sick wife: pressed from without, still he must confer with the doctor and in grief seek remedies for a 'mind diseas'd', 'a rooted sorrow', 'that perilous stuff / Which weighs upon the heart'

(40–5). Shakespeare makes him even extend this humane concern, either literally or with a wry irony that is still not unattractive, to the health of Scotland:

> find her disease,
> And purge it to a sound and pristine health. (51–2)

Along with all of the troubles that he meets, more often than not with sad equanimity, he must also face crucial desertions: 'the thanes fly from me' (49). Like us all, he tells his troubles to the doctor. He has become an underdog, quite another figure from the cornered thug, supported by a gang of sinister loyalty, that he might be. This athlete in evil, as we called him earlier, has had to learn endurance and endure, if we may be forgiven, the loneliness of the long-distance runner. Against such solitude we hardly turn with reproof.

Macbeth opened the scene crying down fear; he goes on with three more denials of fear, one at the end (32, 36, 59); now we are able to see in the repetition an effort to talk down deep misgivings, and the hero again approximates Everyman, ourselves. When Macbeth next appears, just before the battle, it is the same: he opens and closes the scene literally or implicitly denying fear, even though the prophecy of his end seems miraculously fulfilled (v, v, 1–15, 51–2). Meanwhile the queen's death is reported, and the warrior, moved but finely controlled, turns grief into contemplation, with the seductiveness of common thought in uncommon language. The closing battle scene is a series of denials of fear, appealing to both pity and admiration. Some details are instinctively ingratiating. 'They have tied me to a stake; I cannot fly' (v, vii, 1)— oneself as the victim of others bent on cruel sport. 'Why should I play the Roman fool . . . ?' (v, viii, 1)—no moral retreat, no opting out of adversity. 'I will not yield' (27)—the athlete's last span of endurance, fight against all odds.

IV

My intention has been, not to offer a full study of Macbeth or a fresh account of his moral alteration, not to argue that he is a worse man than some have thought (though some analyses seem not to catch what Knights called 'the completeness [of] his final identification with evil') or a better man than other men have thought (though he is remarkably endowed with aspects of personality not ordinarily expected in a man committed to evil), but to describe the apparent impact made upon the imagination by certain deeds, thoughts, and feelings of his. Since there is hardly a need to demonstrate that Macbeth is a villain and that villains ordinarily repel us, the emphasis has naturally fallen upon those elements in him that tend to elicit, in whatever degree, fellow-feeling, pity, favour, or even admiration. Macbeth possibly establishes a subtle kinship by setting in motion certain impulses which we would rather not admit—anomalous siding with the criminal, aggressive ambition, envy, the pleasure of getting away with it (which includes leaving the 'it' unexamined). More frequently the appeal to allegiance is that of states or situations which are neutral in that they may come to good or bad men but which, without analysing the merits of the figure involved, we find it difficult not to fear or pity—the threat of exposure, the anxieties of a perilous position, relentless enclosure by men and circumstances, nightmares and insomnia of whatever origin, the pressing need for greater safety, the pain of miscalculation and the gnawing sense of a bad bargain, any enlargement of the penalties of advanced age, desertion, the unequal struggle, the role of the underdog. Finally, and more important, Macbeth early gives every sign of having a conscience, and later he exhibits qualities and abilities that normally elicit respect or admiration—resourcefulness under severely taxing stresses, readiness for intolerable difficulties, resolution, the philosophic cast of mind, endurance, bravery.

If the general demonstration, as it is summarized here, has merit, it opens the way to several other points. For one thing, it should help explain some rather enthusiastic accounts of Macbeth: that which binds us to him, either the painfulness of what he endures or the qualities that he shares with men we admire, so overwhelms the sense of the ruthless tyrant that we either let this slip out of operative consciousness or take it for granted as not requiring further discussion, and proceed then to erect a rational form for all the feelings of kinship or approval. Shakespeare has so thoroughly attacked the problem of keeping a villain from being a mere villain that at times it has apparently been easy to lose sight of his villainy. On the other hand, the endowing of Macbeth with the power to attract fellow-feeling and even approval makes it unlikely that 'the sympathies of the audience are switched to his enemies'.[17] This is a crucial matter. For if such a switch does take place, then the play does not hold us in an essentially tragic engagement, but carries us into a relationship like that with *Richard III* (a play often used to illustrate *Macbeth*).

To be convinced of Macbeth's retention of our sympathy may seem to imply a denial of our sympathy to Malcolm, Macduff, and the conquering party. By no means: obviously we share their passions whenever these control the action, and we may even cheer them on. Yet we do not remain fixedly and *only* with them, as we do with Richmond and his party in *Richard III*, and with such forces in all dramas with a clearly melodramatic structure. When the anti-Macbeth leaders occupy the stage, we are unable not to be at one with them; but the significant thing is that when his point of view is resumed, Macbeth again draws us back, by the rather rich means that we have examined, into our old collusion. After III, vi, when we first see committed opposition to Macbeth (' . . . this our suffering country, / Under a hand accurs'd!'—48–9), the two sides alternate on the stage until they come together in battle. In one scene we have the rather easy, and certainly reassuring, identification with the restorers of order; in the next, the strange, disturbing emotional return to the camp of the outnumbered tyrant. We move back and forth between two worlds and are members of both. As a contemporary novelist says of a character who is watching fox and hounds, 'She wanted it to get away, yet when she saw the hounds she also wanted them to catch it'.[18]

Macbeth, in other words, has a complexity of form which goes beyond that normally available to melodrama and morality play, where the issue prevents ambiguity of feeling and makes us clear-headed partisans. Whether *Macbeth* goes on beyond this surmounting of melodramatic limitations to high achievement as tragedy is the final problem. It turns, I believe, on Shakespeare's treatment of Macbeth, that is, on whether this retains the complexity that cannot quite be replaced by the kind of complexities that *Macbeth* does embrace. Here, of course, we are in the area of our mode of response to character, where all is elusive and insecure, and we can only be speculative. What I have proposed, in general, is that, because of the manifold claims that Macbeth makes upon our sympathy, we are drawn into identification with him in his whole being; one might say that he tricks us into accepting more than we expect or realize. If it is true that we are led to experience empathy with a murderer and thus to come into a more complete 'feeling knowledge' of what human beings are like (tragic experience as the catharsis of self-ignorance), then Shakespeare has had a success which is not trivial. Yet there remains a legitimate question or two. Let us try this approach. It is not the business of tragedy to let man know that he is only a scoundrel or devil (any more than its business is to let him know that he is really an angel); it is obvious enough that such an experience would be too circumscribed to gain assent to its truthfulness. In so far as he pushes us in that direction, Shakespeare makes the indispensable qualifications. Yet the felt qualifications can be expressed in ways that are less than satisfactory; for instance, 'Macbeth is a villain, but there's also this to be said', or, still more, 'Macbeth is a wonderful man. Oh yes, a villain, of course.' Such flip statements are not found literally in *Macbeth* criticism, but they do represent the tendency to make a unitary assessment and then add an afterthought, that is, to pull the constituent elements apart unevenly instead of holding them together in a fusion not so simply describable.

It is possible that Shakespeare's basic method encourages this tendency. Shakespeare first chooses a protagonist who in action is worse than the other main tragic heroes, and then tends to make him better than other tragic heroes, in effect to make him now one, and now the other. Shakespeare had to protect Macbeth against the unmixed hostility that the mere villain would evoke; perhaps he over-protected him, letting him do all his villainies indeed, but providing him with an excess of devices for exciting the pity, warmth, and approval which prompt forgetfulness of the villainies. If critics have, as Knights protested, sentimentalized Macbeth, it may be that the text gives them more ground than has been supposed, that Shakespeare's own sympathy with Macbeth went beyond that which every artist owes to the evil man whom he wants to realize. We may be driven to concluding that Shakespeare has kept us at one with Macbeth, in whom the good man is all but annihilated by the tragic flaw, by making him the flawed man who is all but annihilated by the tragic goodness—that is, the singular appeal of the man trapped, disappointed, deserted, deprived of a wife, finished, but unwhimpering, contemplative, unyielding. If that is so, Shakespeare has kept us at one with a murderer by making him less than, or other than, a murderer.

This may seem a perverse conclusion after we have been pointing to the 'risks' Shakespeare took by showing Macbeth lengthily arranging the murder of Banquo and by having the murder of Lady Macduff and her children done partly on stage. The risk there, however, was of our separation from Macbeth as in melodrama; the risk here is of an empathic union on too easy grounds. For what is finally and extraordinarily spared Macbeth is the ultimate rigour of self-confrontation, the act of knowing directly what he has been and done. We see the world judging Macbeth, but not Macbeth judging himself. That consciousness of the nature of the deed which he has at the murder of Duncan gives way to other disturbances, and whatever sense of guilt, if any, may be inferred from his later distresses (we surveyed, early in section iii, the passages sometimes supposed to reveal a confessional or penitent strain), is far from an open facing and defining of the evil done—the murders, of course, the attendant lying, and, as is less often noted, the repeated bearing of false witness (II, iii, 99; III, i, 29 ff.; III, iv, 49). Of Cawdor, whose structural relationship to Macbeth is often mentioned, we are told that

> very frankly he confess'd his treasons,
> Implor'd your Highness' pardon, and set forth
> A deep repentance.
>
> (I, iv, 5–7)

Macduff, with rather less on his conscience than Macbeth, could say,

> sinful Macduff,
> They were all struck for thee—nought that I am;
> Not for their own demerits, but for mine,
> Fell slaughter on their souls.   (IV, iii, 224–7)

Cawdor and Macduff set the example which Macbeth never follows; or, to go outside the play, Othello and Lear set examples that Macbeth never follows. Part of Hamlet's agonizing is centred in his passion to avoid having to set such an example. Macbeth simply does not face the moral record. Instead he is the saddened and later bereaved husband, the man deprived of friends and future, the thinker, the pathetic believer in immunity, the fighter. These roles are a way of pushing the past aside—the past which cries out for a new sense, in him, of what it has been. If, then, our hypothesis about the nature of tragic participation is valid, the reader ends his life with and in Macbeth in a way that demands too little of him. He experiences forlornness and desolation, and even a kind of substitute triumph—anything but the soul's reckoning which is a severer trial than the world's judgment. He is not initiated into a true spaciousness of character, but follows, in Macbeth, the movement of what I have called a contracting personality. This is not the best that tragedy can offer.[19]

NOTES

1. See, for instance, Wolfgang J. Weilgart, 'Macbeth: Demon and Bourgeois', *Shakespeare Society of New Orleans Publications* (1946), and its citations, as well as the citations in Kenneth Muir's Introduction to the Arden *Macbeth* (1951 ff.), pp. xlviii ff. Weilgart's ill-written essay, based on Karl Jaspers's *Psychologie der Weltanschauungen* is not uninstructive.

2. For fuller quotations and appropriate comments, see Muir, *op. cit.* pp. lix ff. The Abercrombie quotation is from *The Idea of Great Poetry*, the Knight from *The Wheel of Fire* (Knight carried the idea further in *Christ and Nietzsche*, 1948).

3. *How Many Children Had Lady Macbeth?*, pp. 54–5.

4. Introduction to his edition of *Macbeth* (Boston, 1939), p. xiv.

5. George Clifford Rosser, Critical Commentary, *Macbeth* (1957), pp. 38, 39, 40, 44. This work might be compared with a Catholic schoolboy manual, the Rev. R. F. Walker's *Companion to the Study of Shakespeare: Macbeth* (1947). The often useful application of Catholic doctrine unfortunately keeps giving way to sermons.

6. William Allan Neilson and Charles Jarvis Hill (eds.), *The Complete Plays and Poems of Shakespeare* (Boston, 1942), p. 1183.

7. Cf. Gogol's *Inspector General*, where the meaning 'The way of transgressors is hard' is conveyed exclusively through characters acting in character.

8. *Op. cit.* p. lxxiv.

9. For convenience I shall use the word 'readers' to denote literal readers, spectators at the theatre, viewers, all those who see the play on stage or in print or in any other medium. I use 'we' to denote the hypothetical possessor of characteristic responsiveness.

10. Some critics always defend apparent authority; others redefine the character who has it; still others look for artistic signs that the apparent holder of authority has been subtly disavowed. Thus, one school accepts Gulliver's view of himself and of the Houyhnhnms; another argues that the total structure of Book IV turns the satire against Gulliver. The readers who accept Moll Flanders's view of things resort to various shifts to deal with her inconsistencies; the opposite way out is to treat Moll as a product of confusions in Defoe's own mind.

11. Even when an over-valuing of Brecht's theories puts something of a halo upon the *Verfremdungseffekt* and of a shadow upon *Einfühlung*. The inevitability of *Einfühlung*, whatever its precise character, is indicated by

Brecht's having to rewrite to try to prevent it after it had appeared in responses to his own work. Perhaps, however, we need a new term like 'consentience' to suggest more than 'sympathy' but less than 'identification' or 'empathy', which suffer from popular overuse.

12. *Shakespeare: The Great Tragedies*, Writers and Their Work No. 133 (1961), p. 35. Cf. his statement that 'the Poet for the Defence . . . can make us feel that we might have fallen in the same way' (Introduction, Arden edition, p. 1, and similarly on p. lvi).

13. Gorki's *Lower Depths*, Ibsen's *Wild Duck*, and O'Neill's *Iceman Cometh* are remarkably alike in their portrayal of the need of self-protective illusions; in effect they deny the possibility of the tragic experience of illumination. But recent playwrights like Osborne, Pinter, and Albee choose an opposite course: they make the reader identify with one evil or another by giving him nowhere else to go. They permit no illusions of saving virtue (though they may foster illusions of irremediable defectiveness). This is of course the way of satire, which aspires to much less than the tragic range of personality.

14. This difficulty will of course not exist for critics who believe that Macbeth, though a lost soul, has wrenched some sort of moral triumph from his career.

15. Muir's note on the passage (Arden edition, p. 165).

16. Among the accounts of Macbeth's descent one of the most interesting is that of W. C. Curry, *Shakespeare's Philosophical Patterns* (Baton Rouge, Louisiana, 1937).

17. Muir, *Shakespeare: The Great Tragedies*, p. 36. However, Muir uses the words rather incidentally to name one of the factors that may account for the difficulty of presenting the play successfully on the stage. He may not be strongly convinced that sympathies do switch. At any rate, his words conveniently summarize a point of view probably held widely.

18. Veronica Henriques, *The Face I Had* (1965), p. 38.

19. As Muir says, ' . . . the last two acts are not quite on the level of the first three' (*Shakespeare: The Great Tragedies*, p. 36). This is a passing comment, however, again in the context of the actability of the play. Cf. G. B. Harrison, ' . . . *Macbeth* is in some ways the least satisfactory of Shakespeare's mature tragedies. The last Act falls away . . .' This is from the Introduction to the Penguin *Macbeth* (1937), p. 17. But Harrison uses this statement to introduce the subject of revisions in the text.

Besides the comparisons that have been made, there is another that has elucidatory value. Garrick added to Macbeth's lines a closing speech which in content might have been inspired by the same sense of shortcoming that prevails in the present essay, but which is in the common rhetorical vein of eighteenth-century improvements of Shakespeare:

> Tis done! the scene of life will quickly close.
> Ambition's vain delusive dreams are fled,
> And now I wake to darkness, guilt, and horror;
> I cannot bear it! let me shake it off—
> It will not be; my soul is clog'd with blood—
> I cannot rise! I dare not ask for mercy—
> It is too late, hell drags me down; I sink,
> I sink,—my soul is lost for ever!—Oh!—Oh!

(Quoted in Arden edition, p. xlvi, n. 2.) One wonders whether Garrick was remembering Marlowe's *Dr Faustus*, which *Macbeth* resembles, notably in the great ambition of the hero, in the enormous struggle at the time of the first decisive step, and in the phenomena of psychic strain. Garrick's last four lines might be a précis of Faustus's final hundred lines. But this striking fact underscores the difference in the treatment of the two heroes: Faustus sees the whole truth of his career with utmost clarity, but because of a 'block', as we would say, cannot take advantage of the grace he rightly feels is offered; Macbeth, on the other hand, lacks this clarity and hence is hardly able to advance to the next stage, where the issue is spiritual despair.

ANTITHESIS IN 'MACBETH'

BY

G. I. DUTHIE

In the Introduction to the revised Arden edition of *Macbeth* (1951)[1] Kenneth Muir notes as 'one of the predominant characteristics of the general style of the play' the fact that 'it consists of multitudinous antitheses'. He connects 'this trick of style with the "wrestling of destruction with creation" which Mr Wilson Knight[2] has found in the play, and with the opposition he has pointed out between night and day, life and death, grace and evil'. Muir also refers to Mgr Kolbe,[3] who sees the play as picturing 'a special battle in a universal war', the war between sin and grace, with a 'two-fold contrast . . . —Darkness and Light, as a parable, Discord and Concord as a result'. What I wish to say in the present essay is related to the general conception of antithesis: and, more particularly, it is related to the themes identified and analysed by L. C. Knights in *How Many Children Had Lady Macbeth?* (1933).[4] Knights states[5] that 'Two main themes, which can only be separated for the purpose of analysis, are blended in the play—the themes of the reversal of values and of unnatural disorder. And closely related to each is a third theme, that of the deceitful appearance, and consequent doubt, uncertainty and confusion.' Some of the passages to which I shall refer are discussed by Knights.

In his dramas, Shakespeare thinks of evil in many different ways. Among these is the notion that evil can produce a state of affairs in which a given entity is both one thing and the opposite thing simultaneously. This idea is inherent in, for example, the use of oxymoron. In the church scene in *Much Ado About Nothing*, Claudio rejects the supposedly evil Hero—

> But fare thee well, most foul, most fair! Farewell,
> Thou pure impiety and impious purity! (IV, i, 102–3)

While there is actual oxymoron in the second of these lines, we have, in the first, not an actual oxymoron but what may be called an expanded oxymoron. A person may be spoken of as 'foully fair'—or alternatively with the two elements separated, as 'foul and fair' or (superlatively) 'most foul, most fair'. Now the speaker's meaning is simply that Hero is very beautiful but very wicked, physically most fair but morally most foul. He speaks of physical beauty, however, as if it were to be equated with purity: and impiety is a kind of impurity; so, over and above Claudio's actual meaning, this passage suggests to us that Hero is simultaneously pure and impure, simultaneously one thing and its opposite. And Shakespeare reinforces this impression by means of the chiasmus in the second line. In the verbal patterning, 'impious purity' is the opposite of 'pure impiety', and Hero is in the same moment the one and the other. By rhetorical devices an important idea can be conveyed to audience and readers in addition to the idea that the speaker intends to convey.

In *Macbeth* Shakespeare thinks of evil as involving this conception of a given object or person being both one thing and the opposite; and attention is repeatedly drawn to this by means of phrases which suggest it even though the particular speaker does not (or may not) mean to do

25

anything of the sort. In the introductory scene we are told that the Witches will meet again when the battle is over—'When the battle's lost and won'.[6] On his first appearance in the play (I, iii, 38) Macbeth says 'So foul and fair a day I have not seen': as far as his meaning is concerned, it is foul because of the weather, fair because of his victory—but to us the words have another significance as well. A few lines later Banquo, according to the Witches, is 'Lesser than Macbeth, and greater', 'Not so happy, yet much happier'. The next line explains clearly what they mean, but the lines in question convey an additional impression to us. In II, iii, the Porter, having admitted Macduff and Lennox to the castle, speaks of drink and lechery. Drink both provokes and unprovokes lechery: 'it makes him, and its mars him; it sets him on, and it takes him off... makes him stand to, and not stand to'.[7] Drink is 'an equivocator with lechery'. Equivocation provides an important thematic strand in this play: and an equivocator can, of course, say one thing and mean the opposite, with both senses simultaneously present in his words. There are further examples of the intimate association of contraries. Lady Macduff's little son is 'Father'd... and yet he's fatherless' (IV, ii, 27). Malcolm falsely blackens his own character, and then retracts: and Macduff says

> Such welcome and unwelcome things at once
> 'Tis hard to reconcile. (IV, iii, 138–9)

Of Lady Macbeth in the final act the Doctor says that it is 'A great perturbation in nature, to receive at once the benefit of sleep and do the effects of watching' (V, i, 9–11).

Roused to activity by the Witches, and further encouraged by his wife, Macbeth's own wickedness is one of the factors which produce the state of affairs we are discussing, a state of affairs in which the normal order of things is disrupted. Yet Macbeth himself is capable of appealing to the validity of the normal order of things. He tells the bystanders that he has killed Duncan's grooms. 'Wherefore did you so?' asks Macduff: and Macbeth plunges into a desperate self-justification:

> Who can be wise, amaz'd, temp'rate and furious,
> Loyal and neutral, in a moment? No man.

His point is a simple and intelligible one: he continues—

> The expedition of my violent love
> Outrun the pauser reason. (II, iii, 107–10)

But on one level of imaginative interpretation we note that the Macbeth who tells us that a man cannot be both temperate and furious at the same time has already told us that a day can be both fair and foul at the same time. Evil involves an abnormal relationship between opposites, good involves the normal one. At this point Macbeth, who has been furthering the evil principle, appeals to the good one.[8]

Another frequent conception of evil in Shakespeare's plays is that it produces inversion. He sometimes states this explicitly, as, for instance, in *Timon of Athens* when Timon, having come to regard gold as evil, declares that it

> will make black white, foul fair,
> Wrong right, base noble, old young, coward valiant. (IV, iii, 28–9)

In *Macbeth*, on page after page of the text, the idea of inversion is found in connexion with all three levels with which the tragedy is concerned—personal, political, and cosmic. Lady Macbeth wants her milk to be changed into gall. By means of evil, meditated and executed, Macbeth puts rancours in the vessel of his peace. His castle is surrounded by an atmosphere of holy peace—the 'temple-haunting martlet' nests there: but Macbeth and his lady turn it into a hell, as the Porter-scene makes plain. Confirmed in wickedness, Macbeth, who was originally sought out by the Witches, now seeks them out; and he declares that he will have personal satisfaction

> Though palaces and pyramids do slope
> Their heads to their foundations. (IV, i, 57–8)

In 'this earthly world', where evil so often prevails, we find, according to Lady Macduff, that

> to do harm
> Is often laudable, to do good sometime
> Accounted dangerous folly. (IV, ii, 74–6)

In the kind of Scotland Macbeth creates, 'There's daggers in men's smiles' (II, iii, 139). Malcolm, painting himself as potentially unkingly and a man of vice, asserts that he would 'Pour the sweet milk of concord into hell' (IV, iii, 98). Again: sleep should bring renewed life—to Duncan it brings the reverse. And associated with the murder of Duncan we have a state of affairs in which on the next morning it is dark in daytime, and in which it is possible to recall that on the previous Tuesday a falcon, at the highest point of its flight, was killed by an owl. Shakespeare can reinforce the idea of inversion in the rhetorical sphere also, as when the bleeding sergeant, asked whether a new assault in the battle had dismayed Macbeth and Banquo, replies 'Yes' in a rhetorical pattern which indicates that his reply is a negative (I, ii, 34–5).

The idea that something is simultaneously one thing and its opposite, and the idea that something is changed into its opposite, are of course quite distinct ideas. But, as can be exemplified from various plays, the two ideas are closely associated in Shakespeare's mind. He sometimes puts them together in the same context. In the early stages of *Antony and Cleopatra* we are meant to regard Cleopatra, the corrupter of Antony, as a wicked woman but fascinating in appearance. 'I saw her once,' says Enobarbus,

> Hop forty paces through the public street:
> And, having lost her breath, she spoke, and panted,
> That she did make defect perfection,
> And, breathless, pow'r breathe forth. (II, ii, 233–6)

As she hopped through the street, Cleopatra was doing something unfitting for a queen, but, as she did it, she looked extremely attractive. That is all that Enobarbus means by saying that 'she did make defect perfection'; but the mode of expression suggests an inversion—she made one thing into its contrary. The next line is more complicated. Panting breathlessly, she exuded charm—that is all Enobarbus means. But I think that Shakespeare had a purpose in saying that she *breathed forth* charm. If we take the words simply as words, we find that on the one hand Cleopatra was without breath, and on the other hand she had breath. I cannot avoid the impression that Shakespeare wants us to think in these terms, while, of course, on the uppermost level of meaning 'breathless' does not indicate a total lack of breath, and 'breathe forth' is used figuratively. The two ideas with which we are concerned, then, appear in this passage in two contiguous lines.[9]

In *Macbeth*, when the Witches accost Macbeth and Banquo on the heath and speak to Banquo as 'Lesser than Macbeth, and greater', 'Not so happy, yet much happier', the ritualistic passage which includes these lines terminates with—

> So, all hail, Macbeth and Banquo!
> Banquo and Macbeth, all hail! (I, iii, 68–9)

On the one hand the same person, Banquo, is described as being simultaneously one thing and its opposite: and then, in the same context, we have lines which, by their word-order, suggest the concept of inversion.[10]

I have said that the two ideas are distinct. To say that a day is both foul and fair does not involve inversion: foulness and fairness co-exist in this case. And on the other hand, to suggest that on a certain day light has been turned into darkness by a direct inversion does not involve a coincidence of opposites. Nevertheless there are, in this play and others, some passages which can be seen as containing either or both of these ideas.

When Iago declares 'I am not what I am' (I, i, 66), he simply means that his outward bearing is calculated by him to give the impression of a man different from what inside he really is. The form of words, however, suggests inversion—one thing ('what I am') is changed into its opposite (what 'I am not'). But we may look at the matter in another way, again taking the word-pattern by itself. Iago *is* something ('what I am'—full value should be given to the last two words here), and at the same time he *is not* that something. By the word-pattern we are made to feel that he is simultaneously one thing and its opposite.

Having just learned that he has been made Thane of Cawdor, Macbeth stands rapt. His mind is filled with the thought that he may perhaps murder the rightful king, a thought that terrifies him. So preoccupied is he with this thought, that he is rooted to the spot; his physical functions are virtually suspended. To him at this moment, as he says, 'nothing is but what is not' (I, iii, 141). Only his thought is real to him, and his thought is unsubstantial. That is what he means. But again the wording has a significance when taken by itself. Wilson Knight comments that here 'reality and unreality change places'.[11] Certainly we may think of a double inversion, each of the two things becoming its opposite. Yet it is possible to say that Macbeth's statement conveys (or also conveys) another idea. In the phrase 'what is not' we should give full weight to the last two words. We are concerned with something which *is not*; but at the same time it *is*. It is simultaneously one thing and the opposite.

We may recall the point in *Troilus and Cressida* where Troilus cries out 'this is, and is not, Cressid' (v, ii, 144). In simple terms, this woman whom Troilus has been watching is, on the evidence of his own eyes, his Cressida, who is bound to him by her pledge of love: but her behaviour with Diomed has shown that she is altered, her feeling for Troilus has changed, and she is Diomed's Cressida. In one sense she is Cressida as of old, in another sense she is not. But there is a further idea present also (and in this case the speaker is aware of it, and does mean to convey it): this woman is, at one and the same time, both one thing (Cressid) and its opposite (not-Cressid). And this woman is a single person, 'a thing inseparate' (i.e. indivisible): yet Troilus is forced to the view that this 'thing inseparate' is in fact separable; the indivisible is in fact divisible—it is both at the same time. Troilus is agonizingly aware of the madness of the reasoning ('O madness of discourse . . .') to which his experience of a few moments ago has led him. One is, of course, inevitably led to think and express oneself in a way that seems mad if one is observing and describing a universe from which the coherence of normality has gone. Troilus's experience has led him to think of reality as a chaos in which, if we carry the matter to extremity, everything is both itself and its contrary, as if opposites were identical: all individuality, personal identity, and the distinctness of genera and of species vanish; and the universal coherence, in the context of which, and only in the context of which, our lives have value and significance to us, disappears. Direct inversion produces confusion: this other horror produces it more terribly. And Shakespeare associates the two in *Macbeth* when the protagonist tells the Witches that he will have his own way,

> Though palaces and pyramids do slope
> Their heads to their foundations; though the treasure
> Of nature's germens tumble all together,
> Even till destruction sicken.   (IV, i, 57–60)

King Lear wants the thunder to inflict a horrible fate on the world. He shouts to it—

> all germens spill at once,
> That makes ingrateful man.   (III, ii, 8–9)

And in *The Winter's Tale* we have another parallel:

> Let nature crush the sides o' th' earth together
> And mar the seeds within!   (IV, iv, 470–1)

But the *Macbeth* passage contains an idea peculiar to itself. Lear is speaking specifically of the germens that make human beings, and he wants these to be destroyed. The passage from *The Winter's Tale* relates to all nature's germens. So does that from *Macbeth*: but, though he speaks of destruction, Macbeth thinks of this as coming about through the germens being tumbled all together in confusion. The result of this would be that every species of created thing would lose its individuality[12]—all identities would lose their separateness—and the whole natural world as we know it would be destroyed. Denigrating himself, Malcolm declares that, if he could, he would

> Pour the sweet milk of concord into hell,
> Uproar the universal peace, confound
> All unity on earth.   (IV, iii, 98–100)

In the last two lines he means, no doubt, that he would create conflict all over the world and make it impossible for men and nations to live together in amity. But may not Shakespeare be using the phrase 'confound / All unity on earth' in another sense as well?—if he could, the (allegedly) evil man would, all over the earth, destroy the separateness of every identity so that chaos would come again. Commenting on a passage in *Troilus and Cressida* which we have already mentioned, D. J. Gordon speaks[13] of how 'the doubleness of Cressida—Troilus's Cressida, Diomed's Cressida, every man's Cressida—becomes . . . proof that a thing can be itself and other than itself in the same moment; and this', Gordon goes on, 'denies the principle of oneness, which guarantees being, which rests on the sacred and indivisible *unitas*:

> If there be rule in Unitie itself
> This is not she—   (V, ii, 139–40)

he cries. Being is disrupted and the fabric of the Universe torn.'

It is to such a disruption that we must in fear look forward if our imaginations are schooled by the author to think of something or someone as both lost and won, or foul and fair, or fathered and fatherless, or welcome and unwelcome—or double and single. There is a point where, in an artificial, highly-wrought, and hypocritical speech, Lady Macbeth flatters Duncan. It involves a play on words. 'All our service,' she says to the king,

> In every point twice done, and then done double,
> Were poor and single business to contend
> Against those honours deep and broad wherewith
> Your Majesty loads our house. (I, vi, 15–18)

Here the word 'double' has the usual meaning of 'twice over': and then Lady Macbeth proceeds as if it had had the meaning of 'strong', and uses 'single' as equivalent to 'weak'. We are not here concerned, however, with what she intends to convey, but with something which, beyond her own meaning, her words suggest to us—namely, that under certain circumstances that which is double (in fact twice double) would also be single. I want to stress my 'also'. It is not simply a case of double being turned into single. The double (or twice double) would remain double (or twice double) in one connexion—with reference to the service done; but it would be single in another connexion—in comparison with the honours bestowed. Then, dropping momentarily the notion of the two connexions, we are left with the idea of something being both double and single at the same time, and we may feel inclined to think of these opposites as equated (to speak in one way) or identified (to speak in another).

Evil operates in the course of the play in such a way as to produce the state of affairs I have been describing, and in so far as evil finally triumphs it is with this state of affairs that we are left. But the final triumph of evil is only partial. For Macbeth himself there is no regeneration— nor, I think, for Lady Macbeth either. But apart from this, for Scotland, and in the universe as a whole, there is a re-establishment of normality.

To take the hero first, it is true that, before he dies, Macbeth repudiates the equivocating Apparitions that the Witches had called up for him:

> And be these juggling fiends no more believ'd,
> That palter with us in a double sense. (v, viii, 19–20)

By imaginative extension we might say that he is repudiating the evil which is symptomatized by the co-existence of opposites in the same thing. At least he is able to do this: and he immediately proceeds to his final hand-to-hand combat, in which he shows a kind of nobility. Yet at the moment of his death Macbeth's conduct is absurd as well: he is violently defending something (his life) which he has come to regard as totally valueless to him. So even at the end, as far as he is concerned, opposites co-exist in the same action—the noble and the absurd, the sublime and the ridiculous. As for Lady Macbeth: in the scene in which she appears finally, she is sleeping and 'watching' at the same time. (This reminds us of Banquo's ghost, which had 'no speculation in those eyes / Which [it did] glare with' (III, iv, 95–6), an unnatural state of affairs against which Macbeth, architect of disorder himself, protests.) But almost her last words in the play are 'What's done cannot be undone' (v, i, 66). She is, of course, recalling the past: but, considering her words here by themselves, we may perhaps regard them as suggesting that she now realizes that a thing cannot be itself and its opposite at the same time. She too may here be imaginatively taken as repudiating the evil which is thus symptomatized. At least she is able to do this. Yet in her case too there remains finally the association of contraries. She goes on, 'To bed, to bed, to bed', and these are her last words of all. Again she is recalling the past. But the words themselves suggest the restoration of life through sleep, whereas actually, it appears, she kills herself.

For them there is no regeneration. But for Scotland there is a restoration of the blessings of order, and this is brought about with divine assistance. Help comes from the 'pious' Edward who, by a divine gift, can heal sickness; and the sickness of Scotland is finally healed. 'Things at the worst will cease,' says Ross, 'or else climb upward / To what they were before' (IV, ii, 24–5). The second of these alternatives comes to pass: and the pattern is one of inversion succeeded by reinversion. Duncan is a 'sainted' king (IV, iii, 109): he is killed, and an unnatural night ensues—night encroaches on the province of day—day is inverted into night (cf. II, iv, 6 ff.); and that unnatural night, by reinversion, becomes day again with the help of another 'holy' king. As Malcolm says,

> the pow'rs above
> Put on their instruments. Receive what cheer you may;
> The night is long that never finds the day.   (IV, iii, 238–40)

Towards the end of the scene containing Macbeth's disastrous banquet, he asks his wife 'What is the night?' and she replies 'Almost at odds with morning, which is which' (III, iv, 127). Dover Wilson sees in this 'a symbolical timing of the central moment of the play; borne out by the immediate reference to Macduff who is to usher in the dawn'.[14] On one level this is a true interpretation: but, on the other hand, there is much more evil to come. If there is an immediate reference to Macduff, there is also an almost immediate statement of Macbeth's further dreadful plans. And one may be tempted to see in III, iv, 127 another case of something being at once one thing and the contrary: for at this point, Lady Macbeth implies, night and day are disputing which is which—their identities are not distinct—it is a time of twilight in which, so to speak, night and day are simultaneously present and indistinguishable. Thus evil is still in the air. That is, I think, the main point. But another idea may occur to us in addition: if evil is present, symbolized by the confusion of night with day, the element of day may eventually be separated out and may, in its own single identity, ultimately prevail.

Certainly, taking the play as a whole, there is (not for Macbeth or his lady, but on the social and political plane for Scotland, and in the universe at large) the pattern of inversion followed by reinversion. In the last scene of Act II, in which we have the description of the disorders whereby daytime is dark, and so on, the final lines are spoken by the Old Man. Ross has just taken his leave of him, and the Old Man says—

> God's benison go with you, and with those
> That would make good of bad, and friends of foes.   (II, iv, 40–1)

Though the authenticity of part of this has sometimes been questioned, the couplet excellently fits the design which runs through the whole work. It points forward to the reinversion. I agree with the comments of Watkins and Lemmon.[15] 'God's benison go with you' is certainly spoken to Ross; but then—surely—after that (as these commentators say) 'the old man is alone—alone with us—as he finishes his couplet like the utterance of an oracle. . . . It is a cadence of great beauty, looking forward from the depths of unnatural darkness to the daylight of deliverance which ends the play.' I am sure that this is right—though in these lines themselves the old man is not actually concerned with the imagery of darkness and light, but with the coming reinversion on the moral and social planes. Through the evil which is at the moment triumphant, fair has been inverted into foul, good has been inverted into bad: and, on the social and political plane, friends have been inverted into foes. In the end, a reinversion will come under the direction of God. Perhaps, as we have said, Ross is meant to hear only 'God's benison go with you', and not the rest: but we, the audience, hear it all, and we associate the reinversion with the Divine. And, if we turn to the end of the play, we find Malcolm saying

> We have met with foes
> That strike beside us. (v, vii, 28–9)

The pattern of inversion and reinversion is well illustrated within a limited compass (and specifically in the political sphere) in the scene in England in which, speaking to Macduff, Malcolm first tells of all his unkingly qualities (inverting his true nature), and then unspeaks his self-detraction, reinverting. That Malcolm has a perfectly rational motive for doing this is beside the point, as is the fact that the material for this episode comes from Holinshed. The author makes himself responsible for what he accepts from his source as well as for what he changes; and we are entitled to take it that in this episode Shakespeare has a purpose that conforms with his general dramatic design. It is not only that he has here an opportunity to describe at length the nature of the good king and the nature of the bad king, which relates to the theme of the antithesis between order and disorder: but he is also able to present, by illustration, this process of inversion and reinversion which is so important in the play as a whole.[16] And in the last section of this scene, in another way, he produces the same effect. Ross tells Macduff of the murder of his wife and children. His first announcement of it is a piece of equivocation: the wife and children are 'well' and 'at peace'. In one sense this is false, in another sense true. The one thing and its opposite co-exist in the same words. But, having said that, we may concentrate on the fact that, on the face of it, the statement that Lady Macduff and her children are well is an inversion of the truth: and then, a little later, Ross reinverts, and relates the literal facts of the matter.

At the end, then, political order is restored and universal coherence is re-established, with a beneficent Providence triumphant. All things needful for the regenerated Scotland Malcolm will perform 'by the grace of Grace'; and it is significant that at this closing moment of the drama, in the verbal pattern, the word 'grace' is firmly and unequivocally associated with itself and itself alone.

© G. I. DUTHIE 1966

NOTES

1. Pp. xxxiii–xxxiv.

2. In *The Imperial Theme* (1931, 1951 reprint), p. 153.

3. In *Shakespeare's Way* (1930), pp. 21–2.

4. Reprinted in *Explorations* (1946), pp. 1 ff.

5. *Explorations*, p. 18.

6. Knights (*Explorations*, p. 18) says that both this and the word 'hurly-burly' suggest 'the kind of metaphysical pitch-and-toss that is about to be played with good and evil'.

7. See the revised Arden edition, p. xxxiii.

8. It may be said that Macbeth is here speaking hypocritically for his own purposes. On the other hand, it is possible that his words at II, iii, 107–8 are meant to reflect that side of his nature which genuinely desires order. Throughout most of the play, there is a conflict within the hero between impulses towards and away from order. Cf. note 12 below.

9. Cf. S. L. Bethell, *Shakespeare and the Popular Dramatic Tradition* (1944), pp. 125–6.

10. Shakespeare has a quite different point in reversing the names here from the point he has in doing so with Rosencrantz and Guildenstern in *Hamlet*, II, ii, 33–4.

11. *The Wheel of Fire* (1930, 1949 reprint), p. 153.

12. Knights (*Explorations*, p. 24) refers to III, i, 91–100, where Macbeth lists separate kinds of dogs. 'Macbeth names each one individually': this 'is an image of order, each one in his degree'; it is 'a symbol of the order that Macbeth wishes to restore'. See above, note 8.

13. In *Papers Mainly Shakespearian*, ed. G. I. Duthie (1964), p. 51.

14. *Macbeth* (The New Shakespeare, 1947), p. 142.

15. *The Tragedy of Macbeth* (The Harrow Shakespeare, 1964), p. 104.

16. In *English Studies Today, Second Series* (International Association of University Professors of English, Bern, 1961), pp. 121–2, I have suggested that the inversion/reinversion pattern is symptomatized by the use of the word 'plant' as a 'life-image' at I, iv, 28: as a 'death-image' at III, i, 128; and as a 'life-image' again at V, viii, 65—these being the only occurrences of the word in the play. The pattern of inversion and reinversion is found elsewhere also in Shakespeare—e.g. in *The Taming of the Shrew*, where, at IV, v, 2 ff., Petruchio makes Katharine refer to the sun as the moon, and then makes her refer to it as the sun. See *Annales de la Faculté des Lettres et Sciences Humaines d'Aix*, Tome XXXVIII, Deuxième Fascicule (1964), p. 251.

WHY WAS DUNCAN'S BLOOD
GOLDEN?

BY

W. A. MURRAY

This article[1] is the account of an investigation of the meaning of a single line in the play *Macbeth*, a line which had been for many years a puzzle to me, until, in the course of a quite different inquiry, an answer finally suggested itself out of discoveries made in trying to reconstruct a vanished mental world which was quite familiar to Shakespeare and his audiences. My title refers to the point in the play *Macbeth* just after the discovery of Duncan's murder by Macduff and the slaughter by Macbeth of the two drugged and innocent grooms. When Macduff, in that dagger-pointed atmosphere of suspicion which always follows assassinations, whether of ancient Scottish kings or of modern American presidents, asks Macbeth 'Wherefore did you so?', Macbeth replies:

> Who can be wise, amaz'd, temp'rate and furious,
> Loyal and neutral, in a moment? No man.
> The expedition of my violent love
> Outrun the pauser reason. Here lay Duncan,
> His silver skin lac'd with his golden blood;
> And his gash'd stabs look'd like a breach in nature
> For ruin's wasteful entrance: there, the murderers,
> Steep'd in the colours of their trade, their daggers
> Unmannerly breech'd with gore. Who could refrain,
> That had a heart to love, and in that heart
> Courage to make's love known?

Thirty years ago, when I was studying *Macbeth* in serious detail for the first time, I risked the displeasure of a fierce Scots dominie by asking him why Duncan's blood was golden. The answer which he gave me, and which I am afraid did not satisfy me, was the selfsame quotation from Dr Johnson which is reproduced in the best of modern editions, the Arden *Macbeth*.[2] It is certainly the most complimentary to Shakespeare of a number of similar eighteenth-century notes, and it runs thus: 'It is not improbable that Shakespeare put these forced and unnatural metaphors into the mouth of Macbeth as a mark of artifice and dissimulation, to show the difference between the studied language of hypocrisy and the natural outcries of sudden passion. The whole speech, so considered, is a remarkable instance of judgment, as it consists entirely of antithesis and metaphor.' Johnson's tentative 'not improbable' shows, I think, that he himself thought his explanation something of a last resort, for the speech was a recognized difficulty, and had been freely altered both by actors and by editors.[3]

There was already, by this time, a general problem of Shakespearian meaning, for the Civil War, the Commonwealth, the Restoration, and the Enlightenment had all changed the English language in their various ways, and had profoundly altered the English sensibility.

Accordingly I begin my own solution with a general look at the conditions of Shakespeare's use of language. The stage conditions of Jacobean dramatic art imposed some fairly difficult demands upon the language of the dramatic poet. The prerequisite of success was rapid understanding by the audience. Creation of scene, human situation, emotion and thought, had to be achieved on a bare but intimate stage, in a rapid succession of scenes. These conditions imply, for the successful dramatist, a language of immediate and vivid communication, with adequate resources of subtlety, in which words, images, units of meaning, operate with a minimum of interference; a language which controls the actors, yet offers them as rich an opportunity as possible.

Shakespeare lived in an age when obscurity in a dramatic poem was not a fashionable virtue. He disliked empty bombast, as he himself makes Hamlet tell us: he avoids sterile patterns of rhetoric for rhetoric's sake, except when using them for special effects, as in Brutus' speech to the Roman mob. Although he could, no doubt, presume that a large part of his audience were familiar with formal tricks of style, he is not guilty of exploiting these for the sake of cleverness. Indeed Shakespeare produced that rarity in the history of art, sophisticated work of the highest quality which was at the same time popular.

When we encounter an obscurity, then, like Duncan's golden blood, we should beware of calling it a rhetorical device, or a bombastic Jacobean quaintness—we should look instead to see whether it might, perhaps, be part of some special language of the period. We should at least look for the causes of an immediate effect, an immediate meaning, in the theatre of the first performance.

Although by now we have turned Shakespeare into a world figure, the source of a great academic industry, we are apt to forget that he is one of the *least literary* of playwrights. When Professor Caroline Spurgeon in the 1930's completed her great arithmetical analysis of Shakespeare's imagery, much as one may disagree with her criteria and her classifications, she did show, scientifically, Shakespeare's tremendous sensitivity to the language of the daily life of his time in all its different varieties. It is the stuff of his work. His meaning is embedded in its associations. He assumes that its normal contexts are familiar to his audience. He relies on these, and not just on the stage business or the voices of his actors, for the immediacy and the precision of his communication. Yet he was also a great originator of poetry. He felt free to break and recombine the common associations of words and images, and, as we are increasingly aware nowadays, he was in the best sense an intellectual, vividly alive to mental experiences, and possessed by a complex vision of the real.

I propose therefore to attempt the solution of my small problem within that of a larger one, by reconstructing the special non-literary associations of some of the key images in *Macbeth*, thus recreating something of the original mental framework in which they conveyed their meaning to the audience which heard them for the first time. *Macbeth* is a play especially suitable for this exercise. From Dowden in 1875 to Jan Kott in 1964 every critic of the play has noticed the strong thematic structure of the imagery, for Macbeth is one of Shakespeare's most carefully integrated dramatic poems.

Before I come down to details of the Jacobean material, however, I should like to dwell a little on the important word 'association', and illustrate it with a modern instance or two. If I say to those of you who are about my own age 'It's that man again', most of you will recall not just Tommy Handley, but a whole system of verbal catch phrases and images, to explain which to any outsider we would have to describe quite a lot of recent English history. 'It's that man again' belongs therefore to a group or *matrix* of associations, which I could exploit if I wished and use as a variety of language. In the same way, if I suddenly shout 'There's a beetle', grandmothers and teenage daughters, and for all I know some long-haired sons, may scream, though for very different reasons! Their reasons are different because a *matrix of associations* is a structure in human memories, in time, in a shared social experience, of which its special language is the distillation and the model. Groups of associations differ with age-group and decay with the changes of human life. They appear, they flourish, they vanish or leave traces, in an endless irreversible series. The entertainments of the stage have always been specially apt to make use of the current, even the ephemeral, associations of the language of everyday speech and of the more familiar and topical books, and in this respect the drama of Shakespeare's time is no exception.

What sort of associative matrix, then, do I need for my present purpose with *Macbeth*? It must be one which faded out before the mid-eighteenth century. It must be one which will bring in as many as possible of the main images of the play. It must be one demonstrably topical for an audience of 1606, demonstrably accessible and familiar to Shakespeare, and rich enough linguistically and conceptually to supply him with material for his poetry. The common consensus of critics gives us the main elements which our matrix should combine. From Dowden[4] we may take the 'zymotic poison of sin', the disease of the fallen world, and the imagery of blood. From Monsignor Kolbe[5] we may take imagery of blood, sleep, and the concept of Chaos; from Caroline Spurgeon the imagery of sin as a disease, and the imagery of the human body. The common knowledge we all have of the play will suggest the spirits, witches, and ghosts, the rituals of witchcraft, and necromancy, and Bucknill will remind us of the actual references to medicine.

There happens to be one, and only one, *associative matrix* of the period which combines *all* these elements, and which satisfies our other requirements. It consists of a body of writing connected with, and influenced by, the new medicine of the sixteenth-century German doctor Theophrastus von Hohenheim, who latinized his name as Paracelsus, and whose theories and remedies became a great storm-centre of controversy exactly at this time, so much so that Paul Kocher, an American scholar in this field of history, has written that between 1590 and 1600 every educated person in England must have learned something of his works. King James VI and I himself shows detailed knowledge of them in his *Counterblaste to Tobacco*, and appointed a Paracelsian doctor as one of his own physicians.[6]

Ever since the researches of Bucknill[7] in the last century it has been recognized that Shakespeare had some very precise knowledge of contemporary medicine. His son-in-law, who married Susannah Shakespeare in 1607, was Dr John Hall, in the pages of whose case-books we find *Laudanum Paracelsi* prescribed, and who may well have possessed some of the works. *Macbeth* was written between 1603 and 1605. The main Latin translation of the Swiss-German writings of Paracelsus was published at intervals between 1598 and 1605,[8] and was readily available in England. Its influence was far more rapid and widespread than that of the new astronomy, for it had to do with the health of human beings, and the nature of their psychology, both matters of vital concern. Paracelsus also had as a principle the spreading of medical knowledge amongst laymen, and his followers attempted to do so.

From what I have already written it must be evident that the medical writings of Paracelsus are vastly unlike those of our own medical science. They are, to the modern mind, a strange amalgam of lists of weird remedies, discussions of the nature of disease, speculation about the nature of the soul and its relations with the body, opinions on the Bible's meanings, essays on magic, spirits, witchcraft, cabbalistic signs, astrology and so on. People read these books for all sorts of purposes, from seeking a cure for colic to understanding their wives.

Paracelsus was the first doctor-chemist or iatrochymist: he combined the practice of medicine with that of alchemy, which he understood not as the making of gold, but as the making of remedies to refine and purify and protect the human body from the diseases of mortality. He was deeply religious, indeed mystical in character. His language, drawing on the Bible, and on alchemy, is so rich in images and strange new words that its quality comes across strongly even in translation from his vernacular into Latin. It was a quarry for many poets, both in France and in England, amongst whom were Du Bartas, the friend of James VI and I, Donne, George Herbert, Herbert of Cherbury and Webster. Ben Jonson's *Volpone*, and especially his *Alchemist*, both close to *Macbeth* in date, rely on the audience's familiarity with this type of language.

The world, as Paracelsus conceived it, was extremely complex. It consisted of many varieties of chaos, and many varieties of order. It was a world in which health was a rare neutrality between warring forces, in which everything was in movement either upwards in the scale of being towards perfect order, or downward towards complete disorder. There was no sharp separation between matter and spirit, between living and non-living. Transmutation towards perfection could happen to human flesh as well as to the human soul. Man was a little universe, containing in himself the elements of the whole *Macrocosm*, the great cosmos, a word which Paracelsus himself invented for the needs of his theory.[9] At every point there was a mystical correspondence between Man and the Universe. Man's body had its earthquakes, and the earth its fevers. (See Lennox's speech on the morning after the murder.) Man's body contained all the elements, his spirit contained all the beasts.

Man shared this universe with an inhuman multitude, with gnomes and salamanders, undines, sylphs, and giants. He himself gave rise to spirit forms, to ghosts of the dead, and astral bodies of the living. Man's very blood was thought to have a life of its own, to beget 'spirits as like souls as it can', to flow when a murderer approached, and so on. Chaos produced at every turn new monsters, new diseases, yet the skilled doctor-alchemist, working by what Paracelsus called the light of nature, that burning intuition of truth which sometimes comes to men, could preserve the health and sanity of man, even in the fallen world. He was, indeed, the channel of the physical healing power of Christ.

This world of images and concepts, then, was an important part of the mutual experience of Shakespeare and his audiences. The apparent system which it displayed, the order which it claimed to give to a chaotic mass both of folk belief and religious tradition, had a strong appeal to the growing rationalism of the Jacobean mind—it seemed to serve reason, yet to retain the spiritual world within the realities of everyday life. If the king, James VI and I, may be considered typical of the more learned of his subjects, we may notice that he was the author of a book called *Demonologie*, that he took a profound interest in witches, and that broadly speaking he believed that a denial of the existence of one part of the world of spirit meant a denial of it all. He certainly rejected the Baconian attitude, the conscious split between things of reason and things of faith, from which our modern scientific rationalism developed. Shakespearian minds therefore made no division between what we might call the natural and the supernatural. They accepted miracles. They accepted physical damnation and physical salvation as facts—as facts capable of being experienced and visualized. The structure of their notions of reality was very different indeed from ours. However much, therefore, you may like to think of Shakespeare as though he were an intelligent contemporary, far too bright to be so superstitious, the evidence is perfectly clear that he is NOT a contemporary. He was pre-scientific. The witches in *Macbeth* are not accidental, nor are they pantomime figures. They are part of a unified world of the imagination.

I come now to a few direct demonstrations of the way in which the Paracelsian associations helped to improve the poetic communication of *Macbeth*. Since it is the mark of a good theory to be as inclusive of as widely different data as possible, I shall try to cover in this demonstration all the aspects of the imagery which I have collected from previous critics. I begin with a point of detail, which, though simple, is typical of a class of relationship between the text and these external associations. Paracelsus had a systematic theory of the nature of elemental spirits, which he summed up in his pamphlet on earth and fire spirits, roughly as follows: 'A creature of this kind is more tenuous the denser the matter [Chaos] to which it belongs, and denser the more rarified the matter to which it belongs.'[10] This means that the most tenuous of all spirits are earth spirits, which have to live in the earth-chaos and move through it. As Banquo puts it, when the three weird sisters vanish:

> The earth hath bubbles, as the water has,
> And these are of them. Whither are they vanish'd?
>   *Macbeth*. Into the air; and what seem'd corporal melted
> As breath into the wind.

Shakespeare has made poetry from a fashionable theory of spirit nature, which our more mundane age would no doubt call the inverse density principle of elementals and relegate to a separate section of the department of physics. There are many examples of this type in the play, but more generally useful, in unifying the language of the play, is my next quotation, which helps us to sharpen our perception that Lady Macbeth and the witches are involved in a common group of associations of language. It runs: 'Where the sunlight, there the devils. For the created universe is double, is our world, and is Hell. But to the devils who are in daylight the sun is darkness.'[11] In the play the weird sisters are called by Macbeth 'How now, you secret dark and midnight hags', and they have as their theme lines:

> Fair is foul, and foul is fair:
> Hover through the fog and filthy air.

Their universe is permanently dark, a permanent chaos of earth and air, impenetrable to the eye of heaven, but it is also our universe. Lady Macbeth belongs to the same darkness of hell, to the sightless world of the elements, as she herself is made to say in her horrid dedication of herself to evil, full of physiological images:

> The raven himself is hoarse
> That croaks the fatal entrance of Duncan
> Under my battlements. Come, you spirits

> That tend on mortal thoughts, unsex me here;
> And fill me, from the crown to the toe, top-full
> Of direst cruelty. Make thick my blood,
> Stop up th' access and passage to remorse,
> That no compunctious visitings of nature
> Shake my fell purpose nor keep peace between
> Th' effect and it. Come to my woman's breasts,
> And take my milk for gall, you murd'ring ministers,
> Wherever in your sightless substances
> You wait on nature's mischief. Come, thick night,
> And pall thee in the dunnest smoke of hell,
> That my keen knife see not the wound it makes,
> Nor heaven peep through the blanket of the dark
> To cry 'Hold, hold'.

Paracelsus, discussing the whereabouts of Hell, wrote: 'Either the damned must be below us deprived of all force and delight, or they must be banished into the substance of the elements. For that is the greatest Hell, that they should become the mortal world, and dwell there. Nor could there be a fiercer Hell for an eternal being which has no part in mortality than to be compelled to exist in the world of death.'[11]

Shakespeare, later in the play, will identify Macbeth's castle with hell in the porter scene, which is based on the duality of this world and hell, and will give her the ineffaceable mark of a witch, the secret sign for which the witch-finders were in the habit of looking, and to which she refers in the famous line: 'Out, damned spot! out, I say!' Naturally at the end of her life her eyes are open but sightless. 'Their sense is shut.'

Critics have noticed before that Lady Macbeth re-enacts the Fall of Eve, as Macbeth does that of Adam. If we may classify their Falls like modern attributes of married life, into His and Hers, *hers* is almost immediate and unreasoning, *his* is full of intellectual arguments and struggles of the reason. This corresponds well to the division of qualities between the sexes in the speculative medicine, in which mind was a male quality only. Lady Macbeth, who uses at least one image directly associated with the Fall, resembles Webster's Vittoria Corombona, the White Devil, another opposite of Mary, the mother of redemption, the symbol of compassion, whom Paracelsus called the new Eve. When Lady Macbeth calls upon the spirits to unsex her it is the compassion of the new Eve, and a share in the eternal motherhood, that she chooses to abandon. (Pity, you will recall, appears in the play in the image of a naked, new-born babe, riding the elemental spirits of the wind.)

Macbeth, on the other hand, as I have said, uses much more of the language of reasoning, and with it many more of the technical expressions of my sources. For example, when we hear him describe the dagger in the air:

> Art thou not, fatal vision, sensible
> To feeling as to sight? or art thou but
> A dagger of the mind, a false creation,
> Proceeding from the heat-oppressed brain?

we should recall that for the audience mental images were material, were actually made of a substance with a technical name, which Shakespeare later referred to in *The Tempest* as the 'stuff that dreams are made on';[12] that the light by which we observe was then supposed to be generated in our brains, and to move, carrying the power of perception with it, from the eye to the object. Macbeth's language is the exact language of the speculative medicine. The same is true of the famous description of sleep:

> Balm of hurt minds, great nature's second course,

which identifies sleep with Paracelsus's general balsam of nature,[13] the mysterious power of growth and healing which he used to explain the curing of wounds and disease. Much Paracelsian medicine was devoted to the purgation of poisons which we were supposed to have taken in from the chaos of the world, and to the protection of the patient so that nature itself could heal. (*Homo et medicina unum sunt*—cf. v, iii, 45 where the Doctor seems to echo this.) The most overtly medical speech of Macbeth is significantly one which uses Paracelsian images of purgation, not Galenist images of correction of balance, and implies that Shakespeare's knowledge of medical sources was pretty close and accurate:

> If thou coulds't, doctor, cast
> The water of my land, find her disease,
> And purge it to a sound and pristine health,
> I would applaud thee to the very echo,
> That should applaud again.—Pull't off, I say.—
> What rhubarb, senna, or what purgative drug,
> Would scour these English hence?

The language of Macbeth himself is thus often technical. It also unites a number of our important elements and themes. He uses the imagery of disease, he is at the heart of Chaos. When he consults the Weird Sisters for the second time, he is made to invoke the total ruin of nature in a universal chaos:

> ... though the treasure
> Of nature's germens tumble all together,
> Even till destruction sicken—answer me
> To what I ask you;

and this image is merely the extension of that in which the murder of Duncan was first described:

> Confusion now hath made his masterpiece.
> Most sacrilegious murder hath broke ope
> The Lord's anointed temple ...

which brings me, at length, to the murder of Duncan, to the imagery of blood, of gold and silver, of sainthood and its powers, and the appropriate associative background in my sources. I begin with a rather lengthy quotation from a short work of Paracelsus called *De Sanguine Ultra Mortem*, which means *About the Blood beyond Death*:[14]

For if by Christ's example we are to be raised from the tomb, needs must that we bring with us that blood which we shed on earth. For on that day He will return to each one of us what he possessed on earth, what he took into the earth with him, whether it putrified with him, or whether he was burned, or suffocated, or devoured by birds or wild beasts, or consumed in any other fashion ... And the witness of the Apocalypse itself is the sign of the incorruptible blood, which will be such on the last day. If we shall appear at the last Judgment as we were on Earth, surely we can appear on earth (after our deaths but before that day) should need require it. The Apocalypse is the document on account of which we can deny neither Judgment nor Resurrection. There we shall see the blood, the true blood of Man, without alloy or adulteration, the blood of our natural inheritance, and its definite multitude and quantity, not one drop lacking. Those who go beyond our Faith in philosophizing cannot grasp and understand that the blood which oozes out (from a body when the murderer approaches) is the real blood of that man from whom it flows, as real as the blood which the murderer sheds. For those who lack faith in the Resurrection cannot understand that the *blood is held in the hand of God*, and kept for the time appointed, unless, should there be need meanwhile, it may appear and flow.

This is a passage the language of which is strikingly like that which Donne used in his sermons on the Resurrection, in St Paul's, not so long after the date of *Macbeth*. It may serve to give a common background to many things in the play, from the appearance of Banquo's ghost to Lady Macbeth's 'Yet who would have thought the old man to have had so much blood in him'. This background is essential to our general understanding of the strange qualities of Duncan's blood. Duncan, you will remember, was that rarity of human history, a saintly king, and this implied a special status and power in the world of matter. Edward the Confessor, who also has some images of sainthood in this play, healed with a touch, and invested gold medallions with healing power. Macbeth's awareness of the mystical power of Duncan's blood is clearly evident just after the murder, in the famous image of the reddened sea, which rests upon a common alchemical concept, that of the *tincture*;[15] for the working of which Shakespeare used the very unusual verb 'incarnadine' which means to change into the crimson of flesh:

> Will all great Neptune's ocean wash this blood
> Clean from my hand? No; this my hand will rather
> The multitudinous seas incarnadine,
> Making the green one red.

After the murder, therefore, the audience would instantly take the point that Duncan's blood has become an alchemical tincture, an enormously strong colouring agent made of perfected matter, which has the power of transmuting substances, a notion almost commonplace to them. The poet John Donne, at about this time, and through the influence of the same sources, actually used the image of the tincture to describe the power of Christ to save both *soul* and *body*:

> Hee was all gold when he lay downe, but rose
> All tincture, and doth not alone dispose
> Leaden and iron wills to good, but is
> Of power to make even sinfull flesh like his.

Christ, says Donne, can by his alchemy of the tincture turn even sinful flesh into the everlasting perfection of gold. We have now assembled quite a few of the pieces of background needed to explain the language in which Macbeth speaks of Duncan. I need but one more before I turn again to look at the riddle with which I began. It would be satisfying to discover gold and silver together in this sort of context and fortunately this is possible. From Donne's *Anatomie of the Worlde*, in which he made the dead daughter of his patron, Robery Drury, a symbol of Christian perfection, come the following lines:

> She, of whose Soule if we may say 'twas Gold,
> Her body was the Electrum, and did hold
> Many degrees of that; we understood
> Her by her sight; her pure and eloquent blood
> Spoke in her cheeks, and so distinctly wrought
> That one might almost say her body thought.

In this we have blood given intelligent life; a soul that is made of gold—as nowadays, in a late survival of this kind of language, we still talk of a *heart of gold*; and a body made of Electrum. Electrum was an alloy of gold and *silver*, as well as being, in alchemy, the last stage of matter before perfection. (It is worth noting that this is from a public poem of Donne, and that, although his readers thought it extravagant praise, even blasphemous, they did not fail to understand it.)

Let us turn finally, then, to Duncan's golden blood. Remember Macbeth's character—ruthless ambition, corrupted will, perverted reason, but, above all, a visual faculty subject to the creation of its own hallucinations. After the actual deed he had refused to return to the dead king's room, to arrange the scene against discovery:

> *Macbeth:*   I'll go no more:
> I am afraid to think what I have done . . .
>   *Lady Macbeth:* . . . Infirm of purpose !
> Give me the daggers.

When Macduff shoots at him the pointed question, 'Wherefore did you so?', Macbeth, as Dr Johnson rightly suspected, first puts on the smooth manner which conceals guilt:

> Who can be wise, amaz'd, temp'rate, and furious,
> Loyal and neutral, in a moment? No man.
> The expedition of my violent love
> Outrun the pauser reason.

Then suddenly he finds himself visualizing that which he did not dare to look on. He says, not 'There lay Duncan' which would be more natural, but, with a gesture, '*Here lay Duncan*', and instantly the body of the murdered saint is before his eyes. Like Banquo's ghost or the air-drawn dagger he sees it as real—real but glorified. Its skin shines with the silver light of heaven in his own hellish darkness, and as he watches the blood of the murdered saintly king glows and flows in the presence of the murderer. It is golden, for it is already in the hand of God. It is part of the perfection of heaven. Macbeth's wild line is wrung from him by his vision. His emotion, though it springs from guilt, is real enough, and except for Lady Macbeth the others do not *know* its cause. Lady Macbeth, who is well aware of what is in her husband's imagination, faints at the end of this speech, before he can betray himself. She creates a diversion, but already suspicion has reached the level of action. Donalbain says near the end of the scene,

> ... the near in blood,
> The nearer bloody.

The brothers escape, and Macbeth's judgment on earth has begun.

I think that there is little doubt that many members of Shakespeare's audience would have seen his image in this way. We have direct evidence that, for example, Simon Forman, the alchemist, was an assiduous member of Shakespeare's public, and to him and to his many clients this kind of language must have been very familiar. Although I have chosen, on this occasion, to work with a detail, I consider that it is a significant detail, the kind which raises some general questions. We appear to be entering a period in which Shakespeare is due for another eighteenth-century mauling. Acting versions are becoming less tied to the established text, criticism is become detached from study of the language, and particularly from the complex and frustrating study of linguistic associations. The results are visible in an extreme form in recent stage versions, and in books like Professor Jan Kott's *Shakespeare, Our Contemporary*. I should like to have had time to comment in detail upon his essay '*Macbeth*, or death infected' but I must content myself instead with wondering how Professor Kott avoided noticing that the subject of the play is not a mechanical struggle for power, as he says, nor what he calls the 'Auschwitz experience' but *sacrilegious murder and damnation*, a variant of the Faust theme, in fact. Professor Kott manages to avoid noticing that the play contains a repetition of the Fall, and not ONE but TWO saintly kings. It is, if ever a poem was so, a *traditional Catholic Christian poem*, the moral vitality of which is rooted in an uncompromising medieval faith, and in a pre-scientific view of the nature of reality. Consequently it preserves in a tremendously powerful and well unified set of images one of the greatest forces in Western European culture, a force which, however alien it may be to many of us today, we can afford neither to forget, nor to neglect, for it contains and can still convey, much of the wisdom of human experience.

© W. A. MURRAY 1966

NOTES

1. Originally given in May 1965, as an Inaugural Lecture in the new University of Lancaster.

2. *Macbeth*, Arden edition, Act II, scene iii, p. 68.

3. See the Variorum edition, *loc. cit.*

4. Dowden, *Shakespeare: His Mind and Art* (1875), p. 247.

5. Mgr F. C. Kolbe, *Shakespeare's Way: a Psychological Study* (London, 1930).

6. Theodore Turquet de Mayerne. For Kocher's account of the Paracelsians in England see *Bull. Hist. Med.* (1947), p. 475.

7. Bucknill, *The Medical Knowledge of Shakespeare* (1860), see esp. pp. 12, 23, 44.

8. See Ferguson, *Bibliotheca Chemica* (Glasgow, 1906), and Sudhoff, *Bibliography of Paracelsus* (Berlin, 1894). References to the text of Paracelsus in this article are to the Geneva folio edition of 1658, which was substantially a reprint of the edition of Palthenius, the Latin translation of the originals most likely to have been available to Shakespeare's contemporaries. I refer to the Geneva folio as *Opera Omnia*, followed by volume in Roman and page in Arabic numerals.

9. See Conger, *Macrocosms and Microcosms* (New York, 1922), pp. 55–60, for a summary of Paracelsus' use of these terms, and his place in their history.

10. *De Nymphis, Sylphis, Pygmaeis et Salamandris*, Tractatus II, *Opera Omnia*, II, 392: 'Et quo crassius est chaos, eo subtilior est creatura. Contra, quo chaos est

subtilius, eo crassior est creatura.' The word 'chaos', which for the sake of immediate clarity I have rendered as 'matter', strictly means in this context the surrounding material disorder from which the creature emerges, or is formed, and in which it then moves and has its being.

11. *Philosophiae Sagacis*, Liber IV, *Opera Omnia*, II, 640. See also II, 329.

12. The Paracelsian name was *Ares*, almost exactly Shakespeare's 'baseless fabric of this vision' (*Tempest*, IV, i). See *Opera Omnia*, II, 57: 'Sic etiam proprietas ac natura corporum supercoelestium, ut ex Nihilo plane imaginationem constituant corporalem, quod corpus esse solidum existimetur. Eiusmodi est enim *Ares* ut si lupum speculatio referat, lupus appareat . . .'

13. Main ideas in *Opera Omnia*, I, 170, 130; II, 91.

14. *Opera Omnia*, II, 465 ff.

15. Paracelsus, like other alchemists, seems to have regarded *tinctures* as the agents of transmutation. He regarded man as having two tinctures in his body, one from his animal nature, and one from his divine nature. See *Opera Omnia*, I, 360 and II, 20.

IMAGE AND SYMBOL IN 'MACBETH'

BY

KENNETH MUIR

A good deal has been written about the imagery of *Macbeth* since Caroline Spurgeon showed[1] that the iterative image was that of a man in ill-fitting garments. It has been pointed out, for example, that the image can be interpreted in more than one way and that we need not necessarily suppose that Shakespeare looked on his hero as a small man in garments too large for him: we may rather suppose that the point of the image is that the garments were stolen or that they symbolize the hypocrisy to which Macbeth is reluctantly committed when he embarks on his career of crime. It has also been pointed out[2] that this particular image should be considered in relation to a wider group of tailoring images, of which the imaginary tailor, admitted by the Porter of Hell-gate, may be regarded as a kind of patron.[3]

What is more important is that, since the publication of R. B. Heilman's books on *King Lear* and *Othello*,[4] W. H. Clemen's *The Development of Shakespeare's Imagery* and G. Wilson Knight's series of interpretations, Miss Spurgeon's concentration on a single iterative image, even though numerically predominant, is apt to be misleading. The total meaning of each play depends on a complex of interwoven patterns and the imagery must be considered in relation to character and structure.

One group of images to which Cleanth Brooks called attention was that concerned with babes.[5] It has been suggested[6] by Muriel C. Bradbrook that Shakespeare may have noticed in the general description of the manners of Scotland included in Holinshed's *Chronicles* that every Scotswoman 'would take intolerable pains to bring up and nourish her own children'; and H. N. Paul pointed out[7] that one of the topics selected for debate before James I, during his visit to Oxford in the summer of 1605, was whether a man's character was influenced by his nurse's milk. Whatever the origin of the images in *Macbeth* relating to breast-feeding, Shakespeare uses them for a very dramatic purpose. Their first appearance is in Lady Macbeth's invocation of the evil spirits to take possession of her:

> Come to my woman's breasts,
> And take my milk for gall, you murd'ring ministers,
> Wherever in your sightless substances
> You wait on nature's mischief.

They next appear in the scene where she incites Macbeth to the murder of Duncan:

> I have given suck, and know
> How tender 'tis to love the babe that milks me—
> I would, while it was smiling in my face,
> Have pluck'd my nipple from his boneless gums,
> And dash'd the brains out, had I so sworn as you
> Have done to this.

In between these two passages, Macbeth himself, debating whether to do the deed, admits that

> Pity, like a naked new-born babe
> Striding the blast,

would plead against it; and Lady Macbeth, when she first considers whether she can persuade her husband to kill Duncan, admits that she fears his nature:

> It is too full o' th' milk of human kindness
> To catch the nearest way.

Later in the play, Malcolm, when he is pretending to be worse even than Macbeth, says that he loves crime:

> Nay, had I pow'r, I should
> Pour the sweet milk of concord into hell,
> Uproar the universal peace, confound
> All unity on earth.

In these passages the babe symbolizes pity, and the necessity for pity, and milk symbolizes humanity, tenderness, sympathy, natural human feelings, the sense of kinship, all of which have been outraged by the murderers. Lady Macbeth can nerve herself to the deed only by denying her real nature; and she can overcome Macbeth's scruples only by making him ignore his feelings of human-kindness—his kinship with his fellow-men.

Cleanth Brooks suggests therefore that it is appropriate that one of the three apparitions should be a bloody child, since Macduff is converted into an avenger by the murder of his wife and babes. On one level, the bloody child stands for Macduff; on another level, it is the naked new-born babe whose pleadings Macbeth has ignored. Helen Gardner took Cleanth Brooks to task for considering these images in relation to one another.[8] She argued that in his comments on 'Pity, like a naked new-born babe' he had sacrificed

a Shakespearian depth of human feeling . . . by attempting to interpret an image by the aid of what associations it happens to arouse in him, and by being more interested in making symbols of babes fit each other than in listening to what Macbeth is saying. *Macbeth* is a tragedy and not a melodrama or a symbolic drama of retribution. The reappearance of 'the babe symbol' in the apparition scene and in Macduff's revelation of his birth has distracted the critic's attention from what deeply moves the imagination and the conscience in this vision of a whole world weeping at the inhumanity of helplessness betrayed and innocence and beauty destroyed. It is the judgment of the human heart that Macbeth fears here, and the punishment which the speech foreshadows is not that he will be cut down by Macduff, but that having murdered his own humanity he will enter a world of appalling loneliness, of meaningless activity, unloved himself, and unable to love.

Although this is both eloquent and true, it does not quite dispose of Brooks's interpretation of the imagery. Miss Gardner shows that, elsewhere in Shakespeare, 'a cherub is thought of as not only young, beautiful, and innocent, but as associated with the virtue of patience'; and that in the *Macbeth* passage the helpless babe and the innocent and beautiful cherub 'call out the pity and love by which Macbeth is judged. It is not terror of heaven's vengeance which makes him pause, but the terror of moral isolation.' Yet, earlier in the same speech Macbeth expresses fear of retribution in this life—fear that he himself will have to drink the ingredients of his own poisoned chalice—and his comparison of Duncan's virtues to 'angels, trumpet-tongued' implies a fear of judgment in the life to come, notwithstanding his boast that he would 'jump' it. We may assume, perhaps, that the discrepancy between the argument of the speech and the imagery employed is deliberate. On the surface Macbeth appears to be giving merely prudential reasons for not murdering Duncan; but Shakespeare makes him reveal by the imagery he employs that he, or his unconscious mind, is horrified by the thought of the deed to which he is being driven.[9]

Miss Gardner does not refer to the breast-feeding images—even Cleanth Brooks does not mention one of the most significant—yet all these images are impressive in their contexts and, taken together, they coalesce into a symbol of humanity, kinship and tenderness violated by Macbeth's crimes. Miss Gardner is right in demanding that the precise meaning and context of each image should be considered, but wrong, I believe, in refusing to see any significance in the group as a whole. *Macbeth*, of course, is a tragedy; but I know of no valid definition of tragedy which would prevent the play from being at the same time a symbolic drama of retribution.[10]

Another important group of images is concerned with sickness and medicine, and it is significant that they all appear in the last three acts of the play after Macbeth has ascended the throne; for Scotland is suffering from the disease of tyranny, which can be cured, as fever was thought to be cured, only by bleeding or purgation. The tyrant, indeed, uses sickness imagery of himself. He tells the First Murderer that so long as Banquo is alive he wears his health but sickly; when he hears of Fleance's escape he exclaims 'Then comes my fit again'; and he envies Duncan in the grave, sleeping after life's fitful fever, since life itself is one long illness. In the last act of the play a doctor, called in to diagnose Lady Macbeth's illness, confesses that he cannot

> minister to a mind diseas'd,
> Pluck from the memory a rooted sorrow,
> Raze out the written troubles of the brain,
> And with some sweet oblivious antidote
> Cleanse the stuff'd bosom of that perilous stuff
> Which weighs upon the heart.

Macbeth then professes to believe that what is amiss with Scotland is not his own evil tyranny but the English army of liberation:

> What rhubarb, cyme, or what purgative drug
> Would scour these English hence?

On the other side, the victims of tyranny look forward to wholesome days when Scotland will be freed. Malcolm says that Macbeth's very name blisters their tongues and he laments that 'each new day a gash' is added to Scotland's wounds. In the last act Caithness refers to Malcolm as 'the medicine of the sickly weal',

> And with him pour we in our country's purge
> Each drop of us.

Lennox adds:

> Or so much as it needs
> To dew the sovereign flower and drown the weeds.

Macbeth is the disease from which Scotland is suffering; Malcolm, the rightful king, is the *sovereign* flower, both royal and curative. Macbeth, it is said,

> Cannot buckle his distemper'd cause
> Within the belt of rule.

James I, in *A Counter-blast to Tobacco*, referred to himself as 'the proper Phisician of his Politicke-bodie', whose duty it was 'to purge it of all those diseases, by Medicines meet for the same'. It is possible that Shakespeare had read this pamphlet,[11] although, of course, disease-imagery is to be found in most of the plays written about this time. In *Hamlet* and *Coriolanus* it is applied to the body politic, as indeed it was by many writers on political theory. Shakespeare may have introduced the King's Evil as an allusion to James I's reluctant use of his supposed healing powers; but even without this topical reference, the incident provides a contrast to the evil supernatural represented by the Weird Sisters and is therefore dramatically relevant.

The contrast between good and evil is brought out in a variety of ways. There is not merely the contrast between the good and bad kings, which becomes explicit in the scene where Malcolm falsely accuses himself of avarice, lechery, cruelty and all of Macbeth's vices, and disclaims the possession of the king-becoming graces:

> Justice, verity, temperance, stableness,
> Bounty, perseverance, mercy, lowliness,
> Devotion, patience, courage, fortitude.

There is also a contrast throughout the play between the powers of light and darkness. It has often been observed that many scenes are set in darkness. Duncan arrives at Inverness as night falls; he is murdered during the night; Banquo returns from his last ride as night is again falling; Lady Macbeth has light by her continually; and even the daylight scenes during the first part of the play are mostly gloomy in their setting—a blasted heath, wrapped in mist, a dark cavern. The murder of Duncan is followed by darkness at noon—'dark night strangles the travelling lamp'. Before the murder Macbeth prays to the stars to hide their fires and Lady Macbeth invokes the night to conceal their crime:

> Come, thick night,
> And pall thee in the dunnest smoke of hell,
> That my keen knife see not the wound it makes,
> Nor heaven peep through the blanket of the dark
> To cry 'Hold, hold'.

Macbeth, as he goes towards the chamber of the sleeping Duncan, describes how

> o'er the one half-world
> Nature seems dead, and wicked dreams abuse
> The curtain'd sleep.

The word 'night' echoes through the first two scenes of the third act; and Macbeth invokes night to conceal the murder of Banquo:

> Come, seeling night,
> Scarf up the tender eye of pitiful day ...
> Light thickens, and the crow
> Makes wing to th' rooky wood;
> Good things of day begin to droop and drowse,
> Whiles night's black agents to their preys do rouse.

In the scene in England and in the last act of the play—except for the sleep-walking scene—the darkness is replaced by light.

The symbolism is obvious. In many of these contexts night and darkness are associated with evil, and day and light are linked with good. The 'good things of day' are contrasted with 'night's black agents'; and, in the last act, day stands for the victory of the forces of liberation (v, iv, 1; v, vii, 27; v, viii, 37). The 'midnight hags' are 'the instruments of darkness'; and some editors believe that when Malcolm (at the end of Act IV) says that 'The Powers above/Put on their instruments' he is referring to their human instruments—Malcolm, Macduff and their soldiers.

The opposition between the good and evil supernatural is paralleled by similar contrasts between angel and devil, heaven and hell, truth and falsehood—and the opposites are frequently juxtaposed:

> This supernatural soliciting
> Cannot be ill; cannot be good.

> Merciful powers
> Restrain in me the cursed thoughts that nature
> Gives way to in repose!

> It is a knell
> That summons thee to heaven or to hell.

Several critics have pointed out the opposition in the play between night and day, life and death, grace and evil, a contrast which is reiterated more than four hundred times.[12]

The evidence for this has gone beyond imagery proper and most modern imagistic critics have extended their field to cover not merely metaphor and simile, but the visual symbols implied by the dialogue, which would be visible in performance, and even the iteration of key words. The Poet Laureate once remarked that *Macbeth* is about blood; and from the appearance of the bloody sergeant in the second scene of the play to the last scene of all, we have a continual vision of blood. Macbeth's sword in the battle 'smok'd with bloody execution'; he and Banquo seemed to 'bathe in reeking wounds'; the Sergeant's 'gashes cry for help'. The Second Witch comes from the bloody task of killing swine. The visionary dagger is stained with 'gouts of blood'. Macbeth, after the murder, declares that not all great Neptune's ocean will cleanse his hands:

> this my hand will rather
> The multitudinous seas incarnadine,
> Making the green one red.

Duncan is spoken of as the fountain of his sons' blood; his wounds

> look'd like a breach in nature
> For ruin's wasteful entrance.

The world had become a 'bloody stage'. Macbeth, before the murder of Banquo, invokes the 'bloody and invisible hand' of night. We are told of the twenty trenched gashes on Banquo's body and his ghost shakes his 'gory locks' at Macbeth, who is convinced that 'blood will have blood'. At the end of the banquet scene, he confesses wearily that he is 'stepp'd so far' in blood, that

> should I wade no more,
> Returning were as tedious as go o'er.

The Second Apparition, a bloody child, advises Macbeth to be 'bloody, bold, and resolute'. Malcolm declares that Scotland bleeds,

> and each new day a gash
> Is added to her wounds.

Lady Macbeth, sleep-walking, tries in vain to remove the 'damned spot' from her hands:

Here's the smell of the blood still. All the perfumes of Arabia will not sweeten this little hand.

In the final scene, Macbeth's severed head is displayed on a pole. As Kott has recently reminded us, the subject of the play is murder, and the prevalence of blood ensures that we shall never forget the physical realities in metaphysical overtones.

Equally important is the iteration of sleep. The first statement of the theme is when the First Witch curses the Master of the *Tiger*:

> Sleep shall neither night nor day
> Hang upon his penthouse lid.

After the murder of Duncan, Macbeth and his wife

> sleep
> In the affliction of these terrible dreams
> That shake us nightly;

while Duncan, 'after life's fitful fever . . . sleeps well'. An anonymous lord looks forward to the overthrow of the tyrant, when they will be able to sleep in peace. Because of 'a great perturbation in nature', Lady Macbeth

> is troubled with thick coming fancies
> That keep her from her rest.

The key passage in the theme of sleeplessness, derived apparently from Holinshed and Seneca's *Hercules Furens*, occurs just after the murder of Duncan, when Macbeth hears a voice which cries 'Sleep no more!' It is really the echo of his own conscience. As Bradley noted, the voice 'denounced on him, as if his three names [Glamis, Cawdor, Macbeth] gave him three personalities to suffer in, the doom of sleeplessness'; and, as Murry puts it:

He has murdered Sleep, that is 'the death of each day's life'—that daily death of Time which makes Time human.

The murder of a sleeping guest, the murder of a sleeping king, the murder of a saintly old man, the murder, as it were, of sleep itself, carries with it the appropriate retribution of insomnia.[13]

As Murry's comment suggests, the theme of sleep is linked with that of time. Macbeth is promised by the Weird Sisters that he will be king 'hereafter' and Banquo wonders if they 'can look into the seeds of time'. Macbeth, tempted by the thought of murder, declares that 'Present fears/Are less than horrible imaginings' and decides that 'Time and the hour runs through the roughest day'. Lady Macbeth says she feels 'The future in the instant'. In his soliloquy in the last scene of Act I, Macbeth speaks of himself as 'here upon this bank and shoal of time', time being contrasted with the sea of eternity. He pretends that he would not worry about the future, or about the life to come, if he could be sure of success in the present; and his wife implies that the conjunction of time and place for the murder will never recur. Just before the murder, Macbeth reminds himself of the exact time and place, so that he can relegate (as Stephen Spender suggests)[14] 'the moment to the past from which it will never escape into the future'. Macbeth is troubled by his inability to say amen, because he dimly realizes he has forfeited the possibility of blessing and because he knows that he has become 'the deed's creature'. The nightmares of the guilty pair and the return of Banquo from the grave symbolize the haunting of the present by the past. When Macbeth is informed of his wife's death, he describes how life has become for him a succession of meaningless days, the futility he has brought upon himself by his crimes:

> To-morrow, and to-morrow, and to-morrow,
> Creeps in this petty pace from day to day
> To the last syllable of recorded time,
> And all our yesterdays have lighted fools
> The way to dusty death.

At the very end of the play, Macduff announces that with the death of the tyrant 'The time is free' and Malcolm promises, without 'a large expense of time' to do what is necessary ('which would be planted newly with the time') and to bring back order from chaos 'in measure, time, and place'.

From one point of view *Macbeth* can be regarded as a play about the disruption of order through evil, and its final restoration.[15] The play begins with what the witches call a hurly-burly and ends with the restoration of order by Malcolm. Order is represented throughout by the bonds of loyalty; and chaos is represented by the powers of darkness with their upsetting of moral values ('Fair is foul and foul is fair'). The witches can raise winds to fight against the churches, to sink ships and destroy buildings: they are the enemies both of religion and of civilization. Lady Macbeth invokes the evil spirits to take possession of her; and, after the murder of Duncan, Macbeth's mind begins to dwell on universal destruction. He is willing to 'let the frame of things disjoint, both the worlds suffer' merely to be freed from his nightmares. Again, in his conjuration of the witches in the cauldron scene, he is prepared to risk absolute chaos, 'even till destruction sicken' through surfeit, rather than not obtain an answer. In his last days, Macbeth is 'aweary of the sun' and he wishes 'the estate of the world' were undone. Order in Scotland, even the moral order in the universe, can be restored only by his death. G. R. Elliott contrasts[16] the threefold hail with which Malcolm is greeted at the end of the play with the threefold hail of the witches on the blasted heath: they mark the destruction of order and its restoration.

All through the play ideas of order and chaos are juxtaposed. When Macbeth is first visited by temptation his 'single state of man' is shaken and 'nothing is but what is not'. In the next scene (I, iv) Shakespeare presents ideas of loyalty, duty, and the reward of faithful service, in contrast both to the treachery of the dead Thane of Cawdor and to the treacherous thoughts of the new thane. Lady Macbeth prays to be spared 'compunctious visitings of nature' and in the next scene, after the description of the 'pleasant seat' of the castle with its images of natural beauty, she expresses her gratitude and loyalty to the king. Before the murder, Macbeth reminds himself of the threefold tie of loyalty which binds him to Duncan, as kinsman, subject and host. He is afraid that the very stones will cry out against the unnaturalness of the murder, which is, in fact, accompanied by strange portents:

> Lamentings heard i' th' air, strange screams of death,
> And prophesying, with accents terrible,
> Of dire combustion and confus'd events
> New hatch'd to th' woeful time.

The frequent iteration of the word 'strange' is one of the ways by which Shakespeare underlines the disruption of the natural order.

Passages which older critics deplored, and which even H. N. Paul regarded[17] as flattery of King James, may be seen as part of the theme we have been discussing. Macbeth's curious discourse on dogs is one of these passages. It was inserted not mainly because of James's proclamation on the subject, but to stress the order of nature—*naturae benignitas*—'the diverse functions and variety within a single species testifying to an overruling harmony and design'; and it is used to persuade his tools to murder Banquo. In the scene in England, Malcolm's self-accusations —in particular his confession of wishing to uproar the universal peace and confound all unity on earth—are disorders contrasted with the virtues he pretends not to have and with the miraculous powers of the pious Edward.

Reference must be made to two other groups of images, which I have discussed elsewhere in some detail—those relating to equivocation and those which are concerned with the contrast between what the Porter calls desire and performance.[18] The theme of equivocation runs all through the play. It was suggested, no doubt, by the topicality of the subject at Father Garnet's trial, but this links up with 'the equivocation of the fiend/That lies like truth', the juggling fiends 'That keep the word of promise to our ear/And break it to our hope', and Macbeth's own equivocation after the murder of Duncan:

> Had I but died an hour before this chance,
> I had liv'd a blessed time; for, from this instant,
> There's nothing serious in mortality—
> All is but toys; renown and grace is dead;
> The wine of life is drawn, and the mere lees
> Is left this vault to brag of.

Macbeth's intention is to avert suspicion from himself by following his wife's advice to make their 'griefs and clamour roar upon' Duncan's death. But, as he speaks the words, the audience knows that he has unwittingly spoken the truth. Instead of lying like truth, he has told the truth while intending to deceive. As he expresses it later, when full realization has come to him, life has become meaningless, a succession of empty tomorrows, 'a tale told by an idiot'.

The gap between desire and performance, enunciated by the Porter, is expressed over and over again by Macbeth and his wife. It takes the form, most strikingly, in the numerous passages contrasting eye and hand, culminating in Macbeth's cry—

> What hands are here? Ha! They pluck out mine eyes—

and in the scene before the murder of Banquo when the bloodstained hand is no longer Macbeth's, but Night's:

> Come, seeling night,
> Scarf up the tender eye of pitiful day,
> And with thy bloody and invisible hand
> Cancel and tear to pieces that great bond
> Which keeps me pale.

In the sleep-walking scene, Lady Macbeth's unavailing efforts to wash the smell of the blood from her hand symbolize the indelibility of guilt; and Angus in the next scene declares that Macbeth feels

> His secret murders sticking on his hands.

The soul is damned for the deeds committed by the hand.

It has recently been argued[19] that the opposition between the hand and eye provides the clearest explanation of that division in Macbeth between his clear 'perception of evil and his rapt drift into evil'. Lawrence W. Hyman suggests that Macbeth is able to do the murder only because of the deep division between his head and his hand. The

almost autonomous action of Macbeth's dagger, as if it had no connection with a human brain or a human heart, explains the peculiar mood that pervades the murder scene . . . As soon as he lays down the dagger, however, his 'eye' cannot help but see what the hand has done.

A study of the imagery and symbolism in *Macbeth* does not radically alter one's interpretation of the play. It would, indeed, be suspect if it did. In reading some modern criticisms of Shakespeare one has the feeling that the critic is reading between the lines and creating from the interstices a play rather different from the one which Shakespeare wrote and similar to a play the critic himself might have written. Such interpretations lead us away from Shakespeare; they drop a veil between us and the plays; and they substitute a formula for the living reality, a philosophy or a theology instead of a dramatic presentation of life. I have not attempted to reshape *Macbeth* to a particular ideological image, nor selected parts of the play to prove a thesis. Some selection had to be made for reasons of space, but I have tried to make the selection representative of the whole.

We must not imagine, of course, that *Macbeth* is merely an elaborate pattern of imagery. It is a play; and in the theatre we ought to recover, as best we may, a state of critical innocence. We should certainly not attempt to notice the images of clothing or breast-feeding or count the allusions to blood or sleep. But, just as Shakespeare conveys to us the unconscious minds of the characters by means of the imagery, so, in watching the play, we may be totally unconscious of the patterns of imagery and yet absorb them unconsciously by means of our imaginative response to the poetry. In this way they will be subsumed under the total experience of the play.

And what of the producer? It would be quite fatal for him to get his actors to underline the key images—to make them, as it were, italicize them with a knowing wink at the professors in the stalls or the students in the gallery. All we should ask of the producer in this matter is that he should give us what Shakespeare wrote, and all that Shakespeare wrote, and that he should not try to improve on the script provided by the dramatist.

© K. MUIR 1966

NOTES

1. C. F. E. Spurgeon. *Leading Motives in the Imagery of Shakespeare's Tragedies.*

2. K. Muir (ed.), *Macbeth* (1951), pp. xxxiii, 7.

3. H. L. Rogers has recently argued (*R.E.S.* 1965, p. 44) that the tailor may refer to a man associated in the public mind with the Garnet trial; as Father Garnet went under the name of 'Mr Farmer', equivocator, tailor and farmer were all allusions to the Gunpowder Plot and its aftermath.

4. *This Great Stage* (1948), *Magic in the Web* (1956).

5. *The Well Wrought Urn* (1947), pp. 22–49.

6. *Shakespeare Survey 4* (1951), p. 40.

7. *The Royal Play of 'Macbeth'* (1950), p. 388.

8. *The Business of Criticism* (1959), p. 61. Cf. K. Muir, 'Shakespeare's Imagery—Then and Now', *Shakespeare Survey 18* (1965), p. 55.

9. K. Muir, *Macbeth*, p. lviii, and 'Shakespeare's Soliloquies', *Ocidente*, LXVII (1964), p. 65.

10. More questionably, Cleanth Brooks associates the babe images with the question, much debated in the play, of what constitutes manliness. See, especially, the discussion between Macbeth and his wife in I, vii and between Macbeth and the murderers in III, i. Macbeth, before he falls, declares:

I dare do all that may become a man:
Who dares do more is none.

He is humanized, it has been said, by his fears. When, at the end of the play, he can no longer feel fear, he dies like a hunted beast. This, in turn, links up with the animal imagery, which is of some importance in *Macbeth*, though less prevalent than in *King Lear* or *Othello*.

11. H. N. Paul, *op. cit.* p. 391.

12. F. C. Kolbe, *Shakespeare's Way* (1930), pp. 21–2, Cf. also G. Wilson Knight, *The Imperial Theme* (1931) L. C. Knights, *Explorations* (1946), Roy Walker, *The Time is Free* (1949).

13. Cf. J. M. Murry, *Shakespeare* (1935), p. 333.

14. *Penguin New Writing*, no. 3, pp. 115–26. I am indebted to this article for several points in this paragraph.

15. Cf. Robert Speaight, *Nature in Shakespearian Tragedy* (1955), L. C. Knights, *op. cit.* and G. Wilson Knight, *op. cit.*

16. *Dramatic Providence in Macbeth* (1958), p. 228.

17. *Op. cit.* pp. 367 ff., 392 ff., 359 ff.

18. *Macbeth*, pp. xxvii–xxxii.

19. Lawrence W. Hyman, *Tennessee Studies* (1960), pp. 97–100.

'MACBETH' AND THE FURIES

BY

ARTHUR R. McGEE

This is an attempt to see, as if through Elizabethan eyes, the supernatural background of the play and Macbeth's relation to it. I cannot pretend that this brief study is other than a very rough approximation, because the final impression is really a composite one put together from a wide variety of sources. For good or ill, however, I have ventured into the supernatural world of the Elizabethans because I dislike the 'character sketch' approach to *Macbeth* as much as I dislike the studies of isolated images with their promise of a poetic whole which never quite materializes. Both methods cause fragmentation of the play to such an extent that few commentators nowadays bother much about the Weird Sisters—who or what they are has become more important than what they do. Perhaps a reluctance to associate Shakespeare with a belief in witchcraft is at the root of this malaise. No one can tell whether Shakespeare believed in hanging witches, but can anyone doubt that he felt the same anxiety about them that obsessed so many of his contemporaries? Shakespeare was no iconoclast like Reginald Scot; *Macbeth* would certainly not shake a contemporary audience's belief in witchcraft. I prefer to see in the play the outlines of the same frightful psychic cloud, composed of fear, superstition and religious wrong-headedness, that thundered in the contemporary imagination and destroyed countless thousands of innocent people with its lightning. But can we condemn our ancestors for an over-zealous belief in spiritual evil when we have Eichmanns in our midst? Satan is for many of us an outdated concept but he will linger in our vocabulary at least as long as we remember Belsen.

Since it is generally agreed that *Macbeth* is a study of a man on his way to damnation, it behoves us first to look at the medieval Hell in which the Elizabethans still believed. The importance of the Classics is at once apparent, for the mythological figures of Greece and Rome were one means employed to people Hell—Dante's demons include the Furies, Medusa the Gorgon, and the Harpies, and Milton's devils follow a similar pattern. These additions to Christian demonology were felt to be necessary perhaps because there is comparatively little demonic symbolism in the Bible—apart from the desert demons in Isaiah and the Apocalyptic devils in Revelation. As might be expected, the classical symbols were sometimes hybridized and sometimes completely fused with those of Christianity—Dante's Geryon is drawn from Virgil and from the Apollyon of Revelation; and Robert Burton records that the schoolmen identified the Furies with Apollyon's horde: 'The seventh is a destroyer, Captain of the Furies, causing wars, tumults, combustions, uproars, mentioned in the Apocalypse, and called Abaddon.'[1] But the process did not end there because the mythological figures which were borrowed did not possess stable identities and were almost synonymous. Aeschylus associated his Eumenides with the Harpies and the Gorgons; Virgil's Celaeno is not only a Harpy but 'Furiarum maxima', and she has a prophetic role like the Fates; the Allecto of the Aeneid is 'charged with Gorgon-poisons'; and the Furies of Virgil and Ovid have snakes in place of hair, like the Gorgons.[2] It is little wonder then that Spenser's Celeno is a Harpy/Siren;[3] that Milton wrote of 'harpy-footed Furies', and of 'the blind Fury with the abhorred shears'; and that Shakespeare's Ariel, disguised as a Harpy, assails, Fury-like, the consciences of the 'three men of sin'. Even John Bunyan, though no classicist, availed himself of the same poetic licence by not adhering to the Biblical text in describing his Apollyon. It may be claimed therefore with some confidence that one aspect of medieval demonology was its extension by the imaginative associations which we expect in poetry.

The witches in classical times were involved in these mythological metamorphoses—Lucan's Erichtho and Horace's Canidia have a coiffure of serpents like the Furies.[4] Ovid's Fury, Tisiphone, uses a cauldron in which to make a magic concoction, 'a noisome witch's brew', like his witch Medea.[5] Hecate is closely associated in the Aeneid with the Furies, with Proserpine and Night ('the mother of the Eumenides'); and she was often depicted as carrying a scourge and a torch, as Virgil's Furies do.[6] Thus, following classical tradition, Ben Jonson's witches in *The Masque of Queens* are associated with the Furies, and their Dame has the characteristic snake-coiffure of the Furies and the Gorgons. The association with the Furies and with Hecate is further strengthened by the Dame's invocation:

> You Fiendes, and Furies, (if yet any bee
> Worse than ourselues) You, that haue quak'd, to see
> These knotts vntied; and shrunke, when we haue charm'd.
> You, that (to arme vs) haue yourselues disarmd,
> And, to our powers, resign'd yor Whipps, & brands,
> When we went forth, the Scourge of Men, & Lands . . .
> And thou, three-formed Starre, that on these nights
> Art only power-full, to Whose triple Name
> Thus wee incline; Once, twise, and thrise-the-Same . . .

In an explanatory note Jonson also adds:

And Claud. to his Megaera lib. j. in Rufinum: Who takes the habite of a Witch as these doe, and supplies that historicall part in the Poëme, beside her morall person of a Fury.

Like the medieval devils, Jonson's witches come from hell, and they carry, among other 'veneficall instruments', spindles which are reminiscent of the Parcae.[7] Spenser's associations are similar—his witch, Duessa, appears with Night and with Ate (upon whom Jonson's Dame is also modelled in part), and his hag 'hight Occasion' has Furor as her son.[8] Timothy Bright also placed Hecate in the same context as the Furies,[9] and in *The Buggbear*, a translation from the Italian *c.* 1565, we find this again.[10] Witches/Furies therefore were an aspect of classical demonology which was recognized by the Elizabethans, and this gives point to Coleridge's well-known, but much neglected, intuitive comment: 'The Weird Sisters are as true a creation of Shakespeare's, as his Ariel and Caliban—fates, furies, and materializing witches being the elements.'

It can be further claimed that this classical background is relevant to *Macbeth* because in two respects at least Shakespeare's Weird Sisters do not correlate with the evidence of the witch trials. The first is that cauldrons did not form any essential part of the rituals of witches— Margaret Murray does not even mention them[11] and the few references to them in exclusively Scottish sources do not suggest the use of cauldrons for divination, as in *Macbeth*.[12] But the cauldron of Ovid's Medea and of his Fury, Tisiphone, were readily available in Golding's translation of the *Metamorphoses*—as Henry N. Paul has pointed out.[13] The second feature is that Shakespeare's own references to Hecate at II, ii, 52 and III, ii, 41 (i.e. omitting the disputed 'Middletonian' additions) are not paralleled in contemporary witch practices, because Margaret Murray records no such figure in any trial either in Britain or on the continent. The nearest equivalent to her was the Queen of Phairie or Faerie who is mentioned in the Scottish witch trials. It is interesting to note also that the unknown hand which produced the additions that appear in the Folio followed classical precedent by introducing a Hecate who appointed Acheron as her meeting place with the Weird Sisters.

But the contemporary picture of the witch was not of course only classically derived, for there was a connexion between the witches and the fairies, not only in the popular imagination, but in the witch trials, particularly in Scotland.[14] This may have been due to the fairies' being regarded as devils by some authorities—James I places them in one of four categories which he calls 'Phairie'.[15] Sir Walter Scott, on the other hand, cites Reginald Scot who claimed that as Puck had ceased to frighten people, the fairies had lost their devilish aspects.[16] But for Robert Burton there were two kinds of fairies—water devils and terrestrial devils like 'those Lares, Genii, Fauns, Satyrs, Wood-nymphs, Foliots, Fairies, Robin Goodfellows, Trolls, &c'.[17] Whatever the reason for the close connexion between witches and fairies, Margaret Murray reports that in several witch trials there is demonstrated 'the witches' belief in the superiority of the fairies to themselves in the matter of magic and healing powers'.[18] An example of witch/fairy confusion is a story told by John Aubrey of a certain lord who used the fairies' words 'horse and hattock' and found himself transported to the cellar of the French king's palace;[19] for Margaret Murray records an instance when these same words were uttered by witches as a means of instant transportation.[20] A further case is noted by F. Marian McNeil.[21] Shakespeare himself wrote

> No fairy takes, no witch hath power to charm . . .   (*Hamlet*, I, i, 163)

and

> . . . we fairies that do run
> By the triple Hecate's team . . .
>
>   (*A Midsummer Night's Dream*, v, i, 372–3)

Milton also felt no incongruity in placing 'the pert fairies and the dapper elves' in the same context as his enchanter, Comus (whose mother was Circe), and Hecate. It cannot be said then that the Folio addition at IV, i, 42 'Like elves and fairies in a ring' is as ludicrous as it appears to most commentators—the damage to Shakespeare's creation exists only in the modern mind which makes a rigid distinction between fairies, witches and devils.

There are other reasons too for believing that witches, Furies, devils and fairies were virtually synonymous. One is that all of them were closely associated, even identified, with the owl. In the *Aeneid* the Fury who attacks Turnus transforms herself into an owl, and when Dido is possessed by the Furies and thinks she hears the voice of her dead husband the owl hoots ominously in the night.[22] In *The Golden Ass* of Apuleius the witch Pamphile becomes an owl in pursuit of her lusts.[23] (Also in Book V of the *Metamorphoses* Asclaphus is turned into an owl—a legend similar to the transformation of the baker's daughter which Ophelia alludes to.) Golding himself in his translation interpolates

> . . . a Witch, a cursed odious wight,
> Which in the likeness of an Owl abroad a nights did flie.[24]

When we reach medieval times we find that Paracelsus believed that the owl was a demon-familiar, and it is commonly associated with witches by Middleton, and Jonson, as an atmospheric accompaniment, or as a cauldron ingredient, or as a pet-familiar (Hecate feeds them in *The Witch*). In the Davenant version of *Macbeth* an owl-hoot is interpolated in the first scene to represent the call of the third familiar, which is absent in the Folio. In this connexion Paul records that a 1773 text of *Macbeth* has a plate in which an owl, which he identifies as Harpier, hovers over the witches' cauldron.[25] The evidence of the witch trials, however, is negative—the owl is not mentioned. But Lavater, the Elizabethan authority on ghosts, believed that Satan himself appeared as an owl, and the Jacobean authority on witchcraft, Bernard, takes a similar view.[26] Aldous Huxley records that Satan was referred to as the 'stinking Owl of Hell' by the Capuchin biographer of Grandier of Loudun.[27] For James I the owl had a demonological association, and we can see here the close association with the devils of scriptural origin; for in discussing the appearance of demons James refers to the destruction of Jerusalem in Isaiah xiii and xxxiv, in which the prophet declares 'that it shall not onely be wracked, but shall become so great a solitude, as it shall be the habitackle of Howlettes, and of Ziim and Iim, which are the proper Hebrew names for these Spirites'.[28] And we should notice that this same apocalyptic strain is echoed in Revelation where Babylon will become 'a cage of unclean birds', which certainly included the owl. For Shakespeare owls, fairies, and devils were part of the supernatural pattern:

> This is the fairy-land: O spite of spites!
> We talk with goblins, owls and sprites.
>
> (*Comedy of Errors*, II, ii, 188–9)

From a consideration of the owl symbolism several points emerge. (*a*) Paul's claim that Harpier is an owl can be amply supported.[29] The name Harpier was probably derived from Harpy which as we have seen was associated by Virgil and by Milton with the Furies, and hence again with the owl. The same association occurs in Spenser:

> . . . and after him Owles and Night-rauens flew.
> The hatefull messengers of heauy things,
> Of death and dolour telling sad tidings;
> Whiles sad Celeno, sitting on a clift,
> A song of bale and bitter sorrow sings . . .[30]

(*b*) As the owl was so closely associated with demons, Furies, witches and fairies, this suggests that the hierarchical relation of Satan/demon-familiar/witch was not as clear-cut as the demonologists would have us believe. This can indeed be seen in the contemporary literature. In the *Witch of Edmonton* (1621), for example, which is based on a real-life witch trial, when Mother Sawyer cries

> What is the name, where and by what art learned,
> What spells, what charms, or invocations,
> May the thing called Familiar be purchased?[31]

it is Satan himself who appears in the form of a black dog. In contrast, in *The Sad Shepherd* the witch Maudlin believes she possesses supernatural powers in her own right, but Puck-Hairy, her familiar, reveals that they are due to him. Burton, having discussed the powers of demons, ignores the familiar-mechanism and claims that witches are 'many times worse (if it be possible) than [Satan] himself... Much harm had never been done... had he not been provoked by Witches to do it.'[32] Middleton's Hecate does not acknowledge allegiance to Satan, and is the initiator of mischief in her own right, as is Jonson's Dame in the *Masque of Queens*. Spenser's Duessa lacks a Satan or a familiar. Milton's Comus is not a Satanist, but he refers to his mother's association with the Naiades, whom Burton regarded as water-devils.[33] In *Macbeth* the owl is the demon-familiar Harpier in at least one context, but the wing of an owl was thrown into the cauldron by the witches, an owl which slew a falcon portended the murder of Duncan, the owl hooted all night long when Duncan was murdered, and Lady Macbeth and her husband both heard it; Lady Macduff also refers spontaneously to the owl just before she is murdered. The owl therefore, it seems to me, has a multiple demonic connotation in the play. (c) As the owl was associated with demons in Scripture, it had an apocalyptic significance. This point will be dealt with more fully later.

Yet it is in their powers of operative magic that demon-Furies, witches, and fairies are most clearly seen as interchangeable symbols. For example, causing storms could be ascribed to the Hecate of the Classics, or to Ovid's Medea, or to the medieval demons, or to the contemporary witches, or to the fairies in *A Midsummer Night's Dream*. Similarly, Shakespeare's Sycorax could control the moon, like Hecate, and his fairies have similar powers; Milton's 'faery elves' in *Paradise Lost* hold their revels while the moon draws close to the earth; and Burton affirms the contemporary belief that devils could influence the moon by denying the possibility.[34] That in *Macbeth* 'the moon is down' and 'she goes down at twelve' is surely fraught with supernatural menace when 'secret black and midnight hags' 'celebrate pale Hecate's offerings'. Again, the ability to fly, to become invisible or to disappear entirely, or instantly to transport themselves, or to change into different shapes, is shared by the same agents. Fogs could be produced by the classical witches, by Jonson's and by Spenser's, or by demons who could 'infect the air', or by contemporary Scottish witches; and the fairies' quarrel in *A Midsummer-Night's Dream* has the same effect. Thus the 'fog and filthy air' in the opening scene in *Macbeth* would have been regarded as having been produced by the Weird Sisters. Damage to crops could be done also by witches or demons or fairies.[35] Bedimming the sun (cf. 'dark night strangles the travelling lamp') was within the powers of Ovid's Circe, the Pamphile of Apuleius, and the devils of the Apocalypse; and Shakespeare's fairies could affect the seasons.[36] Madness, diabolic possession, bewitchment, possession by the Furies, were synonymous expressions—James I in particular records that witches could cause insanity[37]—and the owl symbolism is again relevant here, for 'owl-blasted'[38] was a term which could be used to describe all these states of mind. Finally, the Furies, witches, and fairies could be the means of torturing a man's conscience or of inflicting supernatural punishment upon the guilty.

As has been mentioned above, the Furies had been identified with the devils in Revelation, and we have also seen that the Furies had been associated with the witches. Thus as in Shakespeare's time there existed no rigid distinction between these demonic agents, they could be used as synonyms in the language of conscience. Their rôle was like that of Satan himself, who acted as tempter and then, after his victim had succumbed, punished him with God's permission. As Burton says: '... those whom God forsakes, the Devil, by his permission, lays hold on. Sometimes he persecutes them with that worm of conscience, as he did Judas, Saul, and others.'[39]

Our modern psychological approach to Macbeth's guilt falls far short of the full medieval horror in which the victim felt not only the pangs of conscience in our sense, but was faced with an implacable, ubiquitous, supernatural opponent who in the end dragged him down to everlasting punishment in Hell. According to modern commentators the witches tempt Macbeth and then torture him with anxiety in IV, i, and they also contribute largely to the atmosphere of brooding evil. But a Jacobean audience might very well have regarded Macbeth as a man who had succumbed to the Furies and who was destroyed by them. Even Richard Hooker employs this symbolism:

... a guilty mind being forced to be still both a martyr and a tyrant, itself must of necessity endure perpetual anguish and grief; for, as the body is rent with stripes, so the mind with guiltiness of cruelty, lust, and wicked resolutions. Which furies brought the Emperor Tiberius sometimes into such perplexity, that writing to the Senate, his wonted art of dissimulation failed him utterly in this case.[40]

The nightmares which terrify Macbeth are further manifestations of conscience which are readily explicable in modern psychological terms, but to Shakespeare's contemporaries the nightmare was the 'night hag'—a witch or female demon—a belief of which there are literary traces as late as the eighteenth century. And even as early as 1440 Skeat records: 'nyghte mare, or mare, or wytche, Epialtes, vel Effialtes'.[41] ('The Ephialtes or night-Mare', as Sir Thomas Browne called it in his *Pseudodoxia Epidemica*, and to which Sir Walter Scott refers in *The Antiquary*, was the Greek demon of nightmare.)[42] More commonly however, as K. M. Briggs records, ' ... the primitive form of nightmare [was] a mounted, supernatural hag, scouring the countryside with nine demons as her offspring, [as in *Lear*] ... [John] Aubrey calls the hags that ride horses the night mare, and gives a simple charm against them'. We can also see the fairy/witch/demon association in this night spell, recorded in 1651 but probably of earlier date:

> Saint Francis and Saint Benedight,
> Blesse this house from wicked wight;
> From the Night-mare and the Goblin,
> That is hight good fellow Robin;
> Keep it from all evill spirits,
> Fayries, Weezels, Rats, and Ferrets;
> From curfew-time
> To the next prime.

Middleton's Firestone, demon son of Hecate, 'goes on amatory expeditions with the Nightmare'. Milton's 'night-hag' in *Paradise Lost* shows the same close association of the nightmare with witches:

> Nor uglier follow the night-hag, when, called
> In secret, riding through the air she comes,
> Lured with the smell of infant blood, to dance
> With Lapland witches, while the labouring moon
> Eclipses at their charms,

Again, in *The Buggbear*, quoted above, there is a reference to 'hecate the nyght mare'.[43] In Herrick's poem *The Hag* a witch rides abroad at night with the Devil, and this is so like 'the riding of the witch', another folklore synonym for nightmare, that they are indistinguishable. Even Chatterton 'the marvellous boy', could write in the second half of the eighteenth century:

> Hark! the raven flaps his wing,
> In the briared dell below;
> Hark! the death-owl loud doth sing
> To the night-mares as they go.

In the same poem also there is mention of an 'elfin fairy' and 'water witches'—a typical sharing of the demonic context.[44] There seem therefore to be good grounds for believing that not only Macbeth and his wife are tortured in sleep by the Weird Sisters, but that Banquo is tempted by them in this manner, and Malcolm and Donalbain sense their malign influence—they awake from nightmare at the time of Duncan's murder—and Donalbain's reference to

> our fate,
> Hid in an auger-hole

arises from a popular belief that witches could do so.

Macbeth's conscience is therefore more than 'mainly a feeling of fear', as H. B. Charlton has described it;[45] the Weird Sisters have the power to torture him in dreams so that he awakes and cannot find rest, just as they planned to do to the sailor in I, iii. But Macbeth's fear extends beyond his 'terrible dreams' to the living nightmare of the Apocalypse itself. He can persuade himself that what happens after death is unimportant here 'on this bank and shoal of time', he can face the prospect of 'even-handed justice' which will allow his enemies to destroy him, but there wells up in his imagination, against his will, a confused picture of the Last Judgment, such as might have been registered in a child's memory:

> his virtues
> Will plead like angels trumpet-tongu'd against
> The deep damnation of his taking-off;
> And pity, like a naked new-born babe,
> Striding the blast, or heaven's cherubin hors'd
> Upon the sightless couriers of the air,
> Shall blow the horrid deed in every eye,
> That tears shall drown the wind.

These lines were perhaps more meaningful to the older members of an audience who could still remember the paintings of the Dies Irae over the rood-lofts of their churches[46]—such a rood-loft had been removed from the Chapel of Guild in Stratford when Shakespeare's father was chamberlain[47]—or the Mystery plays in which it was a prominent feature until 1580. We should remember also that the Day of Judgment was a favourite theme with the artists of the Renaissance; that in particular it inspired Michelangelo, Dürer, and El Greco—more than 'the eye of childhood' feared 'a painted devil'.

The apocalyptic atmosphere is continued by the Porter and by Lennox's lines:

> The night has been unruly. Where we lay,
> Our chimneys were blown down; and, as they say,
> Lamentings heard i' th' air, strange screams of death,
> And prophesying, with accents terrible,

> Of dire combustion and confus'd events
> New hatch'd to th' woeful time; the obscure bird
> Clamour'd the livelong night. Some say the earth
> Was feverous and did shake.

W. C. Curry has, I think rightly, maintained that demonic forces were at work here,[48] but the context is wider than he claims—the imagery is ultimately derived from Revelation. When we remember also that the demons in Revelation ix had the faces of men (beards presumably) and the hair of women, and that their bodies were like horses with the tails of scorpions, we can see the close association, even identification, of such an image with the bearded witch, the night-hag, the nightmare of folklore, and with the Furies of classical literature.

There are certainly two specific references to the Day of Judgment—'the great Doom's image' at II, iii, 76, which occurs just after Lennox's lines, and 'the crack of doom' at IV, i, 117, before the Weird Sisters finally disappear. To these we may add Malcolm's lines

> I am yet
> Unknown to woman, never was forsworn

which are an echo of Revelation xiv, 4–5:

These are they which were not defiled with women; for they were virgins . . . And in their mouth was found no guile . . .

The juxtaposition of ideas is too striking to be coincidence, and it owes nothing to Holinshed. With this Biblical connexion in mind it is easy to multiply the less direct associations, such as the death of the saintly Duncan, the 'holy angel' flying to the English court, the frequency of the riding images pointed out by Caroline Spurgeon,[49] the 'famine and the ague', and so on. Even the images of blood and darkness which so impressed Bradley can be included, as can the 'scorpions' that sting Macbeth's conscience. (It might also be observed that the whips which the Furies carried could be described as 'scorpions'.)[50] G. Wilson Knight has described the play as 'the apocalypse of evil', but is there any need to coin a phrase when the Biblical Apocalypse will do? To Shakespeare's contemporaries the ultimate horror was Hell, and particularly the Hell of the Last Day. James I, like Banquo, employs this imagery quite spontaneously—in James's case when describing the Gunpowder plot.[51]

At least one contemporary of Shakespeare's saw the Furies, the night-hag, and the Apocalypse in the play—Henry Adamson, who in 1638 wrote:

> Near this we did perceive where proud Macbeth,
> Who to the furies did his soul bequeath,
> His castle mounted on Dunsinane hill,
> Causing the mightiest peers obey his will,
> And bow their necks to build his Babylon . . .
> Who had this strange response, that none should catch him
> That born was of a woman, or should match him . . .
> But yet his sprite deceived him by a mare . . .[52]

The Ghost of Banquo also gains nothing by modernization. If Shakespeare meant the Ghost to be regarded as a hallucination, the obvious way would have been to make Macbeth 'look but on a stool'—as he in fact appears to Lady Macbeth. James I who had written that witches 'can make spirits, either to follow and trouble persons, or haunt certaine houses'[53] would have had no difficulty in regarding the Ghost of Banquo as 'real', nor would an audience which believed in the Witch of Endor, and had read of Hecate's power to raise the dead.[54] And as the Weird Sisters conjure up the Ghost again in IV, i—a fact which Bradley in discussing the objectivity of the Ghost conveniently ignored—the case is surely proved. The appearance of the Ghost not only causes Macbeth to create suspicion in the minds of his thanes, but drives him further into the toils of the witches. As for the 'air-drawn dagger', for the objectivity of which there is no textual warrant, the words of Henry Bullinger are relevant:

Imperial law decreed that they [witches] must be put to death. Therefore let those men consider what they are doing who dispute against these laws and decide that witches who deal only with dreams and hallucinations should not be burnt or put to death . . .[55]

If then witches were believed to cause hallucinations and to raise ghosts, on what grounds can we deny the Weird Sisters these same powers ?

The modern focus on Macbeth's despair is also too narrow, because the Elizabethans saw despair as being also a sin against the Holy Ghost,[56] and as the fatal step towards damnation. Burton describes its symptoms thus: ' . . . fear, sorrow, furies, grief, pain, terror, anger, dismal, ghastly, tedious, irksome, &c. . . '.[57] James I believed that despair was the final stage which preceded the renunciation of baptism that witches had to make, and the signing away of their souls to the devil. Faustus made a formal pact with Mephistopheles, but it has been stressed by H. B. Charlton and M. C. Bradbrook that Macbeth does not undergo the ritual initiation so that his giving his 'eternal jewel to the common enemy of man' is too imprecise to create a parallel with Faustus.[58] But Macbeth's rejection of what is good is in itself a satanic pact—Burton, speaking of despair, remarks: 'Thou hast given thy soul to the Devil, as Witches and Conjurors do, explicitly and implicitly.'[59] Hooker's ideas were similar:

What great advantage Satan hath taken even by the godly grief of hearty contrition for sins committed against God, the near approaching of so many afflicted souls, whom the conscience of sin hath brought unto the very brink of extreme despair, doth but too abundantly show.[60]

Despair, however, was not only the concern of the ecclesiastics. Gaspar in *The White Devil* says

> Hee could not have invented his owne ruine,
> Had hee despair'd, with more proprietie.

And from *The Duchess of Malfi* comes the following:

> *Bosola.* Come, you must live.
> *Duchess.* That's the greatest torture soules feele in hell,
> In hell: that they must live, and cannot die:
> Portia, I'll new kindle thy coales againe,

> And revive the rare, and almost dead example
> Of a loving wife.
> *Bosola.* O fye: despaire? remember
> You are a Christian.

Hieronimo in *The Spanish Tragedy* cries:

> There is a path upon your left-hand side,
> That leadeth from a guilty conscience
> Unto a forest of distrust and fear,
> A darksome place and dangerous to pass:
> There shall you meet with melancholy thoughts,
> Whose baleful humours if you but uphold,
> It will conduct you to despair and death: . . .

It cannot be claimed, however, that the Elizabethan attitude to despair was unequivocal, for the courage of a desperate man could be admired, even though it could be associated with Satan.[61] But on the other hand there is no evidence that the Elizabethans regarded a man who listened to his conscience as being a coward—indeed to have a 'tender' and not a 'cauterized' conscience was a mark of virtue.[62] Macbeth, as a soldier, would be regarded as a man whose conscience was pliable, a 'cheverel conscience' according to Burton,[63] and his ability to look on 'strange images of death' and 'to memorize another Golgotha' foreshadow the final rejection of the promptings of his conscience. Macbeth suffers the anguish of guilt, but his misery is increased by the Witch/Furies who drive him to despair and stifle his repentance. Dante's Medusa, and Sackville's Remorse of Conscience have a similar function.[64] It may be concluded then that Macbeth epitomizes the man who falls into despair to the eternal damnation of his soul, and that, perhaps, the Faustus legend is but another derivative from the same generic condition. Macbeth is like the Weird Sisters who are symbols of despair, but he does not automatically derive powers of satanic magic because of his turning from God. The role of the classical Furies is particularly relevant here—being possessed by the Furies did not make one a Fury, except in the metaphorical sense.

Macbeth's ambition also shows his kinship with Satan, 'So ambitious is he, and greedy of honour (which procured his fall)', in the words of James I.[65] The association of pride with ambition, and both with Satan, is common in the Elizabethan and Jacobean writers, lay as well as ecclesiastical. Hooker says that the Fall of the Angels was caused by pride, and refers to the 'odious name of ambition'; while in Kyd we find 'ambitious villain', 'ambitious proud'; and in Webster 'a saucy and ambitious devil', and

> Whether we fall by ambition, blood or lust,
> Like diamonds we are cut with our own dust.

Burton writes of Adam's 'disobedience, pride, ambition, intemperance, incredulity, curiosity'; and Marlowe's Tamburlaine

> was never sprung of human race,
> Since with the spirit of his fearful pride,
> He dares so doubtlessly resolve of rule,
> And by profession be ambitious . . .

I A   Hell-castle as represented on the stage for
the Passion Play at Valenciennes, 1547

I B   Christ Triumphant before the gate of Hell. Oil painting
by Giovanni Bellini, *c.* 1500

I C   Hearne's print of
Christ's descent into Hell

II Hell-castle as represented in the Doom, formerly in fresco on the church arch in the Chapel of the Holy Cross, Stratford-on-Avon

Raleigh, apostrophizing Death, wrote:

Thou has drawn together all the far-stretched greatness, all the pride, cruelty and ambition of man, and covered it all over with those two narrow words, Hic jacet.

Thus also in *Henry VIII* we find

> . . . fling away ambition:
> By that sin fell the angels. How can man then,
> The image of his Maker, hope to win by it? (III, ii, 441–3)

And Milton wrote:

> He trusted to have equalled the Most High,
> If he opposed; and with ambitious aim
> Against the throne and monarchy of God
> Raised impious war in Heaven and battle proud,
> With vain attempt.[66]

Even in the time of the Romantics this medieval attitude persisted, for Byron scorned 'vile ambition',[67] and Coleridge rebuked a biographer of Milton who referred to his 'ambition', thus:

I do not approve the so frequent use of this word relatively to Milton. Indeed the fondness for ingrafting a good sense on the word 'ambition', is not a Christian impulse in general.[68]

To believe, as we do today, that Macbeth's ambition is an excess of what is a good impulse is wrong—he succumbs to the sin of Satan himself and commits regicide, an act in Elizabethan eyes almost as heinous as the revolt against God. In *The Elizabethan World Picture* E. M. W. Tillyard stressed the importance of the Order of Being to Shakespeare and his contemporaries, and I suggest, with respect, that the picture is incomplete without adding ambition as the force which would destroy it by causing what they most feared—rebellion.[69]

On a play like *Macbeth*, which has such a rich texture and such a complex background, conclusions are necessarily personal and tentative.

(*a*) I find no grounds for believing that the Elizabethans had a single, or simple, literary 'witch-image' (to use TV jargon). On the contrary, witches were associated, identified, confused with the Furies of classical literature, with the biblical demons, and with the fairies of folklore. Hence I believe that Shakespeare was able to combine as one symbol 'the Weird Sisters', 'the goddesses of destinie, or els some Nimphes or Feiries', the 'sort of Witches dwelling in a towne of Murrayland', and 'a certaine witch whom [Macbeth] had in good trust' —all of whom he found in Holinshed—because they were nearly synonymous in his own time. And they continued thus at least until Davenant's version and probably until the age of Lamb and Coleridge.

(*b*) The plasticity of this compound image allowed the incorporation of material from an actual witch trial—that of the notorious North Berwick witches in I, iii—and at the same time permitted the introduction of the allusions to Hecate, and finally her actual appearance, with the fairy associations, in the play (a reinterpretation in longhand, as it were, of Shakespeare's shorthand symbols, such that they again approached the spirit, if not the letter, of Holinshed's narrative).

(c) The Weird Sisters are omnipresent in the play and are responsible for tempting Macbeth, for inciting him to murder Duncan, and they act as agents of remorse and despair like the classical Furies, their aim being to ensure Macbeth's damnation.

(d) They are also responsible for many of the 'natural' phenomena, such as the thunder, lightning, and fog in I, i, the storm on the night of Duncan's murder, and obscuring the sun on the following day. They also produce the more obviously supernatural effects such as the dagger and Banquo's Ghost; and they draw down the moon in II, i, cause the nightmares, and are intimately connected with the owl symbolism and the Apocalyptic atmosphere.

(e) The ambition, the conscience, the remorse, and the despair of Macbeth are to be seen as consonant with the beliefs of Shakespeare's contemporaries, lay and ecclesiastical, and traced to their ultimate sources they lead to Satan, to the Day of Judgment, and to Hell. To interpret the play in terms of the broad popular ideas of modern psychology, as we are all prone to do, and so restrict our inquiry to human character, is to ignore the fact that the mythological demons, the witches, and the fairies—which we may regard as personifications and manifestations of subjective processes—were also looked upon in Shakespeare's time as objective agents in a theological system. Even Timothy Bright, psychologist though he was, subscribed to the religious view of conscience which upheld the essential ambiguity of this symbolism.

Finally, the language of *Macbeth* is written in the idiom of the primitive imagination—the imagination stimulated by the fear of the unknown, of the unknowable. In this language there are metamorphoses instead of substantives, so that there is no longer a dividing line between the literal and the metaphorical, between the objective and the subjective; it is at once vague and precise, real and unreal; what is connoted is more important than what is denoted. It is seminal and it germinates into terror. But we understand this language intuitively, for we have all had nightmares, and if we no longer read the Bible, we still have enough of the apocalyptic feeling to be appalled at the thought of nuclear Armageddon, and to be numb with horror as nature's germens threaten to grow into mushrooms in the sky.

© A. R. McGEE 1966

NOTES

1. *The Anatomy of Melancholy*, ed. Floyd Dell and Paul Jordan-Smith (1955), p. 164.

2. *Aeneid*, III, 246, 252; VII, 341, 346–7. *Metamorphoses*, IV, 475.

3. *Faerie Queene*, II, Canto VII, 23.

4. See *The Masque of Queenes* (*Ben Jonson*, Oxford, 1941), 96–7, footnote *n*.

5. *Metamorphoses*, IV, 500.

6. *Aeneid*, VI, 250, 570–1, 605–7.

7. *Op. cit.* pp. 218–23, 237–9, 214–17, 34–5.

8. *Faerie Queene*, II, Canto IV, 10.

9. *Macbeth* (Arden, 1962), p. lxv.

10. K. M. Briggs, *Pale Hecate's Team* (1962), p. 245.

11. *The Witch-Cult in Western Europe* (1921).

12. F. Marian McNeil, *The Silver Bough* (1957), p. 138.

13. *The Royal Play of 'Macbeth'* (1950), p. 284.

14. Murray, *op. cit.* pp. 14, 238–46.

15. T. A. Spalding, *Elizabethan Demonology* (1880), p. 126.

16. Sir Walter Scott, *Letters on Demonology and Witchcraft* (1830), p. 179.

17. *Op. cit.* p. 168.

18. *Op. cit.* p. 238.

19. *Aubrey's Brief Lives*, ed. Oliver Lawson Dick (1950), p. cvi.

20. *Op. cit.* pp. 105–6.

21. *Op. cit.* p. 137.

22. *Aeneid*, IV, 462–3.

23. *The Golden Ass*, trans. Robert Graves (1950), p. 88.

24. *Op. cit.* p. 266 and footnote.

25. *Ibid.*

26. R. Trevor Davies, *Four Centuries of Witch-Beliefs* (1947), pp. 31, 99.

27. *The Devils of Loudun* (1952), p. 261.

28. *Daemonologie* (1603), p. 57.

29. *Op. cit.* pp. 265–6.

30. See note 3 above.

31. Act II, scene I.

32. *Op. cit.* p. 176.

33. *Ibid.* pp. 167–8.

34. *Ibid.* p. 166.

35. *Lear*, III, iv, 121.

36. *Metamorphoses*, XIV, 368; *Golden Ass*, p. 84.

37. *Daemonologie*, p. 47.

38. Paul, *op. cit.* p. 99.

39. *Op. cit.* p. 938. And cf. Stoll, *Art and Artifice in Shakespeare* (1963 ed.), p. 87.

40. *The Ecclesiastical Polity*, ed. Hanbury (1830), III, 81.

41. *An Etymological Dictionary of the English Language.*

42. Brewer, *A Dictionary of Phrase and Fable.*

43. *Op. cit.* pp. 177, 197, 82, 245.

44. *Minstrel's Song.*

45. *Shakespearean Tragedy* (1948), p. 143.

46. G. M. Trevelyan, *English Social History* (1946), p. 45.

47. Ivor Brown, *Shakespeare* (1949), p. 58.

48. *Shakespeare's Philosophical Patterns* (1937), pp. 79–80.

49. *Shakespeare Criticism 1919–1935* (1936), p. 42.

50. Cf. Brewer.

51. See *Macbeth* (Arden), p. xx.

52. *The Shakspere Allusion Book* (1909), p. 427.

53. *Daemonologie*, p. 47.

54. *Metamorphoses*, VII, 206; *The Witch*, Act V, scene ii.

55. Davies, *op. cit.* p. 5.

56. See Edgar C. S. Gibson, *The Thirty Nine Articles of the Church of England* (1902), p. 484, n. 2; and Paul, *op. cit.* p. 290.

57. *Op. cit.* p. 946.

58. Charlton, *op. cit.* pp. 146–7. M. C. Bradbrook, 'The Sources of *Macbeth*', *Shakespeare Survey 4*, (1951), p. 43.

59. *Op. cit.* p. 956.

60. *Op. cit.* III, 443.

61. Spalding, *op. cit.* p. 46.

62. Bunyan—Faithful (of Shame); Paul, *op. cit.* p. 135.

63. *Op. cit.* p. 940.

64. *Hell*, Canto IX; *The Mirror for Magistrates*, The Induction, 218–31.

65. *Daemonologie*, p. 37.

66. Hooker, *op. cit.* II, 382. *The Spanish Tragedy*, 2, II, 41; 2, IV, 60. *The Duchess of Malfi*, V, V, 91–2. Burton, *op. cit.* p. 114. *Tamburlaine*, II. vi. 11–14. Dover Wilson, *Life in Shakespeare's England*, p. 230.

67. *Childe Harold*, Canto IV, xcvii.

68. *Essays and Lectures on Shakespeare* (1907), p. 290.

69. Cf. Willymat's *A Loyal Subject's Looking Glass* (1604) 'in which he described the prime cause of rebellion as pride, ambition and envy' (Bradbrook, *op. cit.* p. 40).

HELL-CASTLE AND ITS DOOR-KEEPER

BY

GLYNNE WICKHAM

Few scenes in Shakespeare can have provoked more laughter in the theatre and more discomfort in the classroom than *Macbeth*, II, iii. At the centre of this paradox lies the character of the Porter, and in particular the obscenities which punctuate his remarks. These obscenities moreover are inextricably linked to a string of references to hell and the devil. How is this scene to be handled by the actor, and how is it to be handled by the schoolteacher?

The experience of being woken up in the middle of the night out of a deep sleep to deal with some disturbance in the house is as irritating as it is common: it is therefore a situation which if exposed to view in the theatre by a good mimic is certain to provide an amusing spectacle. Macbeth's porter, asleep when he ought to have been awake and on duty, stumbling towards the castle gate still rubbing his bleary eyes and hastily adjusting his costume, arouses a host of personal associations for everyone in the audience and is a sure-fire raiser of laughter in consequence. The fact that in this instance he is suffering from a bad hangover only adds to the fun for adults. Yet it is in this addition that trouble begins; for out of it spring the particular obscenities through which the Porter gives expression in his language both to his predicament and to his feelings. Normally speaking the teacher must reckon both this predicament and these feelings to lie outside the experience of schoolchildren; in consequence, no great effort of imagination is required to understand why many teachers (and some editors) should find themselves perplexed if not embarrassed when faced with the task of explaining this scene to their pupils. To take refuge in the old nostrums of a corrupt passage in the text or, more frequent, of 'comic relief', may ease the embarrassment, but shirks the challenge which the scene presents. Are the references to hell, the devil, drink and lechery to be regarded simply as a rag-bag of swear-words habitual to a coarse, unlettered peasant? Or are they pointers to the true significance of the scene and its function within the structure of the play?

I think it may be useful both to the actor and to the teacher to know that anyone familiar with medieval religious drama is likely to recognize a correspondence between the vocabulary of this scene and that of a similar playlet within the English Miracle Cycles, 'The Harrowing of Hell'. If this story has become unfamiliar, this is partly because it is an aspect of Christian belief which theologians of the Reformation distorted, and partly because modern Anglican opinion prefers to ignore it. Yet I think it is the story which provided Shakespeare with his model for the particular form in which he chose to cast Act II, scene iii of *Macbeth*, and possibly for the play as a whole.[1]

On the medieval stage hell was represented as a castle, more particularly as a dungeon or cesspit within a castle, one entrance to which was often depicted as a dragon's mouth (Plate IA). Its gate was guarded by a janitor or porter. Christ, after his crucifixion, but before his resurrection, came to this castle of hell to demand of Lucifer the release of the souls of the patriarchs and prophets. The setting for this play was either the interior of the gate-house or the courtyard of the castle: Christ's arrival was signalled by a tremendous knocking at this gate and a blast of trumpets. The gate eventually collapses allowing the Saviour-avenger, accompanied by the archangel Michael with his flaming sword, to enter and release the souls held prisoner within. It is in circumstances not unlike these that Macduff knocks at the gate of Macbeth's castle and that Malcolm and Donalbain escape from it in the course of Act II, scenes ii and iii. What did hell look like? How did its door-keeper behave? And where did the authors of the Miracle Cycles obtain descriptive information? The starting point may be found in two of the oldest mimetic ceremonies within the Catholic liturgy, the *Ordo Dedicationis Ecclesiae* and the *Tollite portas* procession to the city gates or church door on Palm Sunday, later elaborated and put to different use in the *Officium Elevationis Crucis*. Karl Young thinks that the inspiration of all these ceremonies is to be found in both the twenty-fourth Psalm, verses 7–10, and the second part of the 'Gospel of Nicodemus', the *Descensus Christi ad Inferos*.[2]

The first six and the last four verses of Psalm xxiv are virtually separate. It is the latter section which bears directly upon the two liturgical ceremonies.

7 Lift up your heads, O ye gates, and be ye lift up, ye everlasting doors : and the King of glory shall come in.

8. Who is the King of glory : it is the Lord strong and mighty, even the Lord mighty in battle.

9 Lift up your heads, O ye gates, and be ye lift up, ye everlasting doors : and the King of glory shall come in.

10 Who is the King of glory : even the Lord of hosts, he is the King of glory.

(Book of Common Prayer)

These words appear in the Latin text of the *Descensus* but as a duologue between Christ and Satan. This dialogue is brought to life in emblematic manner within the *Ordo Dedicationis Ecclesiae*.

A church before consecration was regarded as impure, the dwelling place of Satan and in need of cleansing. Accordingly the bishop approached the building in procession on Christ's behalf, knocked at the West door with his staff three times and said in Latin,

Tollite portas, principes, vestras, et elevamini, portae aeternales, et introibit rex gloriae.

A cleric replies from within the building,

Quis est iste rex gloriae?

This dialogue is repeated three times after which the bishop declares,

Dominus virtutum, ipse est rex gloriae.

As he enters the church the cleric slips out. The church itself is then cleansed by censing. This ceremony can be traced back to the fourth century in Jerusalem.[3]

A full account of the symbolic representation of the Harrowing of Hell derived from the *Elevatio* survives in England from the monastery of Barking, near London. Katherine of Sutton, abbess of Barking from 1363 to 1376, established a ceremony there incorporating the *Tollite portas* verses and lying immediately between the close of Matins on Easter Day and the normal *Visitatio Sepulchri*. At Barking, members of the convent were imprisoned within the Chapel of St Mary Magdalen, thus representing the souls of the patriarchs confined in hell. A priest approaches the door with the words *Tollite portas*; the door is opened and the erstwhile prisoners file out into the church carrying palm branches signifying victory over Satan and death, singing *Cum rex gloriae*. This ceremony also survives from Dublin in two forms.[4]

The authors of the vernacular cycles therefore had a long liturgical tradition behind them as well as the Gospel of Nicodemus to assist them when they came to prepare their play-books of the Harrowing of Hell. The story itself was familiar enough to require little development: ample opportunity existed, however, for the addition of descriptive detail. In this the authors were further assisted by artists in stained glass and by painters who, from Fra Angelico to Bellini and Dürer, had persistently represented Christ with the banner of the cross in his hand standing victorious, like St George above the dragon, before the shattered gates of hell with Satan cringing at his feet (Plate IB).

In *Macbeth*, Macduff enters Macbeth's castle twice, first in II, iii, when Duncan's murder is discovered and Malcolm and Donalbain escape, and again in V, ix, when, as a victorious general, he arrives from the field of battle and addresses Malcolm:

> Hail, King! for so thou art. Behold, where stands
> Th' usurper's cursed head: the time is free.[5]   (v, ix, 20–1)

There is thus no attempt on Shakespeare's part to provide a direct parallel to the Harrowing of Hell within the play of *Macbeth*; but there is ample evidence within the text of the play of a conscious attempt on Shakespeare's part to remind his audience of this ancient and familiar story so that they may discern for themselves the moral meaning of this stage narrative abstracted from the annals of Scottish history. To make this point as forcibly as I think it should be made it is first necessary to reconstruct from the texts and stage directions of the surviving Miracle Cycles the picture of hell and its inhabitants that was familiar to Tudor audiences together with the salient aspects of the story as it was treated on their stages.

Hell itself was represented as a combination of castle, dungeon and cesspit. Of the four surviving English Cycles, Towneley (Play xxv), 'The Deliverance of Souls', follows York (Play 37), The Saddlers, almost verbatim at times: both are derived in large measure from the Middle-English poetical 'Gospel of Nicodemus' of the early fourteenth century.[6] It is from these versions of the play that we learn that hell is equipped with walls and gates like a castle.

TOWNELEY:

> *Belzabub.* Go, spar the yates, yll mot thou the!
> And set the waches on the wall.   (E.E.T.S. lines 120–1)

YORK:

> *Bellial.* We! spere oure ȝates, all ill mot þou spede,
> And sette furthe watches on þe wall.
> (L. Toulmin-Smith, *York Plays* (1885), p. 380, lines 139–40)

This image of Hell-castle is later reinforced in Towneley (lines 146–9) by Belzabub who calls to Satan

> *Belzabub.* Thou must com help to spar
> we are beseged abowte.
> *Sathanas.* Besegyd aboute! whi, who durst be so bold
> for drede to make on us a fray?

In the *Ludus Coventriae* Anima Christi describes hell as 'the logge (*prison*) of helle' (E.E.T.S. p. 305). This is followed by a stage direction which reads: 'The soule goth to helle gatys . . .' which gates Christ further specifies as being a 'derke dore' (*ibid.* p. 306). This image of a prison is consistently maintained in the plays of 'The Fall of Lucifer' and the 'The Assumption' from the same Cycle and is further particularized by Belial (p. 319) as 'helle gonge', i.e. latrine. In the Towneley 'Deliverance' hell is also described as a 'pryson' (by Jesus, line 236) and as 'that pytt' (by Jesus, line 285) and as 'hell pyt' (by Satan, line 360). Prison, pit and dungeon are the words used variously in the Chester cycle to describe hell (Plate II).

What we must visualize is an edifice which, viewed from outside, resembles a castle and, viewed from inside, a sequence of dark dungeons and torture chambers pervaded by stench and heat. This picture, built up from details in the texts of English cyclic plays set in hell, closely resembles the MS. picture of Hell-castle illustrating the Valenciennes Passion Play of 1547 (see Plate I A). Further detail, if we want it, can be found in the Account Book of the Mons Passion Play (1501) where the walls of hell are said to have been 'plastered'.[7] A Scottish castle therefore, through the gates of which a kingly guest has been welcomed by a host who promptly murders him, might be calculated to recall this other, satanic castle with its 'ʒatys of sorwatorie (*torment*)'.[8] Both castles moreover are equipped with a janitor or porter.

The authors of the Cycles found this door-keeper in the poetical 'Gospel of Nicodemus' where, as a character, he already borders on the comic.

> *Dominus.* Wer ys nou þis ʒateward?
> me þuncheþ [*thinketh*] he is a coward.
> *Janitor.* Ich haue herd wordes stronge,
> ne dar y her no lengore stonde;
> kepe þe gates whose may,
> y lete hem stonde ant renne away.[9]

This idea is elaborated upon by the York and Towneley scribes. In both plays the porter acquires a name; significantly it is Rybald, a word defined by *O.E.D.* as meaning 'Scurrilous, irreverent, profane, indecent' and as derived from the French *ribaut*, a menial. A more succinct and apposite description of Macbeth's porter could scarcely be found. In the Towneley play Rybald receives his orders from Belzabub. In *Macbeth*, the Porter's first question is,

> Who's there, i' th' name of Belzebub? (line 4)

We should surely expect him to say 'in the name of my master' or possibly 'in the name of Macbeth'; but, since Macbeth has just murdered Duncan, 'in the name of Belzebub' or 'in the devil's name' is just as appropriate. The knocking has at least put the porter in mind of Hell-gate: his comments put it in our minds too. In the Towneley 'Deliverance' it is Rybald who first answers Christ's knocking.

> *Rybald.* . . . what deviłł is he
> That callys hym kyng over us ałł?
> hark belzabub, com ne,
> ffor hedusly I hard hym całł. (E.E.T.S. lines 116–19)

The 'hideous call' is a fanfare of trumpets followed by the familiar,

Attollite portas, principes, vestras & eleuamini porte eternales, & introibit rex glorie. (Towneley, lines 115–16)

At York and Chester the Latin is followed by a translation, phrase by phrase, into English.

In *Macbeth* the Porter receives no answer to his thrice-repeated 'Who's there?' The knocking continues remorselessly, but the questions are answered rhetorically by the Porter himself. In his drunken condition he stumbles about the stage like a man waking out of a dream who still regards the environment of his dream as more real than that confronting him on waking. Just, as today, one might be woken by one's own telephone and at the same time fancy oneself called to some other 'phone in another house within the fabric of one's dream, so the Porter, dreaming that he is Rybald and in hell, associates the real knocking on Macbeth's castle-gate that has obtruded upon or into his dream with Christ's arrival at hell's 'dark door'. When the Porter asks for the first time who is knocking he is still firmly in his dream-world.

> Who's there, i' th' name of Belzebub? (line 4)

When he asks for the second time he is already beginning to slip out of his dream, for he can't recall the name of any other companion in this diablerie.

> Who's there, i' th' other devil's name? (line 8)

By the time he has repeated this question a third time the chill of dawn is bringing him swiftly back to reality.
> —But this place is too cold for Hell.
> I'll devil-porter it no further: (lines 18–19)

This gate is not shattered: the porter opens it. Macduff enters. The porter asks for a tip.

> I pray you, remember the porter. (line 22)

This remark is ambivalent, for it can be addressed by the actor both to Macduff and to the audience. As in the Porter's dream, it is in two worlds at once; that of Macbeth's castle and that of another scene from another play which has just been recalled for the audience and which the author wants them to remember. If we take the remark in this latter sense, we recollect that it was Jesus who with a loud knocking entered Hell-castle in search of Satan. At this point in *Macbeth* Shakespeare has not yet informed us that Macduff is destined to avenge Duncan's murder, but in his use of the porter he gives us a clear hint of what to expect.

In the next sixteen lines of conversation with Macduff, the porter sobers up and drops every aspect of his earlier hallucination; but in the ribaldry of the language, humour and (where the actor is concerned) gesture, he remains equivocal. When Macduff asks him,

> Is thy master stirring? (line 43)

we are still at liberty to regard him both as Macbeth's servant and as Satan's.

It is then left to Lennox who has entered the castle with Macduff to draw the audience's attention to another strange phenomenon.

> *Lennox.* The night has been unruly: where we lay,
> Our chimneys were blown down; and as they say,
> Lamentings heard i' th' air; strange screams of death,
> And, prophesying with accents terrible,

> Of dire combustion, and confus'd events,
> New hatch'd to th' woeful time, the obscure bird
> Clamour'd the livelong night: some say the earth
> Was feverous, and did shake.
> > *Macbeth.*   'Twas a rough night.
> > *Lennox.* My young remembrance cannot parallel
> A fellow to it.
>
> (lines 55–63)

An older memory, however, might well recall a parallel. In the cyclic plays of the Harrowing of Hell it is the strange noises in the air which alert the devils of impending disaster.

TOWNELEY

Rybald. Sen fyrst that hell was mayde / And I was put therin, / Sich sorow neuer ere I had / nor hard I sich a dyn; /

. . . .

how, belsabub! bynde thise boys, / sich harow was neuer hard in hell.

Belzabub. Out, rybald! thou rores, / what is betyd? can thou oght tell?

Rybald. Whi, herys thou not this ugly noyse?

(lines 89–95)

When Christ arrives at the gates there is more noise including trumpets and knocking.

CHESTER (stage direction)

Tunc veniet Jhesus et fiet Clamor vel sonitus materialis magnus . . .

(line 144)

Still more succinct is the stage direction of the Mons Passion:

Lors se doi(b)t faire en En(f)fer une grande tempeste et la terre doit trambler.

(ed. cit. p. 412)

Lennox might be supplying a literal translation of this last line with his 'some say the earth was feverous and did shake'.[10]

It is Lady Macbeth who completes the picture. It was she who first heard the knocking at the south gate from the direction of England and it is she who, when the bell starts tolling, says,

> What's the business,
> That such a hideous trumpet calls to parley
> The sleepers of the house?
>
> (lines 81–3)

It was Rybald in the Towneley 'Deliverance' who cried out to Beelzebub on hearing Christ's trumpets at Hell-gate

> . . . come ne,
> ffor hedusly I hard hym call.   (lines 118–19) (Plate Ic)

Thunder, cacophony, screams and groans were the audible emblems of Lucifer and hell on the medieval stage. Those same aural emblems colour the whole of II, iii of *Macbeth* and, juxtaposed as they are with thunderous knocking at a gate attended by a porter deluded into regarding himself as a devil, their relevance to the moral meaning of the play could scarcely have escaped the notice of its first audiences.

In the cyclic plays of the Harrowing of Hell, Satan (or Lucifer) is physically overthrown, bound and either cast into hell pit or sinks into it.

CHESTER (stage direction) Iaceant tunc Sathanam de sede sua. (line 168)

TOWNELEY:

> Sathan. Alas, for doyH and care!
> I synk into heH pyt. (lines 359–60)

In the York play the rescued souls leave the stage singing *Laus tibi Domino cum gloria*. Towneley ends with the *Te Deum*. In *Macbeth*, when Macduff has successfully brought Macbeth and his 'fiend-like Queen' to justice, it is Malcolm, the new King-elect, who brings the play to its close in joy and thanksgiving.

> Malcolm. So thanks to all at once, and to each one,
> Whom we invite to see us crown'd at Scone. *Flourish. Exeunt.* (v, ix, 140–1)

Scotland has been purged of a devil who, like Lucifer, aspired to a throne that was not his, committed crime upon crime first to obtain it and then to keep it, and was finally crushed within the refuge of his own castle by a saviour-avenger accompanied by armed archangels. Hell has been harrowed: 'the time is free'.

© G. WICKHAM 1966

NOTES

1. John W. Hales in his *Notes and Essays on Shakespeare* (1884) regarded the Porter as a possible borrowing from the English Miracle Cycles (pp. 284–6). He appears only to have been familiar with *Ludus Coventriae*, the one cycle of the four in which Belzebub is not a character of importance in 'The Descent into Hell'; but he also draws attention to the porter of hell gate as depicted by Heywood in *Four P's* and in the much later anonymous Interlude *Nice Wanton*: see also William Hone, *Ancient Mysteries Described* (1823), pp. 120–47.

This suggestion does not appear to have been carried much further until John B. Harcourt raised it again in 'I Pray You, Remember the Porter', *Shakespeare Quarterly*, XII (1961), 393–402. This important article, which was brought to my attention after the completion of this short essay, anticipates several of the points made in it and draws attention to several other significant details in the scene. The fact that the two articles were written independently of each other and in different continents perhaps serves to strengthen the more important conclusions that are common to them both.

2. *The Drama of the Medieval Church* (1933), I, 149 ff. See also *The Middle English Harrowing of Hell and Gospel of Nicodemus*, ed. W. H. Hulme for E.E.T.S. (1907), pp. lxii ff.

3. Young, *op. cit.* I, 102.

4. *Ibid.* pp. 168 ff.

5. This and other quotations from *Macbeth* are from the Arden edition.

6. See W. H. Hulme, *op. cit.* pp. xviii ff.

7. See G. Cohen, *Le Livre de Conduite du Régisseur et le Compte des Dépenses pour le Mystère de la Passion joué à Mons en 1501* (Paris, 1925), pp. 498, 528.

8. *Ludus Coventriae* (E.E.T.S.), p. 306.

9. Harley MS. Text L, *The Harrowing of Hell*, ed. cit. p. 13, lines 139–44.

10. These extraordinary noises are clearly intended to be associated as much with the murder of Duncan as with the arrival of Macduff and are derived as clearly from the noises associated with the actual moment of Christ's death as from noise associated with the arrival of Anima Christi before the gates of hell. The Harley Text of the *Gospel of Nicodemus* describing this moment reads:

> þe stanes in sonder brak,
> þe erth trembled & quaked,
> with noys als man it spak,
> Slyke mane for him it maked.

(Hulme, *op. cit.* for E.E.T.S., p. 68, lines 705–8)

'HIS FIEND-LIKE QUEEN'

BY

W. MOELWYN MERCHANT

It is surely unnecessary to argue today that Lady Macbeth's invocation of the 'spirits that tend on mortal thoughts', of the 'murth'ring ministers', is a formal stage in demonic possession—though the implications of that statement are rarely if ever pursued. W. C. Curry sufficiently stated[1] the spiritual significance of the invocation in saying that 'Lady Macbeth deliberately wills that [unclean spirits, wicked angels] subtly invade her body and so control it that the natural inclination of the spirit towards goodness and compassion may be completely extirpated'. But even this statement we may regard as slightly evasive and carrying some of the tones of Coleridge's examination of her character:

Hers is the mock fortitude of a mind deluded by ambition; she shames her husband with a superhuman audacity of fancy which she cannot support ... Her speech: 'Come, all you spirits that tend on mortal thoughts,' etc., is that of one who had habitually familiarised her imagination to dreadful conceptions, and was trying to do so still more. Her invocations and requisitions are all the false efforts of a mind accustomed only hitherto to the shadows of imagination ...

'Fancy which she cannot support ... trying to do so ... false efforts', these qualified phrases do less than justice to the force of the invocation at I, v, 40–54; it denies the position which Lady Macbeth holds in the supernatural pattern of the play, her relations to the Weird Sisters and to Hecate; it minimizes the poetic and dramatic organization of scenes iii–vii of Act I.

We should not, perhaps, be surprised that the impact of the demonic invocation is reduced, both in critical reading and in our experience in the theatre. For our emotional attention is deflected, while our immediate understanding is reduced by inadequate attention to the technical force of some of the phrases. In the first place we experience a sharp sexual affront to our sensibility in the two phrases 'unsex me here' and 'come to my woman's breasts,/And take my milk for gall' and it is not insignificant, in weighing this sense of affront, that two classical performances in the role sprang from a conception of great and essentially feminine beauty: Sarah Siddons conceived Lady Macbeth as possessing 'all the subjugating powers of intellect and all the charms and graces of personal beauty ... that character which I believe is generally allowed to be most captivating to the other sex,—fair, feminine, nay, perhaps even fragile'; while Sargent's swift *grisaille* sketch of Ellen Terry in the National Portrait Gallery establishes a like impression of grace and of spontaneity (Plate III). Unless, therefore, Lady Macbeth as 'fiend-like queen' is played in a naïvely 'monumental' way, the demand that her sex be destroyed carries a shocking force.

But in fact the sexual affront is profounder than this immediate experience in performance and relates this scene intimately to its context in the first act. The scene itself (I, v) is close-knit. It opens with Macbeth's letter, ambiguous, allusive, technical: 'they' are as undefined, questionable, as they were in I, i and I, iii; on the other hand a precise phrase, 'they made themselves air', a known power of witchcraft to create a distinct, almost palpable atmosphere into which the initiate may vanish, places and defines their expertise; the pun on 'mortal knowledge' (both 'human' and 'death-dealing') anticipates the 'mortal thoughts' of Lady Macbeth's soliloquy; while the complicity, the intimacy in evil of the two protagonists, is left undefined and unfocused. With the opening of Lady Macbeth's comment on the letter we are referred back to Macbeth's last speech in the previous scene: her grouped antitheses—'Thou wouldst be great . . . but without the illness', 'wouldst not play false,/And yet', 'Rather thou dost fear . . . than wishest should be undone'—precisely echo the thought and grammatical construction of his speech (reflecting an embarrassed dislocation in moral judgment):

> Let not light see my black and deep desires.
> The eye wink at the hand; *yet* let that be,
> Which the eye fears, when it is done, to see.

The ambiguity of her present status and power is extended in the 'spirits' which she would pour into his ear; while the near contempt of her phrase 'the milk of human kindness', that maternal source of compassion, prepares for her own 'unsexing'. The invocation itself proceeds in a formal ritual of demonic possession. The opening lines, in which the entry of the spirits shall unsex her, reflect both the uncertain nature of the Weird Sisters' (I, iii, 45, 'you should be women,/And yet your beards . . .') and the ambiguous rites of witchcraft which may be directed either to fertility or sterility, as we shall see; the transmutation for which she prays, making thick her blood, frustrating remorse and compunction, moves from bodily possession to moral confusion in which purpose and act, will and fulfilment, are disjointed and without 'peace'; finally, in two concluding invocations, 'Come to my woman's breasts', 'Come, thick Night', the moment of demonic possession is given its proper context, palled 'in the dunnest smoke of hell'.

Closer attention is demanded by the phrase, 'take my milk for gall', which has been a continuous editorial problem. From Samuel Johnson to our own day, a favoured solution has been to assume that Lady Macbeth desires simply that the 'murth'ring ministers' 'take away my milk, and put gall into the place', Johnson's paraphrase which Kenneth Muir endorses as 'the best' in his opinion. But this is to mitigate the supernatural force of the whole passage and it is unfortunate that Keightley's tentative solution[2] was not pursued to a proper conclusion: 'Perhaps we should read *with* for "for", taking "take" in the sense of *tinge, infect*, a sense it often bears.' We may deduce from this unnecessary emendation of '*for* gall' that Keightley appears to suppose a wholly physical tainting of the milk with the savour of gall. Had he pressed the 'sense it often bears' further than editors have ventured, he would have reached the wholly acceptable technical interpretation of the phrase, 'bewitch my milk for gall, possess it and complete the invasion of my body at its source of compassion'. There is ample confirmation for this reading and adequate parallels in Shakespeare, fully noted in the glossaries and lexicons. Robert Nares[3] explains the verb:

In the sense of to blast; or to affect violently, as by witchcraft. Sh. says of Herne, the hunter, that

> There he blasts the tree, and takes the cattle,
> And makes milch kine yield blood

and cites Gervase Markham's explanation of 'a horse that is taken',

Some farriers, not well understanding the ground of the disease, conster the word *taken* to be striken by some planet or evil spirit.

C. T. Onions cites the fullest passage (*Hamlet*, I, i, 163) in the sense 'to strike with disease':

> No spirit dares stir abroad,
> The nights are wholesome; then no planets strike,
> No fairy *takes*, nor witch hath power to charm,

while in the two instances from *Lear* (III, iv, 60 and II, iv, 166) Onions glosses the word as 'blasting, malignant influence' and 'blasting, pernicious' ('bless thee from whirlwinds, star-blasting and taking' and 'strike her young bones,/You taking airs, with lameness'). It is of course clear that these instances have in common a sense of cosmic disruption, supernatural evil and the infection of the body by planetary or demonic influences. In the last passage cited, Lear's cursing of Regan (as he had earlier disowned Cordelia by the 'mysteries of Hecate and the night') concludes with terms which recall *Macbeth*: '*Infect* her beauty . . . *blast* her pride.'

That Lady Macbeth, therefore, should consummate the possession of her body by this technical term, 'take my milk for gall',[4] completes the significance of this complex passage. That she should have deplored the natural, instinctively humane impulses of Macbeth a little earlier in the terms, 'too full o' th' milk of human kindness', is of a piece with this disruption of her nature; in the light of this closer examination of her words, the question put with irony by L. C. Knights, 'How many children had Lady Macbeth?', takes on more critical significance. The organic relationship, moreover, between this scene and those on either side (I, iii–vii) can now be more closely established. They deserve more detailed examination than can be given here but two related themes may be taken to make the connexion, that of judgment and justice, and of ministering servants.

Lady Macbeth has presumed to judge her husband, reversing the customary moral categories and taking his humane scrupulosity as merely ineffectual weakness. That this has in fact an element of truth in no way diminishes her moral obliquity in passing judgment. She, in the process of judging him, commits herself, her body and her spiritual functions to a Faustian service; nor is it, in this instance either, any diminution of her moral responsibility that her submission to demonic powers should condemn her in the rest of the play to a merely passive damnation. Macbeth's spiritual degeneration in this first act is both subtler and more scrupulous (and we do not forget here that scrupulosity can be a moral failing as well as a virtue). For Macbeth is involved, from his first contact with the Weird Sisters, in a self-examination dependent on the terminology of divine and human justice. The process begins with his first soliloquy (I, iii, 127–42). The lines,

> This supernatural soliciting
> Cannot be ill; cannot be good

may be felt to have 'the sickening see-saw rhythm' which L. C. Knights finds, confirming the quality of a 'phantasma, or a hideous dream'; it certainly has more profoundly an exploration, in rhetorical, antithetic form, of the status of the Weird Sisters' prophecy. The deep horror of the passage lies in the rational structure—'If ill . . . if good, why . . . ?'—within which the moral problem is explored, united to a mounting emotional tension. The lines from 'Present

fears' to 'what is not' are an almost syllogistic conclusion to a moral argument but carrying
for the attentive reader, in the final lines,

> That function is smother'd in surmise,
> And nothing is but what is not,

an anticipation of Macbeth's ultimate nullity, his conviction that life is a 'tale told by an idiot
. . . signifying nothing'. Yet the moment of rationalized horror in I, iii leads not to emotional
disintegration but to Macbeth's total intellectual control in his response to Banquo at the end
of the scene:

> Think upon what hath chanc'd; and at more time,
> *The interim having weigh'd it*, let us speak—

concerning which Steevens has the wholly just comment: the 'intervening portion' of time is
personified: it (the 'Interim') is represented as 'a cool impartial judge' and so is Macbeth, having
conquered his first revulsion from the 'supernatural soliciting'.[5]

Lady Macbeth, her compact with the 'murth'ring ministers' made firm, employs terms of
judgment with fewer scruples than her husband. In response to Duncan's 'We are your guest
tonight' (I, vi, 25) she replies in the terminology of judicial process:

> Your servants ever
> Have theirs, themselves, and what is theirs, in *compt*,
> To *make their audit* at your Highness' pleasure,

(terms regularly used both for human justice and for the Last Judgment).[6] Five lines later, at the
opening of scene vii, Macbeth returns to his theme of judgment in its most elaborate form.
If Roy Walker[7] is correct in his conjecture that ''t were well/It were done quickly' and 'chalice'
recall the Last Supper and Christ's words to Judas concerning His betrayal—'that thou doest,
do quickly'—then supernatural, 'even-handed Justice' has here its profoundest analogy. The
contrast could scarcely be pointed more strongly between Lady Macbeth's total submission to
her course, with a casual acceptance of the terms of justice between herself and her royal guest,
and Macbeth's extended casuistic examination of the relationship of 'double trust' in which he
and Duncan stand within the context of eternal justice.

A similar contrast in the use of identical terminology may be seen in the image of 'servants'
and 'attendant ministers' which also links these scenes. It begins at Macbeth's personification
of his duties to his royal master as 'children and servants' 'Which do but what they should, by
doing everything' (I, iv, 26), related to Christ's 'unprofitable servants' in St Luke xvii, 10, who
do no more than their duty in doing all. The image is intensified and transferred from the
gracious to the demonic in Lady Macbeth's 'Spirits that *tend on* mortal thoughts' and the
ministers of sightless substance who '*wait on* Nature's mischief'. These verbs, *tend* and *wait*,
applied to evil spirits or angels inevitably recall the biblical terminology of angelic attendance,
'waiting upon God'.[8] The contrast is made most intense in scene vii, after Macbeth's examination of his relation to Duncan as host, kinsman and subject; not only has Duncan these formal,
social claims on Macbeth's integrity; 'his virtues will plead like angels, trumpet-tongu'd', in
the final phrase uniting the angels of the Last Judgment with those 'who stand and wait' at the
throne of God.

At this point in our examination of the dramatic contrast between Macbeth and his wife and their involvement in both good and evil supernature, we may profitably look to other sources of insight into Shakespeare's imagery. Blake clearly considered that the matter of two of his 'colour prints', *Pity* and *Hecate* (both derived in content substantially from *Macbeth*), were intimately related together. They are similar in size (*c.* 17 in. × 21 in. and *c.* 17 in. × 23 in.); they have consistently belonged together since they went first into the collection of Blake's friend Thomas Butts (they are now in the Tate Gallery, with versions elsewhere; Plates IV A, B), and Martin Butlin notes[9] their close identity of theme, for *Hecate* 'is probably a companion print to *Pity* . . . The two subjects were probably chosen to show two aspects of woman in the Fall. The triple representation of the Infernal Goddess Hecate is a traditional symbol of the three phases of the moon, crescent, full and waning.' The Weird Sisters number among the contents of their cauldron 'slips of yew,/Sliver'd in the moon's eclipse', a poisonous ingredient of which K. M. Briggs has extended the significance for this play. For yew is a 'tree of death' while 'Black magic is the magic of sterility; the moon's waxing time has always been counted the time of growth, and the moon's eclipse therefore would be the time of complete negation'.[10] Hecate is of course frequently (in her 'waxing time') associated with fertility,[11] but the associations in this play (and consistently in all Shakespeare's references to her elsewhere) are with destruction, sterility and death. Lady Macbeth's invocation of a demonism which denies her natural sex matches Macbeth's conviction of evil as he prepares (I, i, 50 ff.) for Duncan's murder:

> Nature seems dead, and wicked dreams abuse
> The curtain'd sleep: Witchcraft celebrates
> Pale Hecate's offerings; and wither'd Murther . . .
> Moves like a ghost.

Macbeth's second reference to Hecate is also involved with murder; as he obscurely hints at Banquo's death he sets its atmosphere and accompaniment—the activity of a witch's familiars and of Hecate:

> Ere the bat hath flown
> His cloister'd flight; ere to black Hecate's summons
> The shard-born beetle with his drowsy hums
> Hath rung night's yawning peal.

Blake's brooding, curiously noble figure of Hecate with her court of familiars very adequately depicts 'the goddess of hell and of sorcery', in whose name Lear disclaims all paternal care in Cordelia, by 'The mysteries of Hecate and the night' (I, i, 112); under whose influence the Player King in *Hamlet* is murdered, by a

> Mixture rank, of midnight weeds collected,
> With Hecat's ban thrice blasted, thrice infected—

and who is the appropriate term of abuse for Joan, la Pucelle, 'that railing Hecate' (*1 Henry VI*, III, ii, 64). We do not, then, require Hecate's presence on the stage to establish her presiding power over those in *Macbeth* who owe the same allegiance which Puck acknowledges; the number of those

> that do run
> By the triple Hecate's team
> From the presence of the sun,
> Following darkness like a dream.

This is the demonic company to which Lady Macbeth has committed herself and to which his increasing bloodshed drives Macbeth.

Before this submission to the triple Hecate's force, however, Macbeth, in contemplating his first murder, has a more daunting because more gracious vision; if Duncan's virtues will themselves be trumpeting angels, invoking final judgment against his 'taking-off', 'Pity' will declare his guilt more widely:

> Shall blow the horrid deed in every eye,
> That tears shall drown the wind.

Here we have yet another antithesis in the relation of Macbeth and his 'fiend-like queen'. Her allegiance is to 'mortal' powers who may ultimately hold of Hecate; Macbeth's awareness of submission to 'black Hecate's summons' is of slower growth and interrupted by knowledge of the other supernatural realm of grace. Blake's *Pity*, it is true, is involved in his own private mythology of the Fall but it nonetheless faithfully records the images of Macbeth's vision. The presiding image is that of Psalm xviii (in Coverdale's version):

He rode upon the Cherubyns and did flye; he came flyenge with the winges of the wynde.

Blake conflates the image of the Cherubins who fly *upon* the wind (the female figures, one of whom takes up the naked child) with the 'sightless couriers', the latter word a literal translation of 'angel'. Into this swift motion of grace 'pity' is swept up, the innocent helplessness of the phrase 'naked new-born babe' acquiring power ('striding the blast') from the mounted 'Cherubins'. The relation between Blake's print and Macbeth's speech merits more extended analysis but this would interpret Blake rather than Shakespeare. It suffices at this moment to focus the conflict, which as late as I, vii distinguishes the tugging of sin and grace in Macbeth from the swift demonism of Lady Macbeth. This struggle moreover establishes sharply the superior gravity of Shakespeare's treatment of evil supernature from that of all his contemporaries including King James.[12]

To summarize the argument: Lady Macbeth's willed submission to demonic powers, her unequivocal resolve to lay her being open to the invasion of witchcraft, is held in dramatic contrast to the painful, casuistic deliberations of Macbeth. She takes her appropriate dramatic place in the company of those, on the one hand, whose supernatural status is obscure; are the Weird Sisters witches, norns, fates or hallucinations? Holinshed expressed the historic doubts:

But afterwards the common opinion was, that these women were either the weird sisters, that is (as ye would say) the goddesses of destinie, or else some nymphs or feiries, indued with knowledge of prophesie by their necromanticall science.

Whatever the ambiguity of their status, we have, on the other hand, no doubt of Hecate's significance in Shakespeare's exploration of the supernatural; nor have we doubt (we see the

III   Ellen Terry as Lady Macbeth, sketched by Sargent

IV A   William Blake's *Pity*: a preliminary study

IV B   William Blake's *Hecate*

evidence on stage) of the 'necromantic' desires of Lady Macbeth; we see her bequeath her soul to demonic powers as irrevocably as Faustus. For Hecate broods over this play, whatever the status of the 'interpolated scenes'. The Weird Sisters owe her direct allegiance; Macbeth and Lady Macbeth submit themselves to a less mythical order of damnation, but even in their vision of hell Hecate and her followers belong as of right.

© W. M. MERCHANT 1966

NOTES

1. *Shakespeare's Philosophical Patterns* (Louisiana University Press, 1937).

2. *The Shakespeare Expositor* (1867); cited Furness *in loc.*

3. *A Shakespeare Glossary* (1901 ed., revised and enlarged by Halliwell and Wright).

4. I am grateful to Professor and Mrs Alan Ross (Birmingham) for confirming my conjecture in the following terms:
Take in the sense 'bewitch' presents no difficulties; it is *OED: Take* v. 7*a* and cf. *Take* sb. 3. The suggested translative use of *for* is perhaps more difficult: can *for* in fact mean 'so as to become'? It seems that it can; this sense is effectively *OED: For, prep, and conj.* A 8*b*, as used in *to go for a soldier*, that is, 'to go so as to become a soldier'.

5. Milton uses the word in the same sense, when Eve is first tempted by the fruit which 'Sollicited her longing eye'.

6. For *account (compt)* and *audit* as metaphors for the process of judgment, and more particularly the Last Judgment, cf. Romans XIV, 12: 'Every one of us shall give account of himself to God', and analogous passages which involve the concept of stewardship.

7. Cited by Muir *in loc.*

8. Cf. Revelation VIII, 2: 'And I saw the seven angels which stood before God; and to them were given seven trumpets.'

9. *William Blake*, Tate Gallery Catalogue, 1957, p. 43. Cf. also W. M. Merchant, 'Blake's Shakespeare', *Apollo*, Shakespeare Centenary Issue (April 1964); and Merchant, *Shakespeare and the Artist* (1959), ch. 10.

10. K. M. Briggs, *Pale Hecate's Team* (1962), p. 80.

11. Hecate is not only complex in herself as Triple-goddess (or on occasion quadruple); she varies greatly in significance. As a lunar goddess she was associated with fertility but in literary reference she was more frequently destructive. Elizabethans would be familiar with the passage in Ovid, *Metamorphoses*, XIV, 403-5:

Illa nocens spargit virus sucosque veneni
et Noctem Noctisque deos Ereboque Chaoque
convocat et longis Hecaten ululatibus orat;

which was translated rather vaguely by Golding with no direct reference to Hecate. In *Comus* she was a destructive goddess of riot.

12. This 'gravity' in no way assumes Shakespeare's assent to contemporary attitudes. It does however mark the gulf between Shakespeare's tone and that of the writers available to him. The ephemera and the contemporary accounts of witch trials are for the most part merely credulous and marked by an unpleasant 'curiositas'; works of the authority of *Demonologie* have more sobriety but lean heavily on traditional classics such as the *Malleus Maleficorum*. Shakespeare's dramatic tone is both serious and exploratory.

THE FIEND-LIKE QUEEN:
A NOTE ON 'MACBETH' AND SENECA'S 'MEDEA'

BY

INGA-STINA EWBANK

Not everyone is, perhaps, prepared to say that 'Macbeth without Seneca would have been impossible';[1] but many would agree with Henry N. Paul when he calls Macbeth 'the most Senecan of all of Shakespeare's plays'.[2] Scholars and critics have pointed out affinities with Seneca in the structural and rhetorical features of the play, as well as in those less easily definable aspects which are usually grouped together as 'atmosphere': the presence in action or language, or both, of night, blood and the supernatural.[3] A number of verbal resemblances to lines in Seneca (both the original tragedies and the translations in the Tenne Tragedies) have also been pointed out, and especially Agamemnon, Hercules Furens and Hippolytus (or Phaedra) have thus been suggested as sources for Macbeth. Some critics feel that in preparation for writing Macbeth Shakespeare may have read, or re-read, at least part of Seneca's dramatic works;[4] and one of them thinks that, as most of the verbal echoes are from the Hippolytus and the Hercules Furens—both plays in which 'the protagonist's crimes are accompanied or followed by violent fear and remorse'—this indicates that Shakespeare, in turning to Seneca, paid particular attention to those plays which, compared with the others, he found 'closer in spirit to the theme he had chosen for his next drama'.[5] This may sound too deliberate an imitative process to those who like to think of the workings of Shakespeare's imagination as being less conscious. But the argument can, I think, be supported by the possibility—we are, of course, dealing with possibilities rather than facts—that another Senecan play, the Medea, contributed in a similar way towards the creation of Macbeth: a contribution traceable by some faint verbal echoes and a central thematic similarity.

It has been suggested at various times, and usually with hesitation, that lines from the Medea may be echoed in the witch-broth scene (IV, i) and in Lady Macbeth's appeal to the spirits of murder (I, v, 40–54).[6] I do not think that any verbal resemblances by themselves make up a significant claim for a connexion between the Medea and Macbeth.[7] On the other hand, the Medea seems to me to present a case where Shakespeare, whether from re-reading the play or from his memory of it, found some Senecan dramatic moments a help towards crystallizing and articulating a main motif in his play. From the way in which he uses Seneca at other points in the play, we can tell that—at least at this stage in his career—Shakespeare saw Seneca's plays not as storehouses of plot and character material, but as ways of analysing and defining emotional situations. We can also see that he draws on Seneca at important moments in the play. Thus, for example, it is well known that Macbeth's reaction to the stain of Duncan's blood on his hands—

> Will all great Neptune's ocean wash this blood
> Clean from my hand?—
>
> (II, ii, 59–60)

is an amalgamation of two passages from the *Hippolytus* (lines 715–18) and the *Hercules Furens* (lines 1323–9), respectively. The situations in which those two passages occur are very different between themselves: the first registers Hippolytus' revulsion as he throws from him the sword which he sees as polluted by Phaedra's incestuous desire, the second expresses Hercules' despair as he wakes from his mad fury to find that he has killed his wife and children; and neither, especially not the *Hippolytus* piece, is at all close in plot and character to the *Macbeth* situation. But Shakespeare's imagination must have been stirred by this image as a way of defining someone's realization that an act of sin is irreversible. His own elaboration on the basic image—

> No, this my hand will rather
> The multitudinous seas incarnadine,
> Making the green one red— (II, ii, 60–2)

shows just how vividly it has been stirred. What is more, the 'borrowed' image becomes part of a whole complex of themes in the play. It looks forward to Lady Macbeth's compulsive attempts to wash the 'damned spot', the 'smell of the blood' off *her* hand; and it recurs, as a whole river of blood, to measure Macbeth's departure further and further from Grace:

> I am in blood
> Stepp'd in so far, that, should I wade no more,
> Returning were as tedious as go o'er. (III, iv, 135–7)

These lines, while defining the emotional and moral state of Macbeth at that moment, are yet also, as F. R. Johnson points out,[8] a transmutation of that most famous Senecan tag from the *Agamemnon*, Clytemnestra's *sententia*,

> per scelera semper sceleribus tutum est iter.

I have laboured what may seem obvious, in order to outline my own argument: that, in the writing of *Macbeth*, the *Medea* may have been active in much the same way as we know other Senecan plays to have been; that Shakespeare has seized on a few emotional key-moments in the *Medea*, linked them with other themes and images in the play, and built them into his own moral structure. In drawing attention, then, to what I think may be a neglected source of *Macbeth*, I want not only to suggest another instance of Senecan imitation in the play but also to show another instance of how mature Shakespearian imitation of Seneca contains within itself a reaction away from Seneca.

Shakespeare's narrative source material—Holinshed and Buchanan—provided him both with the outline and with details of the action. It also provided him with the outline of Lady Macbeth, as an ambitious wife urging her initially only partly willing husband on to kill the king. The shaping vision which turned chronicle into poetic drama was one of evil—of, as G. Wilson Knight and many critics after him have shown, evil seen as perversions of the natural state in the individual, the family, the body politic and the universe. The two great thematic speeches which fit Lady Macbeth into this vision are, first, the invocation which follows on her reading of Macbeth's letter about the prophecies of the Weird Sisters—

> Come, you Spirits
> That tend on mortal thoughts, unsex me here;
> And fill me, from the crown to the toe, top-full
> Of direst cruelty! make thick my blood,

> Stop up th' access and passage to remorse;
> That no compunctious visitings of Nature
> Shake my fell purpose, nor keep peace between
> Th' effect and it. Come to my woman's breasts,
> And take my milk for gall, you murth'ring ministers,
> Wherever in your sightless substances
> You wait on nature's mischief. Come, thick night,
> And pall thee in the dunnest smoke of hell,
> That my keen knife see not the wound it makes,
> Nor Heaven peep through the blanket of the dark,
> To cry 'Hold, hold'—   (I, v, 40–54)

and, secondly, the lines with which she whets Macbeth's blunting purpose:

> I have given suck, and know
> How tender 'tis to love the babe that milks me:
> I would, while it was smiling in my face,
> Have pluck'd my nipple from his boneless gums,
> And dash'd the brains out, had I so sworn
> As you have done to this.   (I, vii, 54–8)

In the first speech, Lady Macbeth rejects her very nature as a woman, turns her aim from creation of life to its destruction. The second treats the same theme on a more concrete, intimate and domestic level—and its evocation of natural disorder is all the more horrifying for it. Seneca has one woman whose action, in spirit if not in fact, is identical, and that is Medea.

In the opening scene of her play, Medea invokes Hecate, the goddess of night, hell and magic, to help her revenge herself on Jason by killing the king and the whole royal stock. Studley then makes her also envisage the slaying of her own children—

> Then at the Aulters of the Gods my chyldren shalbe slayne,
> With crimsen colourde bloud of Babes their Aulters will I stayne . . .

whereupon she goes on to ask, in an invocation to her own soul, to be unsexed:

> If any lusty lyfe as yet within thy soule doe rest,
> If ought of auncient corage still doe dwell within my brest,
> Exile all foolysh Female feare, and pity from thy mynde,
> And as th'untamed Tygers use to rage and rave unkynde . . .
>
>   . . . permit to lodge and rest,
> Such salvage brutish tyranny within thy brasen brest.
> What ever hurly burly wrought doth Phasis understand,
> What mighty monstrous bloudy feate I wrought by Sea or Land,
> The like in Corynth shalbe seene in most outragious guise,
> Most hyddious, hatefull, horrible, to heare, or see wyth eyes,
> Most divelish, desperate, dreadfull deede, yet never knowne before,
> Whose rage shall force heaven, earth, and hell to quake and tremble sore. . .

As weyghty things as these I did in greener girlishe age,
Now sorrowes smart doth rub the gall and frets with sharper rage,
But sith my wombe hath yeelded fruict, it doth mee well behove,
The strength and parlous puissance of weightier illes to prove . . .

How wilt thou from thy spouse depart? as him thou followed hast
In bloud to bath thy bloudy handes and traytrous lyves to wast.

(*Tenne Tragedies*, II, 57)[9]

When we penetrate the blanket of Studley's rhetoric here, we find, in close proximity and linked in a similar train of associations, the main ideas and images of the Lady Macbeth passages. We also find ideas and images which, in *Macbeth*, link Lady Macbeth's speeches with the rest of the play. First of all, of course, Medea's lines share with Lady Macbeth's 'unsex me here' speech the framework of ritual incantation—which is handed on, as it were, to Macbeth himself in his invocation to Night before the murder of Banquo (III, iii, 46–50). (Nor may it be altogether irrelevant that, as Macbeth goes to murder Duncan, he envisages witchcraft celebrating 'pale Hecate's off'rings', II, 1, 51–2.) Within this rhetorical pattern, Medea's thoughts move from witchcraft, to royal murder, and to the slaying of her own children, with the courage and cruelty which this requires. The key-line comes in her desire to lose her woman's nature— stressing the 'feare, and pity' which we know are thematic words in *Macbeth*—and a little later this recurs in the cruel paradox that the very fact of her having been the source of life ('but sith my wombe hath yeelded fruict') is being turned into a further reason to kill. But before then we have heard how, unsexed and tigerish, she will do bloody deeds, too terrible (as is the case with both Macbeth and Lady Macbeth) to 'see wyth eyes', and how these deeds, 'shall force heaven, earth and hell to quake and tremble sore', in the kind of universal confusion which Macbeth envisages in the witch-scene, IV, i (lines 50–61). The Medea passage leads up to the central *Macbeth* image of hands bathed in blood—common enough, by itself, in Senecan and Elizabethan tragedy, but significant as the end-product of this particular piece of unnatural 'argument'. There is no reference to milk or giving suck here, to correspond with the second of Lady Macbeth's speeches; but in Act IV of the *Medea*—where indeed 'witchcraft celebrates pale Hecate's off'rings'—there is a scene which is bound to have struck a reader as an emblem of unnatural womanhood and in which a mother's breast is linked with the massacre of her own tender children. Medea, with her breasts bared, sheds her own blood as a sacrifice to Hecate, so that she may harden herself to that massacre:

With naked breast and dugges layde out Ile pricke with sacred blade
Myne arme, that for the bubling bloude an issue may bee made,
With trilling streames my purple bloude let drop on Th'aulter stones.
My tender Childrens crusshed fleshe, and broken broosed bones
Lerne how to brooke with hardned heart: in practise put the trade
To florishe fearce, and keepe a coyle, with naked glittring blade.

(*Tenne Tragedies*, II, 90)[10]

In terms of plot and character *Medea* is a play of sexual jealousy and of terrible revenge taken by a wife on a husband and has as little in common with *Macbeth* as the crude horror of Studley's rhetoric has in common with the poetry of the 'I have given suck' speech. But in terms of tragic emotion the play centres on an obsessed woman perverting her woman's nature in order to do the most unnatural of all deeds, kill her own children—though pity, in the shape of her babes, stands literally before her. It may be objected here that to the Elizabethan imagination Medea was a witch, and that that image would overlay any others in the play. Certainly the Medea of Ovid's *Metamorphoses* (Book VII) was a witch. Ovid, naturally stressing those events in the myth which involve transformations, dwells at length on how Medea aids Jason in getting the golden fleece, how she rejuvenates old Aeson (as Shakespeare remembered in *The Merchant of Venice*, V, i, 13–15) and makes the daughters of Pelias kill their aged father, while he hurries over the events in Corinth in the briefest possible way. Ben Jonson in *The Masque of Queens* used the incantations of Seneca's Medea and of Ovid's side by side.[11] In Cooper's *Thesaurus* the entry on Medea has not a word about her killing of her own children. But the Elizabethan imagination also admitted another Medea image, and that was one of the unnatural woman and damned sinner. Thus in Richard Robinson's singularly pedestrian Mirror-work, *The Rewarde of Wickednesse* (published in 1574), Medea, who is suffering torments in hell, narrates her story from the point of view of 'how I did nature quite forsake'.[12] She acted, she says,

> by Deuillishe ways as women shoulde not doe
> For why they ought with mercye to bee milde,
> and not theyr wicked willes for to pursue. (fol. 3 v)

And in the conclusion of the poem—'the bookes verdite vpon Medea'—we hear, in lines which, for all their crudeness, might remind one of Lady Macbeth's readiness to dash out the brains of her smiling babe, how she

> her Children deare, hath wounde with mortall knife,
> The smiling Babes her body beare, bereft their tender life.

Obviously I am not suggesting that Shakespeare was echoing the poetry, if it can be so called, of Richardson; but these lines show the kind of image the Senecan Medea figure would leave on the imagination. Studley—who in the dedicatory epistle to the 1566 edition of his *Medea* translation presents Seneca as 'yᵗ pearlesse Poet and most Christian Ethnicke'—reinforces the impression which Seneca's original gives: that, though the witch-practices of Medea take up most of Act IV and are referred to throughout, they are peripheral to the real tragic action in which Medea is a wilfully wicked moral agent. Studley constantly 'places' her by the word 'wicked'; without any foundation at all in the original he will sometimes make her speak of her 'wicked will'; and in the struggle between her womanly pity and her desire to kill her children in revenge, he translates Seneca's lines,

> ira pietatem fugat
> iramque pietas, (lines 943–4)

into a morality struggle between vice and virtue:

> Wrath sometyme chaseth vertue out, and vertue wrath agayne.
> (*Tenne Tragedies*, p. 95)

Above all, Studley's version of the last line in the play makes it a fitting end to a tragedy of damnation:

> Beare witnesse, grace of God is none in place of thy repayre.
>
> (*Tenne Tragedies*, p. 98)

As a rendering of Seneca's words, 'testare nullos esse, qua veheris, deos', this has been praised by T. S. Eliot,[13] but it is clearly a twist of the original meaning: a moralistic reading of the nihilist curse of Jason.

The woman damning herself by unnatural acts was, of course, not new in *Macbeth*. In the two speeches quoted, Lady Macbeth performs in ritual a rejection of womanhood which Goneril and Regan had acted out in their deeds, and which speeches about them had drawn attention to:

> Tigers, not daughters, what have you perform'd?
>
> Thou changed and self-cover'd thing, for shame,
> Be-monster not thy feature . . .
>
> . . . howe'er thou art a fiend,
> A woman's shape doth shield thee.   (*King Lear*, IV, ii, 40–68)

When Lear curses Goneril for her unkindness, he strikes at the very essence of her womanhood, unsexing her as Lady Macbeth is to unsex herself:

> Hear Nature, hear; dear goddess, hear.
> Suspend thy purpose, if thou didst intend
> To make this creature fruitful.
> Into her womb convey sterility;
> Dry up in her the organs of increase;
> And from her derogate body never spring
> A babe to honour her!   (I, iv, 275–81)

Yet the unwomanliness of Goneril and Regan differs from Lady Macbeth's not only because they literally reject their father whereas Lady Macbeth symbolically rejects her children; it differs, too, because it is existential—consequent upon their actions of unkindness. In Lady Macbeth it is essential: it is—as in Medea—the deliberate and rhetorically articulated point from which, on her first appearance in the play, all her acts (and, in a sense, those of Macbeth, for in unsexing herself she mothers his deeds) proceed.

Some of the links in the chain of associated images and ideas which connect *Macbeth* with the *Medea* are not very unique or far-fetched. Shakespeare had dealt with rejection of pity, murderous cruelty (exercised on innocent children) and unwomanliness much earlier. Interestingly, however, one of the earliest occurrences in Shakespeare of a combination of these ideas suggests that he already associated the Medea story with a particular kind of destructiveness. In *2 Henry VI* there is the following reference to the story of how Medea slew and dismembered her brother Absyrtus:

> Meet I an infant of the house of York,
> Into as many gobbets will I cut it
> As wild Medea young Absyrtus did:
> In cruelty will I seek out my fame.   (v, ii, 57–60)

It has generally been assumed that the source of this passage is in Ovid's *Tristia*, III, ix.[14] An English source has been suggested by Starnes and Talbert, who quote Cooper's summary of the story in his *Thesaurus*:

... she ranne away with Jason and tooke with her Absyrtus hir yong brother ... Medea seeing that nothing coud stay hir fathers haste, fearing to be taken, kylled the yong babe hir brother, and scattered his lymmes in the way as hir father should passe. With sorrow whereof and long seeking the partes of his yong sonnes bodye the father was stayed and Jason with Medea in the meane tyme escaped out of his realme.[15]

Starnes and Talbert point out that Cooper's version shares with the passage in *2 Henry VI* an emphasis on the *infancy* of Absyrtus which is lacking in Ovid. They also suggest that the 'gobbets' of the Shakespearian passage derive from Cooper's expression 'partes of his yong sonnes body'. But a more direct and plausible source seems to me to be the account of this episode in Seneca's *Medea*, which in the Studley translation reads like this:

> My tender Brother eke, that with my Syer did mee pursue,
> Whom with his secret partes cut of, I wicked Virgin slewe,
> Whose shreaded and dismembred corps, with sword in gobbits hewd,
> (A wofull Coarse to th' Fathers heart) on Pontus ground I strewd.
>
> (*Tenne Tragedies*, p. 61)

Neither Studley nor the original Latin ever mention the boy by name (Seneca, quite clear about his infancy, refers to him as 'nefandae virginis parvus comes'), so the *Medea* cannot be Shakespeare's only source of knowledge for the allusion. But the youth of the boy is stressed just as much as in the Cooper passage, and above all the verbal parallelism in the cutting of the boy's body into 'gobbets'—a favourite Studley word for describing pieces of dismembered human anatomy—suggests that these lines may lie behind Shakespeare's.[16] Anyone who read the *Medea* would be repeatedly reminded of the murder of Absyrtus; Medea refers to it no less than eleven times, and in the end it is her vision of Absyrtus' ghosts which ends her hesitation and drives her to the murder of her own children:

> Alas they [her children] bee mere innocents, I doe not this denay:
> So was my brother whom I slew ...
>
> Yet for my sire and brother, twayne I have, there needes no more ...
>
> My slaughtred brothers ghost it is that vengaunce coms to crave.
>
> (*Tenne Tragedies*, pp. 95–6)

The Absyrtus passage in *2 Henry VI* is the one where Young Clifford discovers his dead father. It is part of a speech which opens with what A. S. Cairncross calls 'a regular Shakespearian group of images': the discovery of a death leads to the idea that chaos has come again.[17] The lines have the ring of mature Shakespeare:

> O ! let the vile world end,
> And the premised flames of the last day
> Knit earth and heaven together;

> Now let the general trumpet blow his blast,
> Particularities and petty sounds
> To cease!
>
> (v, ii, 40–5)

They anticipate Macduff's reaction to the murder of Duncan (*Macbeth*, II, iii, 63–81). It is therefore all the more interesting that the next set of images in the speech—deliberate rejection of pity and the murder of innocent children—

> Even at this sight
> My heart is turn'd to stone: and while 'tis mine
> It shall be stony. York not our old men spares;
> No more will I their babes . . .
>
> Henceforth I will not have to do with pity:
> Meet I an infant of the house of York . . .
>
> (v, ii, 49–57)

is linked with Medea (and, as I have tried to show, probably with Seneca's *Medea*). Though the overt association disappears after this passage, I have a strong feeling that it continues, as it were, underground to enrich the texture of the episodes of *2* and *3 Henry VI* which are consequent on this scene. In the actual killing of young Rutland, which is what the Absyrtus speech anticipates, the 'innocent child' pleads with Clifford for his life, and Clifford replies in words which, on the one hand, suggest Medea's argument of a brother and a father for two sons, and, on the other, look forward to *Macbeth*. Clifford's words,

> In vain thou speak'st, poor boy; my father's blood
> Hath stopp'd the passage where thy words should enter,
>
> (*3 Henry VI*, I, iii, 21–2)

should be compared with Lady Macbeth's,

> Make thick my blood,
> Stop up th' access and passage to remorse.

Young Clifford's ally, Queen Margaret, is often—like Tamora in *Titus Andronicus*—referred to somewhat loosely as a 'Senecan woman'. In the particular chain of associations which I am tracing, that 'tiger's heart wrapt in a woman's hide' adds the notion of murderous cruelty and (virtually) child-murder as manifestation of unnatural womanhood. The baiting of York (*3 Henry VI*, I, iv) is akin to the scene where Medea confronts Jason with his dead sons; and it turns in its climax on the un-womanliness of Margaret:

> How could'st thou drain the life-blood of the child,
> To bid the father wipe his eyes withal,
> And yet be seen to bear a woman's face?
> Women are soft, mild, pitiful, and flexible;
> Thou stern, indurate, flinty, rough, remorseless . . .
>
> But you are more inhuman, more inexorable—
> O, ten times more—than tigers of Hyrcania.
>
> (I, iv, 138–55)

There was clearly no need, either here or in the similar passage in *Titus Andronicus*, II, iii, 136–60 (in which the breast-feeding image also appears, to define Tamora's unnaturalness), to go to the *Medea* for the image of a woman turned tiger; yet, in the context of other Medean associations, it may be worth remembering that in the first of the *Medea* speeches quoted above she sees herself, when unsexed, as one of 'th'untamed Tygers' which 'rage and rave unkynde'.

Various resemblances between *Macbeth* and *2* and *3 Henry VI* have previously been noted,[18] and to these, I think, might be added a common kinship with Seneca's *Medea*. Needless to say, the nature and degree of that kinship are very different: in the *Henry VI* scenes (as in the *Titus Andronicus* one, referred to above) there is that dramatic interest in evil sadistically enjoyed which characterizes the end of the *Medea*—

> This onely is the thing that wants unto my wicked will,
> That Jasons eyes should see this sight as yet I doe suppose,
> Nothing it is that I have done, my travell all I lose,
> That I employde in dyry deedes, unlesse he see the same—
>
> *(Tenne Tragedies, p. 97)*

and which is epitomized in Atreus' words about Thyestes:

> miserum videre nolo, sed dum fit miser. *(Thyestes, line 907)*

Macbeth has none of this quality: evil is presented here, on the one·hand, in terms of its workings in the minds of Macbeth and Lady Macbeth and, on the other, as part of a larger moral and metaphysical pattern. Seneca begins and ends with the mind and deeds of Medea, and although a general destructiveness is one aspect of these—

> Then onely can I be at rest, when every thing I see
> Throwne headlong topsie turvey downe to ruthfull ende with me.
> With mee let all things cleane decay: thy selfe if thou doe spill,
> Thou maist drive to destruction what else with thee thou will—
>
> *(Tenne Tragedies, p. 74)*

he does not, like Shakespeare, through structure and imagery build up a pattern in which the protagonist is seen as one manifestation of universal evil. To take just one example, there is in Seneca none of that inclusiveness of vision whereby in *Macbeth*, after Macbeth's Medea-like words,

> . . . though the treasure
> Of nature's germens tumble all together,
> Even till destruction sicken—answer me
> To what I ask you, (IV, i, 58–61)

the first thing that goes into the witches' brew is 'sow's blood, that hath eaten / Her nine farrow' —a gruesome beast version of Lady Macbeth's symbolical slaying of her own child, linking the wife's destructiveness with the husband's into a coherent whole. On this point, the *Henry VI* plays are much closer to *Macbeth* than they are to *Medea*. Although in these early histories each scene tends to be a climax in itself, Shakespeare is beginning to articulate the chronicle material into a moral pattern. The world in which women turn into tigers and prey on innocent children is the world defined in the emblematic scene in *3 Henry VI* (II, v) where enter a son that has killed his father and a father that has killed his son. From the scene where the queen's side confront the sons of York—*3 Henry VI*, II, ii, a scene thick with references to the atrocities committed by either side, but most of all to the 'butcher'-like killing of 'our tender brother Rutland'—there emerges, in the prince's words, a world in the same moral confusion as that evoked by the witches' 'fair is foul, and foul is fair':

> If that be right which Warwick says is right,
> There is no wrong, but every thing is right. (II, ii, 131-2)

The image of the son who has killed his father and the father who has killed his son is a self-conscious pointing of the pattern; in *Macbeth* the pattern, as so many critics have shown, grows naturally out of a fusion of action and imagery. Macbeth kills his king (and father-figure) Duncan and accuses Duncan's sons of having killed their father and so creates a world where day is turned into night and horses eat each other. And at the centre of this disorder stands Lady Macbeth who in two speeches has unsexed herself and symbolically slain her issue.

In an interesting article on 'The Sources of *Macbeth*' in *Shakespeare Survey 4*, Professor M. C. Bradbrook suggested that Shakespeare got the inspiration for those two speeches from chapter xiii of the *Description of Scotland* prefixed to Holinshed's *Chronicle*:

. . . each woman would take intolerable pains to bring up and nourish her own children. They thought them furthermore not to be kindly fostered, except they were so well nourished after their births with the milk of their breasts as they were before they were born with the blood of their own bellies: nay, they feared lest they should degenerate and grow out of kind, except they gave them suck themselves, and eschewed strange milk, therefore in labour and painfulness they were equal [i.e. with the fighting men] . . . In these days also the women of our country were of no less courage than the men, for all stout maids and wives (if they were not with child) marched as well into the field as did the men, and so soon as the army did set forward, they slew the first living creature that they found, in whose blood they not only bathed their swords, but also tasted thereof with their mouths, with no less religion and assurance conceived, than if they had already been sure of some notable and fortunate victory.[19]

Dr Bradbrook finds in this passage the 'intimate relation between tenderness and barbarity' which she thinks gives us the 'fundamental character of Lady Macbeth as it is embodied in the most frightful of her speeches'. It seems to me very likely that Shakespeare knew the *Description of Scotland*, and that he may have been impressed by the above passage; but I do not think it gives us the fundamental point of those two speeches. The point of the relation between tenderness and war-like courage in the *Description* is that they co-existed, that they were both aspects of womanhood—albeit a primitive or barbaric version of it. The barbarity of those early Scotswomen did not exercise itself at the expense of procreation—it is especially stressed that women with child did not join in the fighting—or of child-nursing. The unnatural paradox of Lady Macbeth's speeches is the fact that she is ready to give up her womanhood to murder, her milk to gall, to kill her smiling babe in order to live up to a destructive oath. These are the qualities epitomized by Medea, and foreshadowed by Albany when he sees, as the outcome of Goneril's rejection of her womanhood, how

> Humanity must perforce prey on itself,
> Like monsters of the deep. (*King Lear*, IV. ii, 47-9)

The last thing envisaged in the *Description* is Scottish humanity preying on *itself*. Nor does *Macbeth* as a whole bear out the Amazonian concept of womanhood which the *Description* suggests. The only other woman whom we see, Lady Macduff, is tender and mild and 'womanly' —the 'dam' for the 'pretty chickens' of Macduff. When Ross tells Malcolm that, if he would return to Scotland, this

> Would create soldiers, make our women fight,
> To doff their dire distresses, (IV, iii, 187–8)

this is the measure of the extremity of a situation which demands extreme means, not a reference to a natural state of affairs. Indeed, Lady Macbeth's essential perversion of womanhood is ironically stressed by the way other characters in the play expect her to conform to its natural mode. Not only does Duncan several times refer to her in terms such as 'most kind hostess', but when the murder of the king has been discovered, Macduff tries to spare her:

> O gentle lady,
> 'Tis not for you to hear what I can speak!
> The repetition in a woman's ear
> Would murder as it fell. (II, iii, 83–6)

But the deepest irony of all is that her woman's nature does in the end steal up on her: she who had sacrificed her womanhood for the deed finds herself destroyed by the memory of the deed. And within the same pattern, Macbeth, who through her has deprived himself of issue, finds himself defeated by the issue of Banquo.

We are here at the point where the ways of Shakespeare and of Seneca utterly part. In Shakespeare's structure, Lady Macbeth's Medea-like action is doubly defeated: first by the self-destructiveness of evil—humanity turning away from woman- and man-hood, into beasts, and thus preying, by the natural order, on itself—and secondly by the positive power of good, as symbolized by the bloody babe (bloody, not because its brains have been dashed out but because of a victorious birth) and by Banquo's issue stretching out to the crack of doom; and as seen in action by the return of Malcolm. While Medea finds her heroic self *through* evil, the two Macbeths lose themselves through evil. Shakespeare's woman unwomanized becomes 'fiendlike' and hence less than a woman; Seneca's becomes a heroine and hence more than a woman. The *Medea* is a study of destruction, an analysis of evil, and there is no suggestion in Jason's concluding curse that 'the time is free'. Shakespeare's vision of evil included a vision of the defeat of that evil, of what G. Wilson Knight has called 'a wrestling of destruction with creation'.[20] We cannot say whether Shakespeare's fiendlike queen would have been possible without Seneca, but we can say that an imaginative understanding of the total meaning of such fiendlikeness—of all the implications of 'unsex me here'—would not have been possible without Shakespeare.

© I.-S. EWBANK 1966

NOTES

1. C. Mendell, *Our Seneca* (Yale University Press, 1941), p. 199.

2. *The Royal Play of 'Macbeth'* (New York, 1950), p. 48.

3. See, for example, J. W. Cunliffe, *The Influence of Seneca on Elizabethan Tragedy* (1893); F. L. Lucas, *Seneca and Elizabethan Tragedy* (Cambridge, 1922); T. S. Eliot's Introduction to *Seneca, his Tenne Tragedies* . . . (The Tudor Translations, 2nd ser., 1927), reprinted in *Selected Essays*; Hardin Craig, 'The Shackling of Accidents', *P.Q.* XIX (1940), 1–19; J. M. Nosworthy, 'The Bleeding Captain Scene in *Macbeth*', *R.E.S.* XXII (1946), 126–30.

4. See Kenneth Muir, *Shakespeare's Sources* (1957), p. 180; and N. Fleming, 'The Influence of Seneca on Shakespeare', unpublished M.A. Dissertation, in the Liverpool University Library (1956).

5. Francis R. Johnson, 'Shakespearian Imagery and Senecan Imitation', *John Quincy Adams Memorial Studies*, ed. J. McManaway (Washington, 1948), p. 44.

6. See Cunliffe, *op. cit.* p. 46; Mendell, *op. cit.* p. 199; Fleming, *op. cit.* p. 201.

7. There are some similarities between the ingredients of Medea's potion (Act IV) and those of the *Hexenkessel* in *Macbeth*; but, as far as classical influence behind this scene goes, it is equally possible (as, for example, Paul thinks: *op. cit.* p. 262) that Shakespeare had in mind the brew prepared by Ovid's Medea (*Metamorphoses*, VII, 215–93). It seems to me impossible to be sure about verbal dependencies here—especially as Seneca presumably himself drew on Ovid. In Elizabethan literature the lines of Ovid's Medea are often conflated with those of Seneca's, and also with those of that other Senecan witch, the Nurse in *Hercules Oetaeus*. An example of this may be found in Prospero's speech in *The Tempest*, V, i, 33–50, which scholars agree shows Shakespeare using Ovid both in the original Latin and in Golding's translation. T. W. Baldwin (*William Shakspere's Small Latine and Lesse Greeke*, 1944, II, 447) thinks that the line 'I have bedimm'd / The noontide sun' shows Shakespeare echoing Golding's version of Ovid's 'currus quoque carmine nostro / pallet': 'Our Sorcerie dimmes the Morning faire, and darkes the Sun at Noone'. In Ovid, Baldwin points out, the sun appears only by allusion, and there is nothing specifically to suggest noon. But, verbally, Shakespeare's line could equally be paralleled—it seems to me—by Studley's version of line 768 in Seneca's *Medea*—'Phoebus in medio stetit': 'I rolling up the magicke verse at noone time Phoebus stay'—which has

both sun and 'noon'; and by Studley's line in *Hercules Oetaeus* (*Tenne Tragedies*, II, 211), in which Deianira describes the effect of the 'magicke vearse' of the Nurse: 'And noonetyde topsy turvy tost doth dim the dusky day', and which has both 'dim' and 'noontide'.

8. F. R. Johnson, *op. cit.* pp. 50–2.

9. I quote from the Tudor Translations edition of *Seneca, his Tenne Tragedies*, II, 53–98. The passage quoted is Studley's rendering of the following lines in Seneca (quoted from the Loeb ed.):

> si vivis, anime, si quid antiqui tibi
> remanet vigoris; pelle femineos metus
> et inhospitalem Caucasum mente indue.
> quodcumque vidit Pontus aut Phasis nefas,
> videbit Isthmos. effera ignota horrida,
> tremenda caelo pariter ac terris mala
> mens intus agitat—vulnera et caedem et vagum
> funus per artus. levia memoravi nimis;
> haec virgo feci. gravior exurgat dolor;
> maiora iam me scelera post partus decent.
> accingere ira teque in exitium para
> furore toto. paria narrentur tua
> repudia thalamis. quo virum linques modo?
> hoc quo secuta es.   (41–54)

Apart from the fact that Studley considerably elaborates upon the manifestations of Medea's wrath (in the lines I have left out), he also adds lines or phrases which suggest that it is the translation, rather than the original, which may lie behind *Macbeth*. Seneca has nothing corresponding to the two first quoted Studley lines, about the slaying of Medea's own children. He does not emphasize the unsexing, as Studley does: above all, it is only fear — 'femineos metus'—not 'pity', that his Medea wants to be free from. The brief Senecan reference to Medea's motherhood—'post partus'—is developed by Studley into a concrete 'sith my wombe hath yeelded fruict' (more akin to Lady Macbeth's 'I have given suck'). Studley, unlike Seneca, makes Medea envisage deeds too horrible to 'see with eyes'. And, finally, there is no immediate Senecan source in this passage for Studley's climactic and *Macbeth*-like image of hands bathed in blood.

10. Studley's rendering of lines 805–10 in Seneca's *Medea*:

> tibi nudato
> pectore maenas sacro feriam
> bracchia cultro. manet noster
> sanguis ad aras; assuesce, manus,
> stringere ferrum carosque pati
> posse cruores.

As in the previous passage, Studley here heavily elaborates, over Seneca, the situation of a woman and mother performing an unnatural deed. Seneca has the grim paradox of the heroine hardening herself to shed 'caros . . . cruores'; but Studley not only introduces the vivid image of the 'tender Childrens crusshed fleshe' but also contrasts this with the emphatic description of the bared breast ('and dugges layde out'). Grim as the artistic effect is, the emotional impact is more powerfully human than is Seneca's magic ritual.

11. See his marginal gloss to *The Masque of Queens* (*Ben Jonson*, ed. Herford and Simpson, Oxford, 1941, VII, 294-5 and 299).

12. *The rewarde of Wickednesse Discoursing the sundrye monstrous abuses of wicked and vngodlye worldelinges . . . With a liuely description of their seuerall falles and finall destruction . . .* by Richard Robinson (1574). As Shakespeare echoes *The Rape of Lucrece* in *Macbeth* (cf. new Arden *Macbeth*, ed. Kenneth Muir, Appendix D), it may be worth noting that, in Robinson's picture of hell, the sinner exhibited immediately before Medea is 'young *Tarquin* rewarded for his wickednesse' of 'Pride and Whoredome' (fols. D3ᵛ–F2).

13. *Tenne Tragedies*, I, xvi, and *Selected Essays*, p. 59. A further indication of the moralizing note in Studley's version of the *Medea* is that he substitutes for the first Chorus, which is an epithalamium, a kind of Mirror-poem on the wrongdoings of Jason and Medea.

14. See T. W. Baldwin, *Shakspere's Small Latine*, II, 429–30, and the notes on this passage in the New Shakespeare edition (ed. J. Dover Wilson, Cambridge, 1952) and the new Arden edition (ed. Andrew S. Cairncross, 1957) of *2 Henry VI*.

15. De Witt T. Starnes and Ernest W. Talbert, *Classical Myth and Legend in Renaissance Dictionaries* (Chapel Hill, 1955), p. 112.

16. For 'gobbets'—which word occurs in the same play at IV, I, 85—H. C. Hart (Arden edition of *2 Henry VI*, 1909) refers to two occurrences in Golding and one in *The Faerie Queene*; but its use here in the Absyrtus context would seem to indicate Studley as a source.

17. New Arden edition, p. 151. The version of this speech in *The Contention*, which Cairncross believes to be a memorial reconstruction, is much more 'Senecan' in the sense of heavily rhetorical; but it has not got the Absyrtus image. Dover Wilson, who is sceptical about Shakespeare's hand in much of *2 Henry VI*, believes that Shakespeare has 'revised pretty thoroughly' (New Shakespeare edition, p. 195) this part of the play.

18. See new Arden *Macbeth*, ed. Kenneth Muir, Appendix D.

19. *Shakespeare Survey 4* (1951), p. 40.

20. *The Imperial Theme* (1931), p. 153. Cf. also Cleanth Brooks, 'The Naked Babe and the Cloak of Manliness', *The Well Wrought Urn* (1949).

SHAKESPEARE AT STREET LEVEL

BY

D. S. BLAND

The end of the eighteenth century and the beginning of the nineteenth saw the production of an enormous number of song-collections (often called 'garlands') designed for the chapman's market. Costing a penny for eight small pages (the first given over to a title-page adorned with a crudely cut and often irrelevant woodcut), a garland would contain the words—but not the music—of perhaps half-a-dozen songs, covering a wide variety of subjects, and appealing to a number of levels of taste: a sentimental love lyric in eighteenth-century clichés, a humorous poem describing an Irishman's adventures in London, a poem in praise of the Battle of the Nile, a sailor's lament at his absence from home, and so forth. These garlands thus throw an interesting light on the state of popular taste at the time.

Reading in a collection of these productions for a purpose remote from Shakespeare[1] turned up the following three songs.[2] So far as I know, they have not been quoted or commented on before. They differ from the broadsheet ballads based on Shakespeare's work which appeared until the end of the eighteenth century.[3] The broadsheet ballads are virtually narrative verse, in spite of the occasional appearance of the words 'To be sung to the tune of . . .'. But the poems in the garlands are more lyrical in shape, even though the garland rarely indicates the tune to be associated with them.

The three poems reproduced here do not call for much comment, but two or three implications can be drawn from them. Only within a social class where first-hand knowledge of the plays was lacking could the plot of *Othello* be twisted to comic purpose and hope to meet with applause. On the other hand, only when the 'Seven Ages of Man' speech had passed into popular currency could it become the basis for 'Paddy McShane'. But the most interesting feature of both 'Othello' and 'Macbeth and the Gipsies' is the combination of accuracy—in the use of proper names, for example—with popular modernization—Cassio as a captain in the Volunteers. The writer[4] not only knows his Shakespeare, but also the level to which he must be reduced to suit the taste of the audience.

The first is from a garland which has no publisher's name or date of publication.

Othello
or
Fine Fleecy Hosiery

O! have you not heard of a story,
    A comical story and true?
If you haven't, and will but attend,
    It's a hundred to one but you do.
It is of a man of some note,
    A comical outlandish fellow;

95

In Venice he lived, as its wrote,
   And his name was Mister Othello.
   Rumpti udity udity, rumpti udiny ido,
   Rumpti udity udity udity, ri, fal, la, de, la, lido.

A gentleman there had a daughter,
   With Othy she's grown very mellow;
He wondered what passion had caught her,
   She sighed for her Blacky Othello.
Now Brabantis had offered his daughter
   A husband a long time before;
She sneezed at the one he had brought her;
   She vowed and declared she'd have Moor.

Then General Othy he came,
   And to Gretna the lady he carried:
Gretna mayn't be indeed the right name,
   But no matter—I'm sure they were married.
No sooner they tightly were tied,
   Than jealousy seizes love's place;
And Othello was so mad with his bride,
   That, egad, he looked black in the face.

A young Captain, Cassio, by luck
   She saw—a fine dashing gay fellow;
His sabre and gorget they stuck,
   In the gizzard of Mr Othello.
After drill now this volunteer gay
   Oft with Mrs Othello drank coffee, sir,
Till Othy thought proper to say,
   'Sweet Desty, don't ask that young officer'.

One evening, this Captain so smart,
   Called in winter as truly 'tis said;
And though he was hot in the heart,
   Yet he'd got a bad cold in the head.
Now as Mr Othello was out,
   And for favours his wife couldn't thank her chief,
To wipe Cassio's acquiline snout
   Desdemona lent her pocket handkerchief.

An Ancient, Iago, love felt,
   And sweet Desty he wished to be kissing;
But finding the fair wouldn't melt,
   Turned to mischief her handkerchief missing;

And bent upon making a row,
    Treated Othy with beer at an oyster house,
Invented the when and the how—
    Then Othello turned wonderful boisterous.

So when he came home, straight he goes
    To Mrs Othello in bed—
And says he, 'Dear, I must blow my nose,
    For I've got a sad cold in the head,
A handkerchief, wife, I expect one'.
    So out from the pillow she tossed it.
'Not this', he exclaimed, 'but the check one'.
    'Oh, curse it', cries Desty, 'I've lost it'.

'You lie', says Othello, 'that's true,
    So nothing remains to be said'.
'I lie !—yes, my dear, that I do,
    For by Jingo, I lie in the bed'.
Cries Othello, 'I vow there's too much light—
    I'll never be called a blood spiller'.
So the General put out the rush-light,
    And killed his wife with the pillow.

Then the blood of Iago he shed,
    Then he fell on his dear Desty's body,
Then Mrs Othello's dead head
    On her shoulders went nidity-noddy.
All this comes from a cold in the head,
    So blind fortune in this matter shows her eye—
Not one of these folks would be dead,
    If they had but worn fine fleecy hosiery.

The second poem appears in two garlands in the White Collection, one published in Edinburgh, and the other in Belfast.[5]

Macbeth and the Gipsies

You've heard of one Gen'ral Macbeth,
    Who was both courageous and bold, sir;
He had 'scaped an unfortunate death,
    If his fortune had never been told, sir.
With Banquo, his friend, he one day
    From battle victorious was coming,
When some gipsies he met in the way,
    Who thought they'd the Gen'ral be humming.
    Rumpti, udity, udity, rumpti, udity, ido.

They promised great things and what not,
    If some silver he would but come down, sir.
From Macbeth two and sixpence they got,
    And they promised his honour a crown, sir.
Banquo's was a different fate,
    But kings were to spring from his body;
And Macbeth went home to relate
    The tale to his wife, like a noddy.

The King he lodged with him one night,
    When Lady Macbeth, the vile slut, sir,
Determined her husband outright,
    His majesty's throat for to cut, sir.
Then in her chemise she turned out,
    And walked in her sleep up and down, sir;
But a doctor the secret found out,
    And told it all over the town, sir.

Then Banquo's grim ghost came to sup,
    When Macbeth had made himself king, sir.
His hair on an end it stood up,
    But his lady could see no such thing, sir.
Next morn to the gipsies he hies,
    Who chickens were making sad slaughter on,
And stealing of turnips likewise,
    As ingredients for their large cauldron.

By no man of woman that's born,
    They said, he could ever be slain, sir.
Nor till on a fine summer's morn,
    Burnham Wood should march to Dunsinane, sir.
Undaunted, says he, I'll now grow,
    My wicked designs never baulking,
For men don't bear children we know,
    And trees they are not fond of walking.

But one day at the door as he stood,
    He beheld a most terrible scene, sir,
For to Dunsinane great Burnham Wood
    Was marching like Jack in the Green, sir.
'Twas an army in bushes all crammed;
    Macbeth fought their Gen'ral Macduff, sir,
And both of they swore they'd be damned
    If ever they cried, Hold, enough, sir.

Macduff was the man for his money,
    The charm it was broke quite asunder;
He came into life very funny,
    So Macbeth was obliged to knock under.
He was killed—so the moral permit,
    Shun gipsies, they are a vile crew, sir;
And murder don't go to commit,
    For you'll surely be hanged if you do, sir.

The last poem occurs several times in the White collection in garlands with Stirling, Kilmarnock and Newcastle imprints.[6]

Paddy Macshane

If my own botheration don't alter my plan,
I'll sing seven lines of a tight Irishman,
    Wrote by old Billy Shakespeare of Ballyporeen.
He said while a babe I loved whiskey and pap,
That I mewled and puked in my grandmother's lap;
She joulted me hard just to hush my sweet roar,
When I slipped through her fingers down whack on the floor.
    What a squalling I made sure at Ballyporeen.

When I grew up a boy, with a nice shining face,
With a bag at my back, and a snail-crawling pace,
    Went to school at old Thwackum's at Ballyporeen.
His wig was so fusty, his birch was my dread,
He learning beat out 'stead of into my head.
Master Macshane, says he, you're a great dirty dolt,
You've got no more brains than a Monaghan colt;
    You're not fit for our college at Ballyporeen.

When eighteen years of age, I was teased and perplexed
To know what I should be, so a lover turned next,
    And courted sweet Sheelah of Ballyporeen.
I thought I'd just take her to comfort my life,
Not knowing that she was already a wife.
She asked me just once that to see her I'd come,
And I found her ten children and husband at home,
    A big whacking chairman of Ballyporeen.

I next turned a soldier, but did not like that,
So turned servant, and lived with great Justice Pat,
    A big dealer in p'tatoes at Ballyporeen.

With turtle and venison he lined his inside,
Eat so many capons, that one day he died.
So great was my grief, that to keep spirits up
Of some nice whiskey cordial I took a big sup,
    To my master's safe journey from Ballyporeen.

Kicked and tossed so about like a weathercock vane,
I packed up my awls, and I went back again,
    To my grandfather's cottage in Ballyporeen.
I found him, poor soul! with no legs for his hose,
Could not see through the spectacles put on his nose:
With no teeth in his head, so death cocked up his chin;
He slipped out of his slippers, and faith, I slipped in.
    And succeeded poor Dennis of Ballyporeen.

© D. S. BLAND 1966

NOTES

1. See D. S. Bland, *Chapbooks and Garlands in the Robert White Collection in the Library of King's College, Newcastle upon Tyne* (King's College Library Publications, no. 3, Newcastle upon Tyne, 1956).

2. There is a fourth, 'Hamlick, Prince o'Denton'. (Denton was a village outside, and is now a suburb of Newcastle.) But it is not in a garland, is very long and written in Tyneside dialect, which would require extensive annotation to make it comprehensible. In spite of the comic twist given to the names of the characters (Ophelia, for instance, becomes 'Feely') it is quite faithful to the plot. I would conjecture that it was composed as a comic recitation for performance in the early music halls, i.e. public houses providing variety turns.

3. As a class the garland seems to rise in popularity as the broadsheet ballad died out, and to precede the nineteenth-century slip-ballad. Apart from the variety of its contents, it is to be distinguished by its 'pocket-edition' format.

4. I say *writer* rather than *writers* because the rhythm, rhyme-schemes and puns of both poems suggest they come from one hand.

5. At least, ostensibly from Belfast. There are other garlands, bearing a London imprint, which are so like the Belfast ones that they must come from a common source, but it is impossible to decide what that source is.

6. Outside London, Newcastle was the biggest single centre for the production of chapbooks and garlands at the turn of the century. The many centres in Scotland, however, were also responsible for a considerable output, and one reason for the large numbers printed in Newcastle was doubtless a sort of Border warfare between English and Scottish chapmen. This would also explain why so many of the Newcastle garlands are straight piracies of Scottish ones.

NEW FINDINGS WITH REGARD TO
THE 1624 PROTECTION LIST

BY

JOHN P. CUTTS

A considerable amount of recent research into early seventeenth-century music manuscripts has not only revealed who were the composers[1] of the music for the King's Men theatre but has also provided clues to the identity of some of the theatre musicians. So it has become necessary to examine much more carefully than has hitherto been possible Herbert's 1624 Protection List (Plate V)[2] for the names of those 'imployed by the Kinge Maties servantẹ in theire quallity of Playinge as Musitions and other necessary attendantẹ'. In particular it is necessary to combine the results of the above research with those of the research into the actors of the company, most exhaustively treated by Professor Baldwin in *The Organization and Personnel of the Shakespearean Company*[3] and by Professor Bentley in volume II of his *The Jacobean and Caroline Stage*,[4] and with the results of Professor Woodfill's research into *Musicians in English Society from Elizabeth to Charles I*.[5]

It is true that Professors Baldwin and Woodfill have each given some passing attention to the music in the theatre, relying heavily on Whitelocke's observations in 1634 that 'the Blackefryars Musicke ... were then esteemed the best of common musitions in London'[6] and on Frederick Gerchow's diary reference to the Blackfriars music.[7] Professor Baldwin suggests musical functions for three names of the 1624 Protection List (Wilson, Toyer and Pallant) and remarks of the others that as far as he knows 'there is no record as musicians'.[8] Professor Bentley adds the identification of one more as a musician, Byland, and cautions about the distinction between a player and a musician not always being very definite.[9] Obviously some theatre musicians would be expected to fill in as minor actors and attendants, especially in those plays which make little use of music.

It is the purpose of this paper to reassess hitherto accepted identifications of musicians in the 1624 List, to provide evidence for further identifications and to begin to explore the possibility that something in the nature of a theatre orchestra existed and how it may have been constituted.

The approaches of Professors Baldwin and Bentley have necessarily been confined to attempts to identify members of the 1624 Protection List either as musicians, actors, or actor-musicians. Professor Woodfill concerned himself with royal musicians in London and with the London waits, without linking up his finds with the theatre.[10] Obviously the various lists of musicians needed to be collated. This process has yielded the information that William Saunders was a musician who by 1634 'for many yeares past' had 'exercised and played with the Citty waights by their good approbacon in service of this City in the tyme of absence of ffrauncis Parke occasioned by reason of his sicknes' (Plate VI).[11] Francis Parke had been appointed a London Wait in 1616; he was dead by 4 February 1641, on which day William Saunders received Parke's place 'by virtue of a grant in revercon to him made the xviij^th: day of September 1634'. Thus

Saunders had 'exercised and played with the Citty waights' many years before 1634, when at Francis Parke's request he was granted the reversion of his place—'the revercon and next avoydance of the said place of the said ffrauncis Parke'. We can assume, therefore, that William Saunders was seeking a position as a London Wait[12] and was deputizing for Parke 'in Consorte with the Citty waights and all other musick'. Whether this alone accounts for his name on the 1624 Protection List or whether he was entered there in his own right we cannot determine.

Interestingly enough the same document of 1634 that promises the reversion of Parke's place to William Saunders mentions that Saunders shared the task of deputizing for Parke with Ralph Trachey,[13] Henry Field[14] and Ambrose Byland,[15] and was to 'receive an equall pte with them of such benefitt and offerings as doe thereby accrue in the roome and stead of the said ffrancis Parke'. Ambrose Byland is included in Herbert's 1624 Protection List. Professor Bentley[16] considers that Byland 'was evidently one of the musicians who served the King's company at the Globe and Blackfriars' and suggests that his 'long career as a royal violinist indicates that he must have been quite a young man when Sir Henry Herbert exempted him from arrest'. Professor Woodfill[17] has shown that Byland was appointed a London Wait in 1631 in 'winde instrumentes and consorts'. Byland was appointed a musician to his Majesty for the violins in ordinary in 1640, a position he surrendered in 1672.[18] Obviously Byland, before he secured a place in 1631 as a London Wait, had, like William Saunders, occasionally deputized for Francis Parke and had been providing music in the King's Men theatre. Although in 1640 he became a King's Musician he did not relinquish his post as City Wait. Each Wait was allowed to have two apprentices[19] and from this it is easy to see how young boys could be giving their musical services to the theatre.

There is even more evidence to link Byland with the theatre. Byland instructed as apprentice John Gamble whose commonplace book, Drexel MS. 4257, has been the subject of considerable recent interest[20] because it contains settings of play songs not extant elsewhere, and only to be explained by Gamble's connexion with theatre musicians. John Gamble, according to Bodleian MS. Wood D 19 (4), 'was bred up to musick in the the [sic] condition of an Apprentice under a noted master called Ambr. Beyland, and after his time was expired, he became a musitian belonging to a play-House in London'. Wood does not mention the name of the theatre, but from the foregoing we can suggest that it was the King's Men theatre. Gamble was certainly close enough to King's Men theatre musicians to know of settings of play songs appropriate only to plays performed in that theatre.

William Saunders and Ambrose Byland certainly begin to make the 1624 Protection List look more meaningful than ever before. Pursuing all possible references to these musicians one uncovers knowledge of others also in the List. Bentley records[21] that on 14 December 1628 the Lord Chamberlain issued a warrant for the apprehension of 'Ambrose Beeland and Henry Wilson fidlers at ye complaint of Mr Hemings'. The two names occur side by side in this order in the Protection List. Both men were violinists. A stage direction in Believe As you List (1631)[22] marks Wilson as a lutenist also. It is possible that Henry Wilson was linked by family with John Wilson, the famous lutenist, a London Wait, King's Musician and composer for the King's Men c. 1614–42,[23] but there is as yet no evidence. All that can be said in favour of such a hypothesis is the tendency for families of musicians to hold a post continuously, son or nephew succeeding father or uncle.[24]

Byland, Wilson and Saunders are fourth, fifth and seventh respectively in the Protection List, all three are principally violinists, though Wilson was also a lutenist. The sixth name, Jeffery Collins, has so far defied identification. Bentley[25] distinguishes Jeffery Collins from the Edward Collins of the 1636 Protection List and this is correct. Jeffery Collins is mentioned in the Longleat Papers as being in 1634 a musician at the Cockpit theatre.[26] Presumably the Blackfriars band of musicians was eked out by musicians from another theatre when the occasion called for it.[27]

Before passing to consider two more in the list, Pallant and Toyer, who have been accepted by Baldwin as musicians, it will be as well to examine other names near this group of musicians, Byland, Wilson, Collins and Saunders. William Chambers is the third name in the list and Nicholas Underhill the eighth.

For William Chambers, Bentley[28] merely notes two burial entries, one in St Anne's Blackfriars for 30 November 1629, the other in St Giles in the Fields for 2 March 1642/3, and thinks the 1629 death item the more likely. William Chambers was included in the 1603 funeral procession[29] as a chorister of Westminster. If this should prove to be the William Chambers of the 1624 Protection List he may have been a singer-musician. William Chambers is listed, as a 'Quirister of Westminster', together with no less a musical dignitary than Walter Porter, a tenor whose *Madrigales and Ayres*,[30] though first published in 1632, contain, as item xxviii, 'An Elogie on the Right Honourable Lady, the Lady Arabella Stewart', indicating that one of the compositions dates as early as 1615. Porter secured a full place as chorister in 1617.[31] He was one of the singers employed for Chapman's Masque to celebrate the betrothal of Princess Elizabeth to the Elector of the Palatinate, 12 February 1612/13.[32]

For the eighth name on the 1624 List, Nicholas Underhill, we now have positive evidence from the Longleat Papers that he was a musician at the Cockpit theatre in 1634.[33] Investigation of the Underhill family helps to suggest why George Rickner, the fourteenth name on the 1624 Protection List, was included there.[34] It is recorded[35] of a *Samuel* Underhill, also a trumpeter, that on 3 October 1636 eleven persons were committed to Newgate 'untill his Majesties pleasure bee knowne, for goeing with one Samuel Underhill a trumpeter who died of the plague, to his grave with trumpettes sounded and swords drawne in the night time in Shoreditch'. The eleven named were Thomas Creswell, Thomas Woodford (Wadd), Edward Bosseley, John Pett, Edward Hodgson, Abraham Rogers, John Carre, George Rickner, George Bosgrave, Adam Rose and William Johnson. By 1 December 1636 a fuller indictment included six more names, Philip Knight, Launcelot Giles, Edward Jupe, Henry Griffin, Francis Langley and John Wilkinson. Of these we know for certain that the following were trumpeters: Thomas Cresswell,[36] Nicholas Wadoll[37] (Woddall, Ward, Wodall, Woodall) listed with Thomas Underhill in 1606,[38] Edward Hodgson and George Bosgrave mentioned together,[39] and Edward Jupe (Juckes, Jewkes, Jurkes, Juxe, Jukes).[40] The event seems to have been a trumpeters' farewell. This information helps to provide some clues to George Rickner's own possible linking with trumpeters. Both Underhill and Rickner took small parts in plays, Underhill as 'Nick' playing Barnavelt's wife in *Barnavelt* (1619) and playing the roles of officer and attendants in *Believe As You List* (1631)[41] and Rickner as 'G:Rick' as a servant in *The Honest Man's Fortune* (1625).[42] What evidence there is would seem to point to the possibility of George Rickner being a trumpeter who played the parts of servants, wives, officers and attendants.

This was the function of William Toyer who was 'Heminges's servant, serving as a musician and necessary attendant'.[43] The stage direction in the First Folio text of *A Midsummer Night's Dream*, v, i records 'Tawyer with a Trumpet before them', and since it is not found in the quartos of 1600 and 1619 Bentley[44] reasonably argues that it 'almost certainly belongs to a revival', that is 1619–23. Thus Tawyer is employed as a trumpeter, musician-attendant, a few years previous to the Herbert Protection List.

Of Robert Pallant there is at present no certain information. Bentley inclines to the belief that he was probably the son of the queen's man of the same name.[45] Baldwin[46] points out that a Robert Pallant had been a musician in *The Seven Deadly Sins* (1593), information which Bentley wisely ignores, for 'The *Book* and Platt, &c' of *The Seven Deadly Sins*, Dulwich MS. xix, as edited in Malone's Supplement (1780), I, 60, has no specific reference to Pallant as a musician. He certainly took the part of 'Warder', 'attendant', 'Captain', and 'Philomela' but is *not* included when musicians are specified—'to them Arbactus & 3 musitions Mr Pope J. Sizler, Vincent, R Cowley'.

John Rhodes, number fifteen on the 1624 Protection List, is almost certainly the musician who was buried at St Giles, Cripplegate, on 22 February 1635/6. Bentley has carefully pointed out the necessity to differentiate him from the John Rhodes, manager of the Fortune and book-seller.[47]

Alexander Bullard, number 20, about whom nothing is as yet known, may possibly be related to John Ballard, recorder player and London Wait 1594–1601,[48] and Richard Ballard, trumpeter.[49]

Edward Shackerly, number 23, is definitely recorded as a 'musition',[50] and as a comic servant in *The Renegado* (1625).[52]

Thus of the twenty-four people mentioned in the 1624 Protection List the following seven can definitely be identified as musicians: Ambrose Byland (violinist), Henry Wilson (violinist and lutenist), William Saunders (violinist and wind instruments), William Tawyer (trumpeter), Edward Shackerly (instrument unknown), Jeffery Collins (instrument unknown) and Nicholas Underhill (trumpeter); and there is a possibility that four more were musicians too: William Chambers (singer), George Rickner (trumpeter?), John Rhodes (instrument unknown) and Alexander Bullard (recorder player: trumpeter?).

The 1624 Protection List would seem to have a potential band of eleven musicians. Interestingly enough this is in fairly close agreement with the Malone conjecture[52] that there were eight or ten musicians in the theatre and with Cowling's suggestion in 1913[53] that 'we may reckon a dozen at most to have been musicians'. Cowling does not arrive at this apostolic number by identifying the musicians from the list but from his assessment, based on the number of music-makers indicated in the stage directions of some plays, that if we suppose all of the musicians to have been employed at once then 'the number could not be less than say two viols, viol da gamba, bass viol, two or three instruments of the lute type, three cornets, three hautboys, three recorders, sackbut, and organ—a total of eighteen musicians'. Cowling assumes that some musicians played several instruments, and that for certain plays additional musicians were engaged.

To what extent the musicians in the 1624 List were 'additional musicians' is, of course, a question, because there is very good evidence that other musicians played in the theatre. Richard Balls, a London Wait 1613–22 and a Prince's Musician, is mentioned in a law suit, Balls *v.* Samptom,[54] as being employed in the theatre as a musician and fortunately one of his theatrical compositions is extant.[55] He trained his nephew, Alphonso Balls,[56] presumably to the same work. John Wilson, succeeding Richard Balls as a Wait,[57] became a composer for the King's Men and succeeded Alphonso Balls as a King's Musician for the lutes and voices.[58] John Adson,[59] brother-in-law to Richard Balls, presumably also worked as a musician in the theatre in his capacity as a City Wait. By 1634 John Adson is listed as a Blackfriars musician.[60] It seems to me that the theatre would need a certain number of musicians as its regular 'music', and would employ extra men for plays which called for more than an average amount of music-making.

NOTES

1. The following composers for the King's Men have been identified since 1951: Robert Johnson, Richard Balls, John Wilson and William Lawes. Robert Johnson was practically unknown when I began work on a Master's thesis in 1951 (see 'The Contributions of Robert Johnson, King's Musician, to Court and Theatrical Entertainments, and the tradition of such service prior to 1642', University of Reading, unpublished M.A. Thesis, June 1953; 'Two Jacobean Theatre Songs', *Music and Letters*, XXXIII, 4, October 1952, 333–4; 'William Lawes's writing for the Theatre and the Court', *The Library*, 5th ser., VII, 4, December 1952, 225–34; 'Jacobean Masque and Stage Music', *Music and Letters*, XXXV, 3, July 1954, 185–200; 'Some Jacobean and Caroline Dramatic Lyrics', *Notes and Queries*, n.s., II, 3, March 1955, 106–9; 'Original Music to Middleton's *The Witch*, and *Macbeth*', *Shakespeare Quarterly*, VII, 2, Spring 1956, 203–9; 'Le rôle de la musique dans les masques de Jonson, et en particulier dans *Obéron*, 1610/11', delivered at Royaumont, Paris, on 11 July 1955 and included by Jean Jacquot in *Les Fêtes de la Renaissance* (Centre National des Recherches Scientifiques, 1956), pp. 285–303; 'The role of music in *The Tempest*. A Study in Interpretation', *Music and Letters*, XXXIX, 4, October 1958, 347–58, paper read at the South-Central Renaissance Convention in Fort Worth, Texas, 8 February 1958; 'Who wrote the Hecate-Scene?', *Shakespeare Jahrbuch*, XCIV, 1958, 200–2; *Musique de scène de la troupe de Shakespeare*, Paris, 1959; 'Robert Johnson and the Stuart Masque', *Music and Letters*, XLI, 2, April 1960, 111–26; '"Speak-Demand-We'll answer"—"Hecat(e) and the *other* three witches"', *Shakespeare Jahrbuch*, XCVI, 1960, 173–6; 'Music and *The Mad Lover*', *Studies in the Renaissance*, VIII, 1961, 236–48, paper read at the Central Renaissance Convention at St Louis, Missouri, 15 February 1958; 'Thomas Heywood's The "Gentry to the King's Head" in *The Rape of Lucrece*, and John Wilson's setting', *Notes and Queries*, n.s., VII, 10, October 1961, 384–7).

2. Plate V. Most reproductions I have seen omit the two postscripts.

3. Cf. T. W. Baldwin, *The Organization and Personnel of the Shakespearean Company* (Princeton, 1927). Hereafter abbreviated to *Baldwin*.

4. Cf. G. E. Bentley, *The Jacobean and Caroline Stage* (5 vols., Oxford, 1941–56). Hereafter abbreviated to *Bentley*.

5. Cf. W. L. Woodfill, *Musicians in English Society from Elizabeth to Charles I* (Princeton University Press, 1953). Hereafter abbreviated to *Woodfill*.

6. Cf. Edmund Malone, *The Plays and Poems of William Shakespeare* (21 vols., London, 1821), III, 113. Hereafter abbreviated to Malone's *Variorum*.

7. *Woodfill*, p. 236.

8. *Baldwin*, p. 120.

9. Cf. G. E. Bentley, 'Records of Players in the parish of St Giles, Cripplegate', *PMLA*, XLIV, 3, September 1929, 799, 801.

10. The 1624 Protection List is not considered by Woodfill at all, nor does he refer to Whitelocke's comments on theatre musicians.

11. I give on p. 107 a complete transcript and facsimile of Repertory 48, fols. 434ᵛ–435, 18 September 1634 (Plate VI). (Repertories of the Court of Aldermen of the City of London.) Saunders was presumably a violinist since Byland and Field, who also deputized for Parke, were violinists.

12. That the London Waits did indeed provide music in the playhouses is evidenced by the complaint of the Aldermen in 1613 (Repertory 31 (1), fols. 44–44ᵛ, 1613):
'Item vpon the humble peticon of Edward Godfrey a man well knowne to this court for his rare and excellent skill in singing is by this court admitted to haue a place

amonge the wayt*e* of this Citty during the pleasure of this court And to be paid out of the Chamber of this Citty such fee and allowance as is allowed to others of the said Company And for as much as great complaint is made of the negligence of the wayt*e* in playing w^thin the Citty in the night*e* And that if either my Lord Maior, the Sheriffe or any Alderman at the mariage of his daughter or other speciall cause haue occasion to vse them, they are then ymployed at play houses And when they come to any Magistrat*e* house of the Citty they demannd vnreasonable for their paynes It is therefore ordered that Sr Stephen Soame, Sr John Garrard, Sr Thomas Lowe, Sr James Pemberton, Sr Thomas Midleton and Sr John Joll*e* Knight*e* and Aldermen calling before them the Citties Waite shall meete and conceaue of certen orders to be observed by them, and what service they ought to doe And the said Committees to certifie this court in writing what they haue done therein and William Raven to warne and attend them.' It would seem that the services of the waits were not available to the Mayor and prominent citizens because the waits were occupied at the time in playing for the playhouses, and it is further implied that the money they received from the theatres was quite competitive. That musicians were willing to pay an annual fee for a licence to play in the theatre would tend to support this latter suggestion ('For a warrant to the Musitions of the king's company, this 9th of April, 1627—£1. 0. 0.', Herber MS., cf. Malone's *Variorum*, III, 112, n. 6).

13. This is the only mention of Trachey I have come across. A Ralph Strachey is listed with John Adson, Ambrose Beeland, Henry Field, Thomas Hutton and Francis Parker as musicians at the Blackfriars in 1634. See the Longleat Papers.

14. Henry Field, a musician for the treble 'violen' and wind instruments, became a London Wait 1610–25 until his death in 1641 (see Repertory 39, fols. 86–86^v; *Woodfill*, pp. 249–50). Henry Field is listed as a Blackfriars Musician employed in *The Triumph of Peace*, 1634 (see the Longleat Papers described by M. Lefkowitz, 'The Longleat Papers', *Journal of the American Musicological Society*, XVIII, 1, Spring 1965, 42–60).

15. Some of Ambrose Byland's work is extant in Bodleian Mus. Sch. MS. d.220.

16. *Bentley*, II, 362–3.

17. *Woodfill*, p. 250.

18. Byland's place was filled by Edmund Flower (see H. C. de Lafontaine, *The King's Music*, London, 1909, p. 249; hereafter abbreviated to *Lafontaine*).

19. Repertory 11, fol. 481.

20. Cf. V. H. Duckles, 'John Gamble's Commonplace Book', University of California, unpublished Ph.D. Thesis, 1 August 1953; Willa McClung Evans, 'The Rose: A song by Wilson and Lovelace', *MLQ*, VII (September 1946), 269–78; and 'Hobson appears in comic song', *PQ*, XXVI, 3 (October 1947), 321–7; John P. Cutts, 'Drexel MS. 4041—Earl Ferrer's MS—a treasure-house of songs of the first half of the Seventeenth Century', *Musica Disciplina*, XVIII (1964), 151–202.

21. *Bentley*, II, 363.

22. *Baldwin*, p. 121; *Bentley*, II, 621.

23. See my article on Wilson quoted last in note 1 for a check list of Wilson's contributions.

24. A brief glance through lists of musicians in *Lafontaine* and *Woodfill* will show this.

25. *Bentley*, II, 409.

26. See note 14 above. Other Cockpit theatre musicians of 1634 who are mentioned as having taken part in *The Triumph of Peace* are: Thomas Hunter, John Lavasher, John Strong (see *Woodfill*, p. 250), Nicholas Underhill and Edward Wright.

27. See also the information on Nicholas Underhill below.

28. *Bentley*, II, 406.

29. *Lafontaine*, p. 44.

30. Cf. E. H. Fellowes, *English Madrigal Verse* (Oxford, 1920), pp. 575–84 and Notes, pp. 626–7.

31. Cf. *Grove*, VI, 885.

32. Cf. K. Douglas-Walker (ed.), *Records of Lincoln's Inn, 1586–1660* (London, 1897–1902), II, 154.

33. See notes 16 and 29 above.

34. Though this does not explain, of course, why George Rickner's name is crossed off the 1624 List.

35. *Bentley*, II, 384. Samuel Underhill is listed in the Longleat Papers as a trumpeter for the Earl of Moorfon (*Lefkowitz*, sic) in *The Triumph of Peace*, 1634.

36. *Lafontaine*, passim.

37. *Ibid.* pp. 43, 47, 48.

38. *Ibid.* pp. 43, 47–9, 51, 54 and 55, and, 'Lists of the King's Musicians from the Audit Office Declared Accounts', *Musical Antiquary* (April 1911), p. 174, Audit Office Declared Accounts Bundle 387, No. 40.

39. *Lafontaine*, p. 88.

40. *Ibid.* passim.

41. *Bentley*, II, 609 and, for 'Nick', II, 516.

42. *Bentley*, II, 547.

43. *Baldwin*, p. 432.

44. *Bentley*, II, 590.

45. *Ibid.* p. 519.

46. *Baldwin*, p. 120.

47. *Bentley*, II, 544–6, and 'Records of Players in the parish of St Giles, Cripplegate', *PMLA*, XLIV (September 1929), 3, 817.

48. *Woodfill*, p. 248. John Ballard (jr?) is listed for 1625 in *Lafontaine*, p. 59, as one of the musicians of 'The Chamber of King Charles'.

49. *Lafontaine*, p. 57.

50. E. M. Denkinger, 'Minstrels and Musicians in the registers of St Botolph, Aldgate', *MLN*, XLVI, 6, (June 1931), 395–8.

51. *Bentley*, II, 561.

52. Malone's *Variorum*, III, 111, 'The band, which, I believe, did not consist of more than eight or ten performers.'

53. G. H. Cowling, *Music on the Shakespearian Stage* (London, 1913), p. 81.

54. Transcribed and published in my *Musique de scène de la troupe de Shakespeare* (Paris, 1959).

55. For Fletcher's *The Mad Lover*, cf. note 1.

56. Repertory XL, fol. 83ᵛ notes that in January 1626 Alphonsus Ball was said to have served with the waits twelve years under his uncle Richard Ball (*Woodfill*, p. 36, n. 4, and *Lafontaine*, p. 66). Alphonsus Ball is mentioned as a King's Musician in 1625 (see *Lafontaine*, p. 59, and *Woodfill*, p. 303).

57. Repertory XXXVII, fol. 21.

58. *Woodfill*, p. 305 and note on p. 313.

59. Cf. *Woodfill*, pp. 44, 45 n., 51.

60. See note 13 above.

REPERTORY 48, fols. 434ᵛ–435, 18 September 1634 (see p. 101).

William Saunders/to continew in/service with ye/Citty weights

Item this day vpon the humble peticon of William Saunders Citizen and Musicon of London *who for many yeares past hath exercised and played with the Citty* waights by their good approbacon in service of this City in the tyme of absence of ffrauncis Parke occasioned by reason of his sicknes and extreame paine with the stone in the bladder And at the humble suite of the said ffrauncis Parke this Court doth graunt leave that the said William Saunders may in all respects Continew his service in Consorte with the Citty waights and all other musick in place of the said ffrauncis Parke during the tyme of his sicknes and inhability to pforme the same through his said greiffe at the Charge only of the said ffrancis Parke and may doe his service in the night waches as heretofore he hath done with Ralph Trachey Henry ffeild and Ambrose Bee[—]lland and receive an equall pte with them of such benefitt and offerings as doe thereby accrue in the roome and stead of the said ffrancis Parke And this Court doth graunt vnto the said William Saunders the revercon and next avoydance of the said place of the said ffrauncis Parke To have hould exercise and inioy the same place with all fees pffitts and Comodities therevnto due and of right belonging Soe long as he shall well and—honestly vse and behave himselfe theirein saveing to all and every other personne and personns his and their right and interest in and to the same by force and vertue of any former graunt made thereof by this Court And soe alwayes and vpon Condicon that he the said William Saunders at such tyme as he shall come to clayme and⟨—f. 435⟩ inioy the benifitt of this his graunt be thought and adiudged by this Court fitt apt and hable for the due execucon thereof and not otherwise/

REPERTORY 55, fols. 63ᵛ–64, 4 February 1640/1 (see p. 102)

Sanders admitted one of the Citty Weights./
Item this day Willm̃ Sanders Cittizen and Musicon of London by virtue of a grant in revercon to him—made the xviijᵗʰ day of September 1634 is by this Court admitted one of the Citty Weights in place of ffrancis Parker deceased To have hold exercise and enioy the same place with all fees profitts and Comodities therevnto due and of right belonging Soe long as hee shall well and honestly vse and behave himselfe therein And was here sworne for the due execucon thereof accordingly./

SHAKESPEARE PRODUCTIONS IN THE UNITED KINGDOM: 1965

A LIST COMPILED FROM ITS RECORDS BY THE
SHAKESPEARE MEMORIAL LIBRARY, BIRMINGHAM

JANUARY

13   *The Winter's Tale:* Adam House Theatre, Edinburgh. *Producer:* IDA WATE.

27   *Richard II:* The Playhouse, Nottingham. *Producer:* JOHN NEVILLE.

FEBRUARY

Not known   *Twelfth Night:* David Lewis Theatre, Liverpool. *Producer:* ALAN SPENCER.

2   *King Lear:* Oxford University Dramatic Society at the Playhouse, Oxford. *Producer:* PETER BAYLEY.

8   *Twelfth Night:* Civic Theatre, Chelmsford and on tour. *Producer:* CHARLES VANCE.

12   *A Midsummer Night's Dream:* Tavistock Repertory Company, Tower Theatre, London. *Producer:* JESSICA TAYLOR.

16   *Much Ado About Nothing:* National Theatre Company, Old Vic Theatre, London. *Producer:* FRANCO ZEFFIRELLI.

16   *The Tempest:* The Playhouse, Sheffield. *Producer:* COLIN GEORGE.

16   *Henry IV, Part I:* Empire Theatre, Sunderland. *Producer:* ANTONY CARRICK.

23   *Macbeth:* Everyman Theatre, Liverpool. *Producer:* JOHN RUSSELL BROWN.

MARCH

1   *Macbeth:* Colchester Repertory Theatre. *Producer:* Not known.

1   *Macbeth:* Theatre Royal, Lincoln. *Producer:* ALAN VAUGHAN WILLIAM.

2   *Twelfth Night:* Everyman Theatre, Cheltenham. *Producer:* IAN MULLINS.

3   *A Midsummer Night's Dream:* The Playhouse, Salisbury. *Producer:* DEREK MARTINUS.

8   *Romeo and Juliet:* Marlowe Society, Arts Theatre, Cambridge. *Producer:* GARETH MORGAN.

9   *The Winter's Tale:* Birmingham Repertory Theatre. *Producer:* BRAHAM MURRAY.

9   *The Merchant of Venice:* Castle Theatre, Farnham. *Producer:* ANTONY TUCKEY.

9   *Romeo and Juliet:* Leatherhead Theatre. *Producer:* JORDAN LAWRENCE.

9   *King Lear:* Northampton Repertory Theatre. *Producer:* KEITH ANDREWS.

9   *The Winter's Tale:* Empire Theatre, Sunderland. *Producer:* JOSEPH O'CONOR.

10   *The Taming of the Shrew:* Belgrade Theatre, Coventry. *Producer:* ROBERT CARTLAND.

10   *Henry IV, Part I:* People's Theatre Arts Group, Newcastle-upon-Tyne. *Producer:* TOM EMERSON.

11   *Romeo and Juliet:* Arts Theatre, Ipswich. *Producer:* DAVID PERRY.

12   *Romeo and Juliet:* Royal Academy of Dramatic Art, Vanbrugh Theatre, London, and on tour. *Producer:* DAVID GILES.

16   *The Merchant of Venice:* Citizens' Theatre, Glasgow. *Producer:* ERIC JONES.

17   *Love's Labour's Lost:* Royal Academy of Dramatic Art, Vanbrugh Theatre, London. *Producer:* DAVID GILES.

23   *Hamlet:* Bristol Old Vic Company, Theatre Royal, Bristol. *Producer:* ALVIN RAKOFF.

23   *The Tempest:* Civic Theatre, The Arts Centre, Leeds. *Producer:* MARGARET RHODES.

23   *The Tempest:* Library Theatre, Manchester. *Producer:* COLIN GEORGE.

23   *As You Like It:* Victoria Theatre, Stoke on Trent. *Producer:* PETER CHEESEMAN.

29   *The Tempest:* Royal Academy of Dramatic Art, London, at the Opera House, Harrogate. *Producer:* JOHN FERNALD.

APRIL

7   *Love's Labour's Lost:* Royal Shakespeare Theatre, Stratford-upon-Avon. *Producer:* JOHN BARTON.

16   *The Merchant of Venice:* Royal Shakespeare Theatre, Stratford-upon-Avon. *Producer:* CLIFFORD WILLIAMS.

MAY

11   *A Midsummer Night's Dream:* Flora Robson Playhouse, Newcastle-upon-Tyne. *Producer:* JULIAN HERINGTON.

11   *Macbeth:* Palace Theatre, Watford. *Producer:* GILES HAVERGAL.

14   *The Taming of the Shrew:* Maddermarket Theatre, Norwich. *Producer:* IAN EMMERSON.

19   *The Comedy of Errors:* Royal Shakespeare Theatre, Stratford-upon-Avon. *Producer:* CLIFFORD WILLIAMS.

24   *Henry IV, Part II:* People's Theatre, Arts Centre, Newcastle-upon-Tyne. *Producer:* JOHN LILBURN.

27   *Twelfth Night:* Harrow School. *Producer:* JEREMY LEMMON.

27   *Henry V:* Royal Shakespeare Theatre Company, Aldwych Theatre, London. *Producers:* JOHN BARTON and TREVOR NUNN.

JUNE

No date   *Antony and Cleopatra:* Royal Academy of Dramatic Art, Vanbrugh Theatre, London. *Producer:* HUGH MORRISON.

No date   *Hamlet:* Ludlow Festival and on tour. *Producer:* COLIN GEORGE.

10   *As You Like It:* New Shakespeare Company, Regent's Park Open-Air Theatre, London. *Producer:* HAROLD LANG.

22   *Richard II:* York University, King's Manor, York. *Producer:* IAN STUART.

JULY

1   *Timon of Athens:* Royal Shakespeare Theatre, Stratford-upon-Avon. *Producer:* JOHN SCHLESINGER.

5   *As You Like It:* Oxford Stage Company at the Shakespeare Institute, Stratford-upon-Avon. *Producer:* CHRIS PARR.

6   *Othello:* Royal Academy of Dramatic Art, Vanbrugh Theatre, London. *Producer:* ELLEN POLLOCK.

10   *A Midsummer Night's Dream:* Amateur Dramatic Club, Cambridge, at Alveston Manor Hotel, Stratford-upon-Avon.

16   *Hamlet:* Richmond (Yorks.) Theatre. *Producer:* COLIN GEORGE.

AUGUST

Not known   *Measure for Measure:* Dryden Society, at the A.D.C. Theatre, Cambridge. *Producer:* DAVE BENNETT.

10   *Coriolanus:* Berliner Ensemble at the National Theatre, London. *Producers:* MANFRED WERKWERTH and JOACHIM TENSCHERT.

19   *Hamlet:* Royal Shakespeare Theatre, Stratford-upon-Avon. *Producer:* PETER HALL.

23   *Macbeth:* Traverse Theatre Festival Productions, at the Assembly Hall, Edinburgh. *Producer:* MICHAEL GELIOT.

SEPTEMBER

6   *Antony and Cleopatra:* Youth Theatre, at the National Theatre, London. *Producer:* MICHAEL CROFTS.

13   *Troilus and Cressida:* Youth Theatre, at the National Theatre, London. *Producer:* PAUL HILL.

22   *Measure for Measure:* Nottingham Playhouse. *Producer:* JOHN NEVILLE.

27   *Twelfth Night:* Library Theatre, Manchester. *Producer:* OLIVER NEVILLE.

27   *Antony and Cleopatra:* Oxford Playhouse. *Producer:* FRANK HAUSER.

28   *A Midsummer Night's Dream:* Tower Theatre, Canonbury, London. *Producer:* ROBERT PENNANT JONES.

28   *Hamlet:* Sheffield Playhouse. *Producer:* COLIN GEORGE.

OCTOBER

11   *A Winter's Tale:* Queen's Theatre, Hornchurch. *Producer:* ANTONY CARRICK.

12   *The Taming of the Shrew:* Marlowe Theatre, Canterbury. *Producer:* ANN STUTFIELD.

12   *Henry IV, Part I:* Victoria Theatre, Stoke on Trent. *Producer:* JONATHAN DUDLEY.

13   *The Merchant of Venice:* Bristol Old Vic Company, Theatre Royal, Bristol. *Producer:* JOAN KNIGHT.

14   *Romeo and Juliet:* Royal Academy of Dramatic Art, Vanbrugh Theatre, London. *Producer:* HUGH MORRISON.

17   *Othello:* Phoenix Theatre, Leicester. *Producers:* CLIVE PERRY and PHILLIP COLLINS.

25   *Hamlet:* Perth Theatre. *Producer:* DAVID STEUART.

NOVEMBER

1   *Henry IV, Part I:* Everyman Theatre, Cheltenham. *Producer:* IAN MULLINS.

8   *Twelfth Night:* Palace Theatre, Watford. *Producer:* GILES HAVERGAL.

9   *Twelfth Night:* Civic Theatre, Chesterfield. *Producer:* COLIN MCINTYRE.

9   *Twelfth Night:* The Playhouse, Liverpool. *Producer:* TONY COLEGATE.

19   *Henry V:* Norwich Players at the Maddermarket Theatre, Norwich. *Producer:* IAN EMMERSON.

29   *Richard III:* Everyman Theatre, Liverpool. *Producer:* TERRY HAND.

DECEMBER

20   *Hamlet:* Royal Academy of Dramatic Art, Vanbrugh Theatre, London. *Producer:* ROGER JENKINS.

THE ROYAL
SHAKESPEARE COMPANY 1965

BY

JOHN RUSSELL BROWN

In 1960 when Peter Hall became Director of the Shakespeare Memorial Theatre at Stratford-upon-Avon he spoke of forming a company. He wanted a policy. He did not want each production to be a shot at a target chosen by its director in the light of his own limited experience and to serve his individual career. He did not want to provide vehicles for star actors with established reputations and established mannerisms. He talked about creating a real company with its own distinctive character, whose members could gain strength from each other and from a common purpose. Nothing like this existed in England but Peter Hall persuaded a great number of persons to work with him so that in five years he has achieved the best part of his ambition.

Now the Stratford programme can display the company's wide-ranging activity. There are 'artists under long-term contract', associate directors and associate designers, teachers engaged for speech, singing, music and movement. The public is assured that the company 'develop in private in their studio the agility and freedom that Shakespeare's plays demand'.

A broader organization has been formed: Peter Hall is now Managing Director with two fellow Directors, Peter Brook and Michel Saint-Denis. New functionaries have been introduced, as Artistic Controller, Theatre Club Organizer, Literary Manager, Advisory Dramaturg. A London theatre has been provided for presenting contemporary plays and a further showing for those from Stratford which the public likes best. The company has its own Graphic Design Consultant, and three, instead of an original one, Publicity and Publications Officers. Expenditure must have been great, but it has purchased a company. The plays presented at Stratford during 1965 have unity of style. In the previous year a single group of three directors had worked in collaboration on each of seven productions and thus achieved a unity, but this year, when five directors were responsible independently for the five plays by Shakespeare, the company's style has been just as evident. (And the five new plays were more obviously varied in their demands—three comedies and two tragedies—than the seven history-plays of 1964.) Everywhere in the Royal Shakespeare Theatre, there are signs of Peter Hall's successful creation of a company.

To talk of Shakespeare in Stratford, or in other places where the company has toured, is to talk of the Royal Shakespeare Company. It has won such respect that when one of its productions cannot be acclaimed the critics are apt to say that it is puzzling or challenging. The Stratford season is now accepted as an intelligent experiment, and a review must try to appreciate a corporate and developing achievement.

Apparently the company has been taught to scrutinize every word in a play so that they know, always, what they are saying. This policy is not far-fetched, but the rigour of its application is rare enough to be accounted original and even revolutionary. Ageing varnish no longer obscures

Shakespeare's brilliance. Generalizing and debilitating resonance and overblown fullness of phrase have been rinsed away; and most individual quirks and flourishes of elocution. There is no compensating pursuit of a pure diction—everyone sharing the same vowel sounds and treating consonants with equal respect—but the words are alive, as far as the actors understand them.

Here the gains are great. The audience follows by-ways of plot and can appreciate the manipulations of Claudius or the craftiness of Shylock. Passages of verbal complexity no longer lie heavy and undigested, but shine with energy; nothing is 'too picked, too spruce, too affected, too odd, as it were, too peregrinate'. The actors communicate to their audience the pleasure of the chase, and seem proud of their dexterity—so Dromio of Syracuse ransacks the world to describe a kitchen wench, or Hamlet answers Osric, in his own tongue, or Moth spars with Armado. When Bassanio and Portia quarrel about the interchange of rings in the last scene of *The Merchant of Venice*, their rhetorical nimbleness, in answering each other's expostulations, gives the temporary discord a hint of playful and spirited harmony; underlying their strife and verbal animation, there is collusion, and so a scene that is stubbornly artificial on the printed page achieves its illusion of psychological subtlety.

Passages less pyrotechnical fare less well. For moments of consideration or deep feeling the primary rule of understanding every word will not take the actors far enough. Here the company seems to have two resources. Firstly to take everything lightly, adding an energy and comic timing which have only a quick-fading gloss of irreverence to recommend them above the older varnish of impressive 'verse-speaking'. In *The Comedy of Errors*, a production revived from earlier seasons, this is more acceptable than elsewhere. But the gloss, even here, obscures inherent contrasts, and so weakens the whole play. The first scene, with little action and long, unambiguous speeches, has been broken up to be made funny and more lively: the Duke has a comic Vizier (Plate VIII A); and rhetorical elaboration is pushed towards comedy. 'The pleasing punishment that women bear' and 'such as seafaring men provide for storms' both raise laughter; and, by breaking the sentence after 'inquisitive' and stressing that word's twentieth-century connotations of mere impertinence to the exclusion of its usual Elizabethan ones of serious investigation, 'became inquisitive after his brother' yields two rounds of laughter. The wit, extravagance and agitation which are the production's main attractions do not break out from early pretensions of order, dignity and feeling, nor are these suggested among the various and dispersed eruptions of the final scene. And, consistently, contrasts are also abandoned in the whirling world of the main action; the lyrical

> Sing, siren, for thyself, and I will dote:
> Spread o'er the silver waves thy golden hair . . .   (III, ii, 46 ff.)

becomes a sharp expostulation or reproof. The same resource is notable in *Love's Labour's Lost*, turning or pushing the dialogue in early scenes towards facetiousness, and introducing such comic business as a pair of pedagogue's spectacles for the King of Navarre and persistent fluttering, primping and snickering for the court of the Princess of France.

The last act of *Love's Labour's Lost* illustrates the other main vocal resource: an obvious weighting of dramatic implication at the cost of rhythmical and metrical coherence. For several seasons this has been evident at Stratford, leading to a portentous *Measure for Measure* and *Julius Caesar*,[1] and a collection of unsubtle politicians in the history plays of 1964.[2] The portentous style is given to the last speeches of the Princess of France, especially 'I ... will ... be ... thine', and to many of Armado's; these scenes have a studied or self-conscious impression out of keeping with the pressure of events, the run of the versification, and the shallow-minded performances of the greater part of the play. Occasional straining for dramatic effect suggests that the director, John Barton, had chosen a general theme that he wished to emphasize and made the actors extend their normal delivery of the lines to impress it upon the audience. Berowne's soliloquies and longer speeches give the same impression: Charles Thomas, who plays this role, does not use a wide range of vocal effect in other plays, but here an easy vigorous performance becomes vocally showy. In other plays a punching or emphatic delivery seems to have been introduced to bolster up ineffective incidents. In *The Merchant of Venice* Portia's casket scene with Bassanio has an overall energy, a stagey forcing of tone, that is out of keeping with the situation and the grace and wit of Shakespeare's versification. When Horatio talks about the 'palmy state of Rome' in *Hamlet*, I, i, he changes his restrained speech for larger emphasis, as if the director had had to inject some sort of impetus at the cost of consistency of character.

At other times dramatic effectiveness is joined with a precise psychological realism, a fresh awareness of character and situation. This serves best in verbally simple and short speeches, giving new-found allusiveness and power. David Warner, playing Hamlet, wins the greatest number of these trophies. 'Come to Hecuba', during the First Actor's Pyrrhus speech, expresses his involvement in the image of a grieving queen and also a weariness with the uses of the world —with Polonius' interference, with the words, with his own involvement; the inflection of the line is reinforced with a movement which is almost comically helpless and weary. When pursued by Rosencrantz, Guildenstern and the officers, his 'Here *they* come' is illuminated with a contemporary inflection that marks 'they' as a composite description of restrictive and uncomprehending authority; the speech is far more than the simple identification that it seems to be on the printed page. In the following dialogue with Claudius:

> *King.*   Therefore prepare thyself;
> The bark is ready, and the wind at help,
> Th'associates tend, and everything is bent
> For England.
>   *Hamlet.*   For England!
>   *King.*   Ay, Hamlet.
>   *Hamlet.*   Good!   (IV, iii, 43–6)

Hamlet's last word is spoken sharply, his hand striking the prayer desk at which he has been kneeling; and again the inflexion is taken from contemporary behaviour. Besides the obvious irony there is a flashlight exposure of Hamlet's situation, his tense nerves and distrust of honest words; he mocks the king with his own platitudes and defies him to no immediate good purpose. Later, when the gravedigger displays a skull with 'This same skull, sir, was, sir, Yorick's skull, the King's jester', Hamlet's simple question, 'This?', carries such a shock of precognition —an incipient sense of the need to meet death in personal terms—that the word 'this' seems totally eloquent, a reluctant confrontation of destiny. In these instances David Warner's delivery is so dramatically alive in the use of the simplest verbal means that he challenges many commonly held concepts of Shakespearian 'poetry'.

Other actors in the company attempted this psychological realism so that verbal interpretation was often new—sometimes to the degree of oddity—and frequently illuminated dramatic situation provocatively. Brewster Mason as Claudius, for example, discarded the usual apoplectic delivery of 'Give me some light. Away!' after *The Mousetrap* has been sprung; he spoke the line quietly, as a challenging reproof. The fright, on which Hamlet has just remarked ('frighted with false fire'), is represented by a silent unsteadiness as he rises from his throne to approach Hamlet; and the courtiers, led by Polonius, are those who raise the general consternation obviously called for by the sudden emptying of the stage. This Claudius is cunning and dangerous even when temporarily cornered or affronted; and Hamlet's following 'Why let the strucken deer go weep . . .' seems to reflect his own excitement rather than the behaviour of his uncle. When Timon listens for the first time to Flavius' account of his friends' worthlessness, Paul Scofield also avoids melodramatic emphasis: 'Is it true? Can't be?' is carefully spoken in level tones, the important crisis marked with a quick turn of the head and a movement across and down stage; increased tension is shown by maintaining his customarily erect carriage. (There is a careful consistency in these readings, as if the actors were testing each line by their grasp of the character as a whole.) So, too, Eric Porter as Shylock subdued 'Cursed be my tribe if I forgive him' (I, iii, 46–7) from the usual proud threat of vengeance to a satirical comment made for his own pleasure. At their best a fresh appraisal of the dramatic situation is involved in these new readings, for Shylock's assurance at this juncture also marks the unreflecting self-absorption of Antonio and Bassanio. When the Prince of Aragon makes a long pause after reading the motto on the silver casket, before announcing in considered tones 'And well said too' (II, ix, 37), the audience is reminded of the danger incurred by daring to respond to the riddle that protects Portia. In the trial scene, when Portia as Balthazar asks 'Is he not able to discharge the money?', Bassanio's quick and ringing 'Yes' (IV, i, 205), before proceeding with the rest of his speech in a more reasoned tone, marks an impulsiveness of nature that is consistent in Peter McEnery's portrayal and also the nervous tension that affects everyone during the trial of his friend's life. During the formal proceedings of this trial scene, Shakespeare has provided some opportunities for an alert vocal realism.

But when consideration or deep feeling is expressed in long speeches the company at Stratford is much less at ease; it is here that the actors resort to forcing the tone or glossing over the words with liveliness and comedy. This is a serious limitation—for Shakespeare frequently sustained thought and feeling in rhetorical elaboration—and it has become increasingly apparent in the last two or three years. The directors sometimes seem well aware of it, but their remedies are not radical enough. Shylock gains a measure of effectiveness by increasing tempo progressively in the last half of his 'Hath not a Jew eyes?' speech, and at the end of the scene he adds an impassioned cry in unintelligible Hebrew: but these devices are mere patching and propping, mere expediency. So, too, Hamlet at the end of the scene with the ghost hastily builds a vocal climax on

O cursed spite
That ever I was born to set it right

with a newly oratorical flourish, a bow and a sweep of his cloak. And after the concluding line of his last lengthy soliloquy, 'My thoughts be bloody, or be nothing worth' (IV, iv, 66), which is spoken slowly with a falling inflexion of self-absorption, he breaks off into grandiloquent gesture and a broad and quickening exit. When Claudius reaches the prayer scene (III, iii), his significant soliloquy which recognizes

'tis not so above:
There is no shuffling; there the action lies
In his true nature

suffers damaging cuts—presumably because the tense and realistically judged vocal style of this Claudius cannot sustain the lengthy rhetorical elaboration.

This company pays too little attention to metrical accuracy and coherence. A realistic and dramatically effective moment is often given too great precedence. If the lines—

Soft you now!
The fair Ophelia.—Nymph, in thy orisons
Be all my sins rememb'red—   (III, i, 88–90)

are spoken for their own metrical, rhythmic and tonal qualities in contrast with those of the preceding lines, they must surely be spoken softly, flowingly, with a concluding long phrase. Indeed any actor who chooses to interpret 'Nymph' and 'orisons' satirically, will find that the run of front vowels make them hard words to stress, to punch or bite; and he will have to fight against syntax and metre to escape a growing ease—almost a relaxation—in the concluding words. David Warner, however, takes violent grasp of the speech so that his Hamlet addresses Ophelia with growing volume and power and with a whirling movement away. (It is no defence of this reading to say that Hamlet is near mad or feigning madness, for Shakespeare has elsewhere used similar means to indicate violent expression for violent feeling; metre, syntax, sound and rhythm can signal both high and low.) Another example of momentary disregard of the implicit stage-directions of Shakespeare's versification is found in the same scene with Ophelia's compact and ordered soliloquy; here Glenda Jackson breaks rhetorical and metrical regularity by shouting out loud, as if to the spying king and father, the words 'The observ'd of all observers'; so the break which Shakespeare has provided in the following 'quite, quite down' is lost, and calculation rather than hard-won control and sentiment becomes dominant.

The company that over-rides metrical considerations for a moment's effective drama also neglects metrical coherence. As each line loses its proportional relationship to its fellows so regular lines provide no resolution, irregular ones have little tension; metrical finesse disappears and intervening prose offers little constraint; and the sustaining power of metre and rhythm is lost in those long rhetorical speeches which are often the pillars of dramatic structure. The company seems afraid of metrical restraint; but if the psychological realism which it has just rediscovered was controlled by the 'frame' or 'measure' of the verse-form its charge would appear the greater. Impressions of emotion and of willed and unwilled changes of motive grow in contrast to a firmly established norm of speech, and develop if the actors learn to depend upon rhythmic design.

Paul Scofield is the only actor who obviously attempts metrical truth and coherence and his performance of Timon has authority and an impression of power. His scenes with other characters, where duologue and mutual control are obligatory, were the weakest passages.

In range of feeling or boldness of conception Scofield cannot rival Peggy Ashcroft's triumph of the earlier season, but his sustained truthfulness and clarity can do so and are, perhaps, more necessary for the long role and discursive narrative of *Timon of Athens*. Both these artists come to the Royal Shakespeare Company with successful careers already behind them and if they seem to bring with them qualities that are not being nurtured in their fellow actors at Stratford important lessons may possibly be learnt.

Perhaps the time has come to persuade an overtly musical director—such as Sir John Gielgud, for whom both Peggy Ashcroft and Paul Scofield have previously created notable performances, or George Rylands, or David William—to come to Stratford and attempt to collaborate. To be given a proper chance to prove its worth the new realism must be used together with a sure and detailed response to the metrical and poetic qualities of Shakespeare's writing. Sir John's earlier collaborators have shown that the fusion of styles is practicable.

The stage-settings for all the plays at Stratford successfully follow earlier experiments. *The Comedy of Errors* and *Love's Labour's Lost* are readily accommodated on an unchanging set, each providing a large, inclined, open acting-area that gives full scope to the processional entries and elaborate regroupings demanded by these early plays. For the other three productions an equally wide stage area is backed by simple variable structures. John Bury's set for *Hamlet* has a space at the back and centre of the stage for 'discoveries' of actors and properties that are then moved forward, and two large panels obliquely at each side which can vary mood or location by changing from large openings to stone walls, book-cases or painted frescos. Ralph Koltai's sets for *Timon* and *The Merchant* are comprised of three-dimensional units that move transversely to regroup as structures of very different formal emphasis and colour. Whereas the *Hamlet* sets provide points of realism—real books in book-cases, real wood for panelling—these two sets are formally abstract with some symbolistic details such as suggestions of large key-holes and hour-glasses for Venetian scenes in *The Merchant*.

The chief departure this season was a stronger use of colour, in place of a brown-and-black neutrality for most of the 1964 history plays. Black is dominant in *Hamlet*, very dark green for *Love's Labour's Lost*, yellow, white and sharp blue for the first half of *Timon*, blood-red, orange and stone for the Venetian scenes and sky-blue and white for the Belmont scenes in *The Merchant*. The effect is powerful but too single-minded. *Love's Labour's Lost* cannot move from lightness and warmth to a chill evening; the tall, dark, tangled forms of giant yew hedges that flank the stage have from the very outset suggested that 'the scene' could all too easily 'begin to cloud' (v, ii, 710). The young men dressed in black do not express 'Flat treason 'gainst the kingly state of youth' (IV, iii, 289) but fit harmoniously into the dark green background of the set. So Hamlet's clothes, 'all in black', seem appropriate to the solid fabric of Elsinore, rather than a remarkable 'cloud' or 'nighted colour' (I, ii, 66–8). Stark purity of colour in the Belmont scenes and sharp outlines against the blue cyclorama made for coldness and intensity, so that the wit became forced (especially in I, ii) and the gentler expressions of sentiment lost.

While formally the Stratford way with stage design can present plays with Elizabethan fluency, the tonal variations and subtleties of Shakespeare's dramaturgy are not so satisfactorily served as in previous years when strong colour was carried chiefly in costumes and moveable properties. The designers need to use more tact, or subtlety, in colour—or perhaps more complexity—if their sets are to be other than neutral in colour.

Policy with regard to stage-business has become clearer with the 1965 productions. In the history plays its plentiful introduction seemed dependent on a general interpretation—a decision to emphasize everything that was military, painful and violent. But business proliferates just as much without such purpose in 1965. First it serves a detailed realism, providing a sense of actuality for both actor and audience. Most damagingly this is introduced when a scene is wholly dependent on words and acting: so Portia sips wine with Nerissa in I, ii of *The Merchant* (see Plate VII A), and so do Claudius and Laertes when they are plotting the death of Hamlet. Of course lines can sometimes be pointed by the gestures involved, but too often the concern of the business and the motives for engaging in it are too far removed from the 'necessary question of the play'. *Timon of Athens* III, ii is set in a barber's shop (see Plate IX B) and has been given elaborate by-play which submerges the textual contrast between Lucius and the three 'strangers', and deflects interest from the personal hypocrisy to trivial social indulgences. When Shylock calculates the proposed loan on an abacus (see Plate VII B), the stage-business is either too naïvely connected with the text, making it appear that Shylock cannot multiply a thousand by three, or else underlines, unsubtly, that he is pretending to be an innocent in high finance. Perhaps the main trouble is that business is always liable to seem trivial in comparison with the wider implications and strong verbal statements of the drama. Directors need to use greater economy. And sometimes they need greater weight; the masque in *Timon* should not deteriorate so easily into sleazy vamping as it does at Stratford (see Plate IX A).

Peter Hall's production of *Hamlet* uses business most elaborately and with strongest purpose. The manner in which Polonius keeps Claudius supplied with appropriate papers for state business usefully helps the impression of an administrative Head of State and his chief servant; Gertrude appearing without a wig for the closet scene illustrates and lends force to Hamlet's reference to a 'matron's bones' (III, iv, 83). But all this business also brings a slow-paced fussiness; Polonius looking up references in books; Laertes packing books for Paris; Polonius sipping and savouring his wine; the royal party sheltering under a black canopy because it is raining at Ophelia's funeral; the introduction of several different thrones for Claudius and Gertrude according to the precise location and business of a scene. The notion of having Gertrude vomit a stream of yellowish fluid as she dies may appear to offer a way of making her death by poisoning obvious to every member of the audience without relying on individual or ensemble acting; but so much is happening around her at the same time, and the duel is so elaborate in a succession of weapons and ingenious confrontations, that many of the audience simply fail to notice that this piece of business is effected in the very centre of the stage.

How far should a director impose a unity on a production, and of what kind? Should he start rehearsals with a clear interpretation of text? On these questions the Royal Shakespeare Company has no single opinion. Obviously a simple thematic concept governs John Barton's production of *Love's Labour's Lost*, for individual performances and stage setting alike announce that a solemn recognition of death's inevitable demands is the final purpose of the performance; everything must give way to this. The director of *The Comedy of Errors*, Clifford Williams, has aimed at a mood or attitude; liveliness, absurdity and plenty of marginal capers in a Pirandello world of masquerade: his object seems to have been to keep the fantasy in check with moments of realistic intonation and confrontation; certainly no theme emerges. For *The Merchant of*

Venice the director, Clifford Williams, announced his dependence on intuitions and individual expertise in a programme note:

He must wipe the slate clean and start as with a new play. He must repress memories of previous productions and resist academic influences. He must value each scene for what he can find in it and not for what others have found in it.

The result is a lack of size, of overall strength; a Shylock who only occasionally dominates and whose affairs have nothing but a plot-connexion with the affairs of Belmont. For *Timon of Athens*, John Schlesinger has contented himself with elaborate pictures—as far as he can make opportunity—for displaying a *dolce vita*, a world of stupid, fashionable people; and he has left his chief actor to create a psychologically subtle interpretation of the protagonist. Again the production lacks structural strength: the scene with Apemantus and the fool is cut entirely so that the concern with usury is unnecessarily obscured; the masque is devalued; and Timon's bankruptcy is due to personal failings rather than a serious attitude to wealth and trust. However, the movement from the easy satire of Timon's palace to a *Godot*-like bareness in the second half, presided over by a single gnarled tree, gave obvious theatrical bearings to audiences used to London theatre: from the Establishment Club to Beckett's imagination.

For *Hamlet*, Peter Hall has taken the firmest control. He has sought to illuminate Elsinore as a place of power, corruption, efficiency, lack of feeling and danger; and in doing this he has encouraged a serious Polonius of political capability, an Ophelia who is calculating when sane, and embarrassing when mad, an astute and cold Claudius, a ruined Gertrude, a menacing Osric. And from David Warner he has brought a performance of a disillusioned and therefore 'apathetic' prince (the word is Hall's own). This Hamlet shows no hope and almost no feeling on 'I will watch tonight'; his 'would the night were come' is petulant; and at the end he acts almost in a daze, fulfilling a function more like an automaton than a hero; in slow motion he pours a giant goblet of poisoned wine over the prostrate body of the King and uses his last moments of life to kiss lovingly and privately the medallion of his father. As a director, Peter Hall has boldness and originality; the creator of a real company believes in maintaining an individual concept for a play. He finds one that is grounded in a notion of contemporary society and character; and he applies it strictly and consistently to surprise his audience and attempt a revaluation by main force. Undoubtedly *Hamlet* took the critics unprepared and is the most interesting and revealing production of the season.

© J. R. BROWN 1966

NOTES

1. See *Shakespeare Survey 16* (1963), 144.   2. See *Shakespeare Survey 18* (1965), 150–1.

THE YEAR'S CONTRIBUTIONS TO
SHAKESPEARIAN STUDY

1. CRITICAL STUDIES

reviewed by NORMAN SANDERS

In a useful article reviewing the trends in Shakespeare criticism during this century, Irving Ribner[1] looks ahead to a new generation which may recognize that even in seemingly contradictory approaches there has been room for reconciliation in terms of a common larger tradition. When faced by the critical deluge occasioned by the quatercentenary, it is difficult to share Ribner's optimism. For, while a large number of articles do certainly complement each other in their illuminations of scenes, speeches, and whole plays, there are also those which assert conclusions among which there is even less chance of reconciliation than there is between Coriolanus and the tribunes. Symptomatic of such fundamental division between critics—and, one suspects, whole groups of critics—are two papers which appear in a single memorial volume and scowl adjacently. In one, Kenneth Myrick[2] claims that a Christian reading of *Lear* is the only kind that makes sense and, in the light of popular religious handbooks of the period, argues that the dark view of man found in the play is 'normal in Elizabethan Christianity'. However, it is just this dark view of man that Nicholas Brooke[3] takes to constitute the greatness of the play which he sees as asserting with superb energy a perfectly complete negation in which there are good and bad values which can have no reference beyond themselves and for which there are no ultimate sanctions. Brooke also develops his view at greater length in a monograph on the play[4] in which he follows the five-act structure because 'the experience of the play, the sense of its significance, develops the sequence of events; and to deprive the events of that sequence and to discuss them as if they were simultaneous, is to falsify the nature of the drama'. The method pays off, for there is worthwhile comment on almost every phase of the action, and some perceptive analysis of the effect of individual lines and key words. The last two chapters stress heavily the continual repudiation of comforting ideas, and elsewhere in the book the play's Christian overtones are seen to be established 'by direct exploration of nature itself, and not by assumption from . . . the New Testament'. Brooke will allow only a Nature which has no moral order, and the small comfort of 'the perpetual vitality of the most vulnerable virtues' in an indifferent world.

Sears Jayne[5] would go along with many of Brooke's views; he sees the play as harshly pagan— 'a purely human jungle without the benefit of clergy, or deity, or of any other religious solace' in which the characters wander, owning a need to love and an inability to give it. In a typically eloquent essay, full of perceptive comment on the play's world and the special character of its

---

[1] 'Shakespeare Criticism 1900–1964', *Shakespeare 1564–1964*, ed. Edward A. Bloom (Brown University Press, 1964), pp. 194–208.

[2] 'Christian Pessimism in *King Lear*', *ibid.* pp. 56–70.

[3] 'The Ending of *King Lear*', *ibid.* pp. 71–87.

[4] *Shakespeare: 'King Lear'* (Studies in English Literature, 15; Edward Arnold, 1963).

[5] 'Charity in *King Lear*', *Shakespeare 400*, ed. James G. McManaway (Holt, Rinehart and Winston, 1964), pp. 277–88.

9-2

action, Maynard Mack[1] notes the modernity of *Lear*, and locates its meaning as being of this world where man, in order

> to realize his humanity, to become anything more than a well-clothed animal . . . has to act as if there were a moral order behind the thunder, and yet he must make his choice, if he makes it, knowing that it will never necessarily be vindicated—not, at any rate, in the light of this world . . . There is no certainty or there could be no merit.

The patience which Mack stresses in his article is also analysed by Raymond Jenkins[2] who sees it as the necessary ingredient of the self-knowledge that Lear ultimately attains. Sharon German[3] isolates the themes of silence and speech and their relationship to truth, and Mohit Sen[4] the tension between feudal authority and bourgeois appetite. In other articles on various aspects of the play, S. N. Ray[5] rather weakly examines the importance of the Fool's role; Thomas P. Harrison[6] usefully compares the similarities in character, imagery and situation between *Lear* and *Titus Andronicus*, stressing those qualities which are uniquely Shakespearian; M. J. C. Echeruo[7] comments on the way in which the play's dramatic intensity is in part a product of the functional imagery; and William Elton[8] relates the term 'good years' (v, iii, 24) to the play's themes.

The whole question of the relationship of Shakespeare's tragedies to Christian belief is raised by both Irving Ribner[9] and Roy Battenhouse.[10] While Ribner is willing to admit that, although the world view of Shakespeare, his audience and his civilization is basically Christian, the non-Christian's aesthetic experience of the plays need be no different from that of the Christian viewer; Battenhouse is adamant about the necessity of an accurate knowledge of Christian theology as well as an adequate theory of tragedy for any critic who wishes to examine the plays as Christian tragedies. In one of the most substantially scholarly books to appear on all of the tragedies during the period under review, Virgil K. Whitaker[11] also takes up the question of the Christian approach to Shakespeare as an integral part of his thesis that

> Shakespeare was at one with his dramatic contemporaries. Even in his greatest plays their habits of workmanship appear, and we will understand him better if we first recognize the implications of this fact and then ask why, and in what ways, he differed from his fellows and surpassed them.

---

[1] '"We Came Crying Hither": An Essay on Some Characteristics of *King Lear*', *Yale Review*, LIV (1964), 161–86.

[2] 'The Socratic Imperative and *King Lear*,' *Renaissance Papers 1963* (South-eastern Renaissance Conference, 1964), pp. 73–84.

[3] 'The Upward Passage in *King Lear*', *Forum*, v (1964), pp. 10–15.

[4] 'Betwixt Damnation and Impassioned Clay: The Dialectics of *King Lear*', *Osmania Journal of English Studies* (*India*), IV (1964), 77–88.

[5] 'Lear's Fool', *Shakespeare: A Book of Homage* (Jadavpur University Press, 1965), pp. 159–66.

[6] '*Titus Andronicus* and *King Lear*: A Study in Continuity', *Shakespearean Essays*, ed. A. Thaler and N. Sanders (Tennessee University Press, 1964), pp. 121–30.

[7] 'Dramatic Intensity and Shakespeare's *King Lear*', *English Studies in Africa*, VI (1963), 44–50.

[8] 'Lear's "Good Years"', *Modern Language Review*, LIX (1964), 177–8.

[9] 'Shakespeare's Christianity and the Problem of Belief', *Centennial Review*, VII (1963), 99–108.

[10] 'Shakespearean Tragedy as Christian: Some Confusions in the Debate', *ibid.* pp. 77–98.

[11] *The Mirror Up To Nature: The Technique of Shakespeare's Tragedies* (The Huntington Library, California, 1965).

He insists that Shakespeare was 'intellectually a Christian' who accepted the beliefs of his age so that 'these beliefs govern the structure of his plays and are therefore a necessary key to their meaning'. His discussion of the dramatist's techniques is placed against an impressive study of both Elizabethan tragic practice in general and critical theories of the time in two opening chapters which are meticulously documented and contain the best classification of tragic types I know. Basically, Whitaker sees Shakespeare's practice as akin to Sidney's theory in that his aim was not only to present an action but also to provide an exemplum, the value of which lay in its truth to fundamental principles of human conduct. At the heart of Shakespeare's practice lay an awareness of moral order as it operates in man, and the concept of man as a rational creature ordained to a supernatural end. Thus the magnitude of the tragedies, for Whitaker, is to be found in the basic importance of moral choice—'in an action that determined the outcome of a great man's life with respect to his full potentialities as a man'. The plays illustrate the operation of Grace, of repentance, of the necessity for patience, and of deserved and undeserved suffering as part of God's plan and as man's means to salvation. In his discussion of these ideas, Whitaker has some truly perceptive comments on the technical aspects of the plays, particularly on traditional and specifically Shakespearian devices, and on the *personae* as symbols, forces and characters.

Yet despite the wide-ranging implications and fertile suggestions this general discussion contains, the analyses of individual works emerge as curiously limited in range. *Hamlet* fails ultimately owing to its author's inability to reconcile the system of Christian thought, which figures so prominently in the language, to the action as a whole; *Lear* is a genuinely Christian tragedy of redemption and stands in its perfection beside *Macbeth*, which is a tragedy of damnation showing a man's violation of the laws of nature and of God; *Othello* is but partially successful, its hero's deeds linked to passion psychology but not to the moral laws of nature and nations. The real limitations of Whitaker's approach, however, emerge in his essays on *Antony and Cleopatra* and *Coriolanus*. Because there is seen to be no relation between their heroes' inner conflict and the laws of heaven, and because Nature and God have disappeared in them, these two plays are judged to represent a falling-off in those qualities which make Shakespeare unique in his age. If it is true that *Antony and Cleopatra* constitutes the supreme challenge to the Shakespeare critic, then Whitaker's account of it as a collection of brilliant scenes and purple passages places him below the top rank. But whether this is true or no, the chapters on the individual plays are a real disappointment after the opening sections of the book.

Terence Hawkes,[1] in another general book, also approaches the plays from their contemporary background. In a brilliant opening chapter, he discusses the tension between a supra-rational intuitive faculty and reason as it existed in Shakespeare's age, and the various guises under which it had appeared in Aristotle, Aquinas, medieval thought, and Reformation theology; and in particular the form it took in Ficino's writings, the influence of which is central to Hawkes's argument. Because of these two possible ways of knowing to which Neoplatonism had had the effect of adding moral elements, man was faced 'with a moral choice between two now *opposed* ways of thinking, to both of which he was committed by his very nature'. Hawkes sees the tragedy of this situation, however, as residing not in whatever alternative was chosen, but in the fact that a choice was required—a choice which forced the question of 'what is real?' to

[1] *Shakespeare and the Reason* (Routledge and Kegan Paul, 1964).

which Shakespeare's protagonists have to find an answer. Using his dual concept, he discusses the four great tragedies and the problem plays, showing how the reason/intuition, appearance/reality motifs are written into them. As we would expect, *Hamlet* responds well to such an examination, with the Claudius world being seen as characterized by the employment of reason as a weapon of linguistic and philosophical perversion, and opposed to Hamlet's madness which 'may be said to be the dramatic expression of a form of mental activity higher and farther reaching than that of reason'. In his development of this idea in the latter half of the play in terms of reality opposed to an appearance, Hawkes has much to say that is illuminating, particularly about its connexion with the imagery of cosmetics, acting, mortality, and with stage happenings; but one is struck by his—perhaps unintended—conviction of Hamlet's almost total possession of the right way—a conviction which leads him to interpret the line 'My thoughts be bloody or be nothing worth!' as 'intuitive groping after reality'. As he traces the different handling of this dichotomy between two ways of life through the other tragedies, Hawkes manages not only to demonstrate its central importance to all of them, but also is able to convey the special atmosphere of each. The structural simplicity of *Othello* is reflected in the view of the play's balancing of the intuitive Desdemona and the rational Iago as the hero is torn between his responses to both. The metaphorical density of *Macbeth* is conveyed by a subtle demonstration of how all its antithetical structures spring from the matrix of the appearance/reality division. *Lear* is seen as the end of the cycle which *Hamlet* began, with its dual plot mirroring at every level the interconnexions between intuition and reason, appearance and reality. By not pretending to give a final analysis of the tragedies, Hawkes is able to present one fundamental aspect of them with well-nigh definitive thoroughness. Certainly, one may disagree with certain judgments and emphases (e.g. the overstress on the non-physical nature of Othello's and Desdemona's love, or the scant treatment of the central image of blood in *Macbeth*); but admiration is far more frequently elicited by genuinely fresh insight into such things as the false concept of 'manliness' in all the plays, or the sex-change motif in *Macbeth*, or the Cordelia–Fool relationship. Altogether it is a most fertile and useful book.

There have been many studies of individual tragedies and special aspects of them. *Hamlet* as usual gets the lion's share of attention with a book-length introductory study and numerous articles and chapters.[1] In his book on the play, Kenneth Muir[2] provides first, a useful handrail through the wood of *Hamlet* criticism, in particular that which has concerned itself with the imagery, and notes rightly that 'the imagistic structure of the play is much more complex than an isolation of . . . one group of images would suggest'.[3] Muir arranges his study of the play around the hero's relations with the different characters with whom he comes in contact, and each discussion is marked by an eschewing of futile scholarly debate, and an extreme clarity in seeing exactly what happens at each point and what is being talked about. He sees the change that Hamlet undergoes as being both dramatically well-contrived and psychologically accurate; and deftly conveys the 'wholesome sense of the mystery of human personality' in a hero neither idealized nor condemned. Other writers deal with various special aspects of the Prince and the

[1] Elder Olson discusses the hermeneutics of drama, and argues an ignorance of them in many critics of this play (see *Modern Philology*, LXI, 1964, 225–37).

[2] *Shakespeare: 'Hamlet'* (Studies in English Literature, 13; Edward Arnold, 1963).

[3] See also Muir's 'Imagery and Symbolism in *Hamlet*', *Etudes Anglaises*, XVII (1964), 352–64.

play. In one of two articles, Fredson Bowers,[1] after considering various alternative theories, demonstrates logically from an analysis of plot development that Hamlet's tragic error consists in the fact that his emotional drive is too strong to allow him to leave revenge to heaven in accordance with Christian doctrine. J. K. Walton[2] also develops a detailed study of the narrative structure and draws upon recurrent themes, particularly that of self-defeat, to define 'the undefeated constancy of Hamlet himself'. Paul A. Jorgensen[3] would agree with much of Bowers's view of the hero, but stresses that a man can also win his way to God's will through an understanding of his own hidden thoughts and feelings as well as through resignation.[4] Also emphasizing the individual element is G. K. Hunter[5] who sees the Prince as moving forward by an enormous and convulsive effort 'to the heroism of the individual, without abandoning the older social and religious framework of external action'; and Rosemary Stephens[6] who selects those features which delineate Hamlet's disillusionment with society; and Sydney Mendel[7] who compares Hamlet's reactions with those of Gregers Werle in *The Wild Duck*.

Three other authors concentrate on some of the implications of Hamlet's situation: Hardin Craig,[8] seeing his action as one of justice not revenge, argues that the Prince's denunciations of himself as inactive are misleading simply because his whole being is absorbed in his enterprise; and William T. Hastings[9] and Barbara Burge[10] focus their attention on the outward appearance and the inward reality of man's identity. The former concludes that the play is an inspired 'hoax' with the artistic tension being between the established nobility of the hero and the unworthy nature of his procrastination; and the latter, that Hamlet perceives that if he is to be true to himself, his actions must be equal to his thoughts because 'a thing is what it is because of the person who is thinking about that particular thing'. Patrick Cruttwell[11] also considers two possible extremes in viewing Hamlet and suggests that it is the continuous incongruity of both character and setting that holds the clue to the moral problems which the play and hero present. Jon S. Lawry[12] illuminatingly sets Hamlet and his problems alongside those of Hal and Prospero.

Some detailed attention has also been paid to the final act of the play: two writers scrutinize the graveyard scene and its connexions with the action as a whole, both seeing it as crucial to the change Hamlet has undergone. Peter G. Phialas[13] contends that Hamlet's Christian faith in

---

[1] 'Dramatic Structure and Criticism: Plot in *Hamlet*', *Shakespeare 400*, pp. 207–18.

[2] 'The Structure of *Hamlet*', *Hamlet: Stratford-upon-Avon Studies 5*, ed. J. R. Brown and B. Harris (Edward Arnold, 1964), pp. 44–89.

[3] 'Hamlet's Therapy', *Huntington Library Quarterly*, XXVII (1964), 239–58.

[4] Jorgensen has a companion piece to this in his '*Hamlet* and the Restless Renaissance', *Shakespearean Essays*, pp. 131–44.

[5] 'The Heroism of Hamlet', *Hamlet: Stratford-upon-Avon Studies 5*, pp. 90–109.

[6] '*Hamlet*: Shakespeare's Play of Disillusionment', *Forum*, V (1964), 45–55.

[7] 'The Revolt Against the Father: The Adolescent Hero in *Hamlet* and *The Wild Duck*', *Essays in Criticism*, XIV (1964), 171–8.

[8] 'Hamlet as a Man of Action', *Huntington Library Quarterly*, XXVII (1964), 229–38.

[9] 'Is *Hamlet* a Hoax?', *Shakespeare 1564–1964*, pp. 38–49.

[10] '*Hamlet*: The Search for Identity', *Review of English Literature*, V (1964), 58–71.

[11] 'The Morality of Hamlet—"Sweet Prince" or "Arrant Knave"?', *Hamlet: Stratford-upon-Avon Studies 5*, pp. 110–28.

[12] '"Born To Set It Right": Hal, Hamlet, and Prospero', *Forum*, V (1964), 16–24.

[13] 'Hamlet and the Grave-Maker', *JEGP*, LXIII (1964), 226–34.

a hereafter has been qualified rather than replaced by Stoicism, and B. L. Reid,[1] viewing the scene as one that is generalizing 'because of its extensiveness in space and time, its cross-cutting of social strata, its ambulatory, horizontal movement . . . its closeness to the plane of earth', makes the similar point that the hero acts out the limits of his human power in the eye of God, once he has 'fallen into register with the human condition'. In his second article on the play, Fredson Bowers[2] also argues for the hero's submission to providence by instancing his resistance to the opportunity to escape his fate, represented by Horatio, and his buying noble regeneration in Christian terms. The actual dramatic techniques by which Shakespeare makes us accept the sea-change are analysed by J. Gold[3] in a close reading of the letter to Horatio.

The other characters in *Hamlet* have also been subject to individual scrutiny. Baldwin Maxwell[4] takes Gertrude's part line by line and concludes that she is a weak, vacillating woman subservient to external emotional and moral stresses, and acting independently only once in the play, this being in the final scene; and M. D. Faber[5] psychoanalyses Claudius's self-destructive tendencies in the light of his *penchant* for drink and his symbolic death. On the second family of the play, there are some instructive remarks. With all the authority of a current editor of the piece, Harold Jenkins[6] examines the 'nunnery scene' and its implications for both participants; and, by clearing the air around some disputed readings, character interpretations, and stage directions, he defends Ophelia against many of the accusations which have been levelled at her, and shows how the scene is closely linked thematically with the other situations out of which Hamlet's tragedy develops. Carroll Camden[7] agrees with Jenkins on the importance of the Hamlet–Ophelia relationship, and, while excellently documenting the girl's madness by reference to contemporary accounts of love-melancholy, rather strains some of the lines of her songs to make them apply to Hamlet rather than Polonius. Much more persuasive on the songs' underlying significance with regard to Gertrude and Hamlet is a good paper by Peter J. Seng.[8] The character of Polonius is looked at by E. M. de Hostos[9] who claims a greater complexity for him than is usually allowed.

The roles of politics and philosophy in the play are considered by E. A. J. Honigmann[10] and Morris Weitz[11] respectively. The former gives an expert analysis of the political activities in Denmark, and shows that they 'afford a useful example of the complex of elements in the "world" of the play and of their osmotic relationship'; the latter pans earlier critics of the play in their attempts to reduce it to some one philosophic theme on the evidence of plot, soliloquies, or imagery, and stresses that it is in the tone that one finds what the play is about—namely, the celebration of the mystery of human life, not in the myth and ritual pattern, but in the more basic secular pattern of life as a series of questions to which there are no certain answers. Several

[1] 'The Last Act and the Action of *Hamlet*', *Yale Review*, LIV (1964), 59–80.
[2] 'The Moment of Final Suspense in *Hamlet*: "We Defy Augury"', *Shakespeare 1564–1964*, pp. 50–5.
[3] 'Hamlet's Sea Change', *English*, XV (1964), 53–5.
[4] 'Hamlet's Mother', *Shakespeare 400*, pp. 235–46.
[5] 'Two Studies in Self-Aggression in Shakespearean Tragedy', *Literature and Psychology*, XIV (1964), 80–96.
[6] *Hamlet and Ophelia* (Annual Shakespeare Lecture of the British Academy; Oxford University Press, 1963).
[7] 'On Ophelia's Madness', *Shakespeare 400*, pp. 247–55.
[8] 'Ophelia's Songs in *Hamlet*', *Durham University Journal*, LVI (1964), 77–85.
[9] 'Hamlet', *Shakespeare Jahrbuch*, 100 (1964), 227–31.
[10] 'The Politics in *Hamlet* and "The World of the Play"', *Hamlet: Stratford-upon-Avon Studies 5*, pp. 129–47.
[11] '*Hamlet*: Philosophy the Intruder', *Philosophy in Literature* (Wayne State University Press, 1963), pp. 43–67.

papers consider the play's infinite stylistic variety: Madeleine Doran,[1] while saying nothing new, usefully considers the great range of language within the dramatic action; and R. A. Foakes[2] relates the modes of speech to character, action and theme, finding a correspondence between their variety and that possessed by Hamlet himself in his many roles and voices. Also on the relationship between speech and personality is Adrien Bonjour's[3] close reading of Claudius's opening speech, which he claims may be taken in no way as a 'valid indictment of Hamlet'. One special aspect of the style, the sensitivity to natural beauty and its relation to the theme of mutability is wanderingly dwelt on by Norihiro Nabeshima;[4] and the quibble on the word 'king' and 'body' is explicated by G. N. Murphy[5] by reference to E. H. Kantorowicz's *The King's Two Bodies*.

The huge volume of commentary that has grown up around the play is almost as illuminating about human nature as the play itself. In recognition of its bulk and the difficulty it presents there have been some guides through the wilderness. Stanley Wells[6] provides a judiciously annotated selection of the principal critical and scholarly works; and T. J. B. Spencer[7] wittily sets some current political evaluations in a perspective of English and continental interpretations of the hero and the play over the centuries. Two individual critics of the play are assessed: G. L. Kittredge with too uncritical an eye by Kenneth Myrick,[8] and T. S. Eliot whose recently recanted and too much noticed opinion is verbally stamped on by V. Chatterjee.[9] In an interesting article, M. Grivelet[10] makes it clear that *Hamlet*'s impact on French writers in this century has been literary rather than theatrical.

The other great tragedies have received a less voluminous amount of criticism. John R. Brown,[11] in his book on *Macbeth*, provides a first-rate introduction to the play. The early part of his study presents with admirable clarity and well-digested scholarship much of the necessary information on the text, sources, supernatural elements, and the contemporary dramatic and social backgrounds. The hard core of his book, however, lies in his discussion of what he calls the 'presentation', which is a perceptive account of how the impact of the play is made by the interaction of its various parts, all of which are seen in theatrical terms:

By management of the interchanges of dialogue, by provision of opportunities for the actor to display all his powers with, and sometimes against, the words, and also by more literary poetic effects, Shakespeare has realised Macbeth upon the stage in depth and width of consciousness.

His scene commentary illustrates how the varying settings, groupings, stage-movements, timing, and changes of dramatic focus reveal the 'very depths of the beings of the protagonists, the

---

[1] 'The Language of *Hamlet*', *Huntington Library Quarterly*, XXVII (1964), 259–78.
[2] 'Character and Speech in *Hamlet*', *Hamlet: Stratford-upon-Avon Studies 5*, pp. 148–62.
[3] 'The Test of Poetry', *Shakespeare Jahrbuch*, 100 (1964), 149–50.
[4] 'A Sensitivity to Beauty in *Hamlet*', *Anglica* (Japan), V (1964), 41–52.
[5] 'Corpus Delicti', *Shakespeare Quarterly*, XV (1964), 447–8.
[6] 'A Reader's Guide to *Hamlet*', *Hamlet: Stratford-upon-Avon Studies 5*, pp. 200–7.
[7] 'The Decline of Hamlet', *ibid.* pp. 185–99.
[8] 'Kittredge on Hamlet', *Shakespeare 400*, pp. 219–34.
[9] 'T. S. Eliot and the Problems of Hamlet', *Shakespeare: A Book of Homage*, pp. 118–26.
[10] 'La mort d'Hamlet. Shakespeare dans les lettres françaises depuis le début du siècle', *Études Anglaises*, XVII (1964), 628–45.
[11] *Shakespeare: 'Macbeth'* (Studies in English Literature, 14; Edward Arnold, 1963).

interactions of their outward life and their inward life in its repetitions, assumptions, contradictions, fantasies, uncertainties, instincts, hesitations, subterfuges'. L. C. Knights,[1] in his attempt to bring out the universal significance of the play as 'an imaginative unfolding of what is inherent in evil action of a particular kind', also stresses the fusing of the inner reality and the outer world. Other writers consider aspects of the play which contribute to the overall effect as described by Brown and Knights. For example, Toshikazu Oyama[2] isolates the confusion at various levels of the hero's consciousness, particularly in relation to the imagery of the theatre; and D. J. Brindley[3] discusses the natural, sexual, moral, and spiritual value reversals. The broad movement of the piece is seen by Ruth L. Anderson[4] to be the highly conventionalized and common Elizabethan one of nobility-ambition-crime-fear-tyranny-brutishness-destruction, which Shakespeare had used earlier in *Richard III*. The question of 'equivocation' and its relationship to the two main characters is dealt with by Frank L. Huntley[5] against the background of its contemporary real-life manifestations. And the Porter scene as a whole is examined by H. B. Kulkarni[6] who sees it as 'a sonic fulcrum exerting its pressure . . . upon the whole play'.[7]

Unlike the other major tragedies, *Othello* is curiously resistant to investigations of its total impact; for, despite their initial good intentions, critics so frequently find themselves concentrating on one or two of the three main figures. Grasping the problem besetting those commentators who have tried to avoid this dilemma by reading the play as Christian allegory, Robert H. West[8] notes the many biblical allusions and echoes, but concludes that the overall effect implies neither Eden nor Judgment, Christ nor Godhead. The play's basic dual scheme emerges in various forms. Jan Kott[9] sees two paradoxes in Iago's rightness about the malignity of the world that he has created, and Desdemona's being a victim of her love which testifies against rather than for her. V. A. Shahane[10] documents the equilibrium of opposites seen in terms of both Christian and economic imagery. For Stephen A. Shapiro,[11] the duel is a psychological one between Othello's love and hate for his wife which is resolved ironically in the kissing and killing of the final scene. Also psychologically orientated is F. Grelon's[12] analysis of the hero's jealousy in relationship to that of Claudio, Posthumus, and Leontes. Othello is seen as the possessor of the traditional heroic virtues, by R. Marienstras,[13] at the time of their decline in estimation, but which are nevertheless affirmed in the play. Iago exercises his fascination, his motive being, as Harry Levin remarks,[14] the focus of much *Othello* criticism; and on this topic

[1] 'Poetry and Philosophy in *Macbeth*', *The Literary Criterion (India)*, VI (1964), 49–61.

[2] 'Macbeth, the Withered Murder: A Study of his Tragic Consciousness', *Anglica (Japan)*, V (1964), 53–71.

[3] 'Reversal of Values in *Macbeth*', *English Studies in Africa*, VI (1964), 137–43.

[4] 'The Pattern of Behaviour Culminating in *Macbeth*', *Studies in English Literature*, III (1963), 151–74.

[5] '*Macbeth* and the Background of Jesuitical Equivocation', *PMLA*, LXXIX (1964), 390–400.

[6] 'Sound and Significance in *Macbeth*', *Osmania Journal of English Studies (India)*, IV (1964), 35–46.

[7] Daniel A. Amneus has an interesting note on Ross as a possible composite character; see 'The Cawdor Episode in *Macbeth*', *JEGP*, LXIII (1964), 185–90.

[8] 'The Christianness of *Othello*', *Shakespeare Quarterly*, XV (1964), 333–44.

[9] 'Les deux paradoxes d'*Othello*', *Etudes Anglaises*, XVII (1964), 402–21.

[10] 'The Two Worlds of *Othello*', *Osmania Journal of English Studies (India)*, IV (1964), 47–65.

[11] 'Othello's Desdemona', *Literature and Psychology*, XIV (1964), 56–61.

[12] 'Shakespeare et la jalousie', *Etudes Anglaises*, XVII (1964), 390–402.

[13] 'La degradation des vertus héroïques dans *Othello* et *Coriolan*', *Etudes Anglaises*, XVII (1964), 372–90.

[14] '*Othello* and the Motive-Hunters', *Centennial Review*, VII (1963), 1–16.

P. K. Guha[1] retreads the old ground to endow him with a passion for disinterested mischief and moral perversity. Just how disinterested this mischief can be is demonstrated by Ernest A. Strathman[2] who examines his good advice given to Roderigo in I, iii; and by Joseph T. McCullen[3] who concentrates on his expert use of proverbs for the purposes of persuasion. Two articles seem to support Terence Hawkes's contentions about Iago mentioned above: John W. Harris[4] stresses the mental characteristics of his villainy, and Paul A. Jorgensen[5] analyses the two key words *know* and *think* as they are used by both Iago and Othello at various points in the play; and the two concepts of appearance and reality lying behind these words are seen as crucial by Ann L. Hayes.[6]

Shakespeare's earlier love tragedy is examined from various viewpoints as a conflict of generations. Thomas G. Tanselle[7] considers the methods by which Time is established in *Romeo and Juliet* both in relationship to important ideas and to the youth/adult tensions; David Laird[8] contrasts the styles and values of the utterance of the lovers and their parents; and John A. Hart[9] illustrates how the romantic love of the protagonists is in stark contrast to the non-romantic people surrounding them. Norman Holland[10] gives an interesting psychoanalytical analysis of Romeo's dream in V, i. *Romeo and Juliet* is also used by James Sutherland[11] as an example to illustrate how the stylistic unity in a given play comprehends and reconciles a large number of different kinds of writing.

A number of critics consider aspects of the tragedies more generally. In a lecture containing all the clear perception that we expect of its author, W. Nowottny[12] ranges over the whole tragic canon and attempts to isolate 'what makes each tragedy itself', and while most of her comments on individual plays are necessarily brief, all are worth reading for their seminal quality. The role of character in the plays also gets some attention: both Robert Ornstein[13] and Nicholas Brooke,[14] in first-rate articles, insist upon the importance of viewing characters as part of the theatrical experience, with the latter stressing Shakespeare's employment of 'the maximum range of theatrical possibility', and the former noting that 'Shakespeare's vision of character is, in essence, moral, and the perfect clarity of that vision is blurred only when we attempt to explain by means of psychological hypothesis'. Hardin Craig[15] claims that Shakespeare followed the traditional and natural method of inferring character from the various issues arising from compulsion

---

[1] 'Iago's Motive', *Shakespeare: A Book of Homage*, pp. 167–89.

[2] 'The Devil Can Cite Scripture', *Shakespeare 400*, pp. 17–23.

[3] 'Iago's Use of Proverbs for Persuasion', *Studies in English Literature*, IV (1964), 247–62.

[4] 'The Sickness of Iago', *The Literary Criterion (India)*, VI (1964), 62–7.

[5] '"Perplexed in the Extreme": The Role of Thought in *Othello*', *Shakespeare 400*, pp. 265–75.

[6] 'Othello', *Carnegie Studies in English*, VIII (1964), 53–67.

[7] 'Time in *Romeo and Juliet*', *Shakespeare Quarterly*, XV (1964), 349–62.

[8] 'The Generation of Style in *Romeo and Juliet*', *JEGP*, LXIII (1964), 204–13.

[9] 'Romeo and Juliet', *Carnegie Studies in English*, VIII (1964), 17–31.

[10] 'Romeo's Dream and the Paradox of Literary Realism', *Literature and Psychology*, XIII (1963), 97–104.

[11] 'How the Characters Talk', *Shakespeare's World*, ed. James Sutherland and Joel Hurstfield (Edward Arnold, 1964), pp. 116–35.

[12] 'Shakespeare's Tragedies', *ibid.* pp. 48–78.

[13] 'Character and Reality in Shakespeare', *Shakespeare 1564–1964*, pp. 3–18.

[14] 'The Characters of Drama', *Critical Quarterly*, VI (1964), 72–83.

[15] 'Character and Event in Shakespeare', *Renaissance Papers 1963*, pp. 31–40.

of events. In a brace of excellent essays, Robert B. Heilman considers two major themes of the tragedies and the variations Shakespeare worked upon them. One[1] is a sensitive examination of the degree and development of self-knowledge in Othello, Lear and Macbeth, which indicates that with each handling of the theme Shakespeare had 'a stronger conviction of man's preferring or needing other satisfactions than those of mastering the truth of self'; in the other[2] he traces the forms that the concept 'manliness' may take in individual fulfilment, with two possible poles of forbearance or ruthless retaliation, patience or aggression. One form of such aggression is discussed by Horst Oppel[3] in his examination of the ambiguous nature of Herculean rage and its *modus operandi* in some of the tragic heroes. Less centrally, Heinrich Straumann[4] analyses the dramatic function of the 'honest man' figure (Kent, Horatio); and R. W. Ingram[5] expertly shows how music and its imagery is made an 'aural definition of some major implications of the tragic theme' in *Hamlet*, *Othello* and *Lear*. Also on the subject of the tragic themes of *Macbeth* and *Lear*, C. D. Narasimhaiah[6] has some interesting comments; as does Thomas B. Stroup[7] as he discusses the 'testings of man upon the stage of the world' in Elizabethan tragedy generally.

In his scrutiny of the Shakespeare canon, D. A. Traversi[8] has reached the Roman plays in his most recent book, the bulk of which is devoted to a line by line reading of *Julius Caesar*, *Antony and Cleopatra* and *Coriolanus*. In his introductory section he considers those generally acknowledged qualities which make these plays constitute a group, and suggests that they are also a special amalgam of the power issues of the English history plays and the superhuman tragic individual inwardness of the great tragedies. In their new welding, both of these elements undergo modifications in Traversi's analysis, so that the clarity of the former becomes blurred and the heroes' fatal weaknesses in the latter now overshadow the more admirable qualities in their Roman counterparts. In the chapters on the separate plays the method of close analysis following the order of scenes certainly makes for heavy reading, but they are full of the kind of acute and sensitive perceptions which one has come to expect of the author. One may instance as immediately striking his anatomization of the unattractive traits in Brutus' character, or his delineation of the nature of the Roman world in *Antony and Cleopatra* and the poetic methods by which it is conveyed, or, perhaps best of all, the analysis of the blundering yet sensitive responses of Coriolanus to the bewildering forces surrounding and influencing him; as well as the countless unerring swoops on to valuable insights into word, phrase and line.

Yet despite its manifold virtues, the book provokes two large disagreements in this reviewer. First, the method used gives us no overall view of the plays: when we start each of Traversi's essays we are familiar with the play as it stands, and after reading each we are in the same position with the addition of a valuable running commentary. What we do not have, unless we are

---

[1] ''Twere Best Not Know Myself: Othello, Lear, Macbeth', *Shakespeare 400*, pp. 89–98.

[2] 'Manliness in the Tragedies: Dramatic Variations', *Shakespeare 1564–1964*, pp. 19–37.

[3] 'Vom gerechten und ungerechten Zorn der tragischen Gestalten Shakespeares', *Shakespeare Jahrbuch*, 100 (1964), 173–90.

[4] 'Der redliche Mensch: Horatio-Kent-Pisanio', *ibid.* pp. 191–208.

[5] 'Hamlet, Othello, and King Lear: Music and Tragedy', *ibid.* pp. 159–72.

[6] 'Ideas of Self, Sin, Social Impulse, and Moral Regeneration in Shakespeare's Plays', *The Literary Criterion* (India), VI (1964), 94–110.

[7] 'The Testing Pattern in Elizabethan Tragedy', *Studies in English Literature*, III (1963), 175–90.

[8] *Shakespeare: The Roman Plays* (Stanford University Press; The Bodley Head, 1963).

Theise are to Certifie no[te] That Edward Knight, William Mawbirk, William Chambers, Ambrose Byland, Henry Wilson, Jefferey Collins, William Sanders, Nicholas Underhill, Henry Clay, George Vernon, Roberte Mallant, Thomas Tuckfield, Roberte Clarke, ~~George ~~ John Rhodes, William Mago, and Anthony Knight, are all imployed by his Ma[ies]ties servant in theire quallity of Playinge or Musitions and other necessary or Attendants, And are att all tymes and howers to bee readie with theire best endevors to doe his Ma[ies]ties service (Duveringe the tyme of the Revells) In w[hi]ch tyme there are none of them here to bee arrested, or deteyned under arrest, imprisoned, Pressed for Souldiers or any other molestacion Wherby they may bee hindered from doinge his Ma[ies]ties service, without leave furste had and obteyned of the L[or]d Chamberlyne of his Ma[ies]ties most hono[ra]ble household, or of the Maister of his Ma[ies]ties Revells. And if any shall presume to interrupt or deteyne them or any of them after notice hereof given by this my Certificate hee is to aunswere itt att his utmost perill. Given att his Ma[ies]ties Office of the Revells under my hand and Seale the xxviij[th] Day of Decemb[er] 1624.

(left margin) And Edw[ard] Ashborne w[i]th Carver & Alexander Bullard, William Toyer, William or Easborne.

To all Mayo[rs], Sheriffs, Justices of the Peace, Bayliffs, Constables, Knight Marshalls men, and all other his Ma[ies]ties Officers to whom it may or shall ~~apperteyne~~ apperteyne.

(signature)

A certificate *(interlined: graunted)* to Edward Shatterly not to bee arrested or imprisoned Duveringe the tyme of the Revells, the 29[th] of November 1624.

A certificate graunted to Richard Sharpe the 29 of Decemb[er] 1624 not to bee arrested or imprisoned Duveringe the tyme of the Revells.

V Herbert's 1624 Protection List

VI   Repertory of the Court of Aldermen of the City of London, 18 September 1634

VII A   Janet Suzman as Portia and Patsy Byrne as Nerissa, sitting at a table with drinks (i, ii)

VII B   Peter McEnery as Bassanio and Eric Porter as Shylock, discussing the loan (i, iii)

'THE MERCHANT OF VENICE', ROYAL SHAKESPEARE THEATRE, 1965
Directed by Clifford Williams, settings by Ralph Koltai

VIII A   Timothy West as Ægeon and Donald Burton as the Duke, with his Vizier (I, i)

VIII B   Ian Richardson as Antipholus of Syracuse with Michael Williams as his
Dromio, talking of Luce (III, ii)
'THE COMEDY OF ERRORS', ROYAL SHAKESPEARE THEATRE, 1965
Directed by Clifford Williams, costumes by Anthony Powell

IX A   The Masque

IX B   The Barber Scene (III, ii)
'TIMON OF ATHENS', ROYAL SHAKESPEARE THEATRE, 1965
Directed by John Schlesinger, settings by Ralph Koltai

X A　Paul Scofield as Timon, in his cave　　　'TIMON' OF ATHENS, ROYAL SHAKESPEARE THEATRE, 1965

X B　David Warner as Hamlet, in the 'To be or not
to be' soliloquy (III, i)

'HAMLET', ROYAL SHAKESPEARE THEATRE, 1965
Directed by Peter Hall, settings by John Bury,
costumes by Ann Curtis

XI A   Hamlet and Ophelia (Glenda Jackson) at the
Play (III, ii)

XI B   Hamlet and Gertrude (Elizabeth Spriggs) on
the Queen's bed (III, iv)

XII A   Gertrude, Claudius (Brewster Mason), Hamlet and Polonius (Tony Church) in I, ii
'HAMLET', ROYAL SHAKESPEARE THEATRE, 1965

XII B   Brewster Mason as Boyet reads Armado's letter to the Court (IV, i)
'LOVE'S LABOUR'S LOST', ROYAL SHAKESPEARE THEATRE, 1965
Directed by John Barton, settings by Sally Jacobs

willing to compose an appendix to each chapter, is the results of the author's total reading. Possibly one *should* not expect such a critical shifting around of the play's original counters, but surely we do. Secondly, despite all his subtle responsiveness, Traversi seems to bring to his criticism, particularly of *Caesar* and *Antony and Cleopatra*, his own yardstick for judging the characters and their actions, so that while he gives due attention to, say, what is warm and admirable about Brutus, or to the grandeur of the love poetry, he does not really allow either of these things to affect his final judgment of the characters concerned and consequently of the play's final impact to which they contribute. Time and again one feels that, in his seeking for a moral standard, Traversi misses what Shakespeare always seems to have been aware of (in perhaps a similar search)—namely, the mysterious contradictory powers in human life which defy definition even during the act of defining.

R. A. Foakes[1] also sees the later tragedies as different in tone from the earlier ones, asserting that in them there is a shift away from Christian order to one in which the absolutes of good and evil are inextricably mixed, and where the stress is on the wholeness of the individual. And one aspect of the wholeness—self-knowledge—and the difficulty of attaining it is discussed by Robert Heilman[2] with reference to *Coriolanus* and *Antony and Cleopatra*. It is the complexity of the protagonists of the latter play which continues to perplex. Laurens J. Mills[3] traces the tragedies of the two lovers and their interrelation. While his book illuminates many aspects of the play, and is excellent in pointing out the often underestimated 'Roman' qualities in Antony, he misses completely the true variety of Cleopatra who emerges from this study as a self-interested sensualist quite devoid of morality, and who learns something of virtue (i.e. Roman virtue) just prior to her death. Certainly the play incorporates a Sunday-school lesson; but it also contains a great deal more. Adrien Bonjour,[4] in rejecting S. L. Bethell's theological interpretation of the same play, is a good deal nearer to the truth in his defence of Cleopatra's psychological consistency[5] and the depth and spiritual substructure of her love—a topic on which R. A. Foakes[6] has much of interest to say in his discussion of the intensity of the lovers' erotic vision; as does Brents Stirling[7] in his commentary on the queen's scene with Seleucus. The paradox in Antony's character is pointed out by David Berkeley[8] who claims for him, particularly in the death scene, an inscrutability in matters of intention. It is in the death scenes of both characters, however, that Sheila M. Smith[9] finds certainly a sense of failure, but also both an absence of sordidness and an emotional splendour. Some special features of the play which are also analysed are the morality-type unity of its structure by Thomas B. Stroup;[10] the tripartite handling of the theme

---

[1] 'Shakespeare's Later Tragedies', *Shakespeare 1564–1964*, pp. 95–107.

[2] '"From Mine Own Knowledge", A Theme in the Late Tragedies', *Centennial Review*, VII (1963), 17–38.

[3] *The Tragedies of Shakespeare's Antony and Cleopatra* (Indiana University Press, 1964).

[4] 'Shakespeare and the Toil of Grace', *Shakespeare 1564–1964*, pp. 88–94.

[5] Marion A. Taylor also defends Cleopatra's psychological consistency as the mistress of a married man; see '"Not Know Me Yet?"', *Forum*, V (1964), 63–6.

[6] 'Vision and Reality in *Antony and Cleopatra*', *Durham University Journal*, LVI (1964), 66–76.

[7] 'Cleopatra's Scene with Seleucus: Plutarch, Daniel, and Shakespeare', *Shakespeare 400*, pp. 299–311.

[8] 'On Desentimentalizing Antony', *Notes and Queries*, n.s., XI (1964), 138–42.

[9] '"This Great Solemnity": A Study of the Presentation of Death in *Antony and Cleopatra*', *English Studies*, LXV (1964), 163–76.

[10] 'The Structure of *Antony and Cleopatra*', *Shakespeare 400*, pp. 289–98.

of disunity on the character, family, and state levels by Lawrence E. Bowling;[1] the various types of conflict by Cynthia K. Whitney;[2] and David Kaula[3] works out the ways in which the 'public image the characters strive to create . . . is closely related to their sense of time'.

An article which should be read as a corrective to Traversi's view of *Julius Caesar* is L. C. Knights's[4] perceptive and clearheaded essay which deals with Shakespeare's handling of the relationship between idea and action in public life, by reference to Brutus' dilemma, and their close connexion with personal morality. Norman Sanders[5] also discusses an aspect of politics in the play. A personal rather than political centre of the piece is detected by Norman Rabkin[6] in the identity between Caesar and Brutus, so that Shakespeare 'turns what promised to be a tragical history into a revenge play', by his experiments with structure and convention. Caesar himself receives some attention: J. Bruneau[7] usefully compares Shakespeare's treatment of the character with previous representations; and Douglas Peterson[8] in discussing some of Shakespeare's departures from Plutarch[9] gives a simple explanation of Caesar's lines on his deafness by pointing to their proverbial meaning: 'when we hear a thing that liketh us not we say I cannot hear on that side'.

There have been two excellent articles on *Coriolanus*. One is by R. F. Hill,[10] who examines how the syntactical and rhetorical ordering shapes the violent oppositions in this 'study of intransigence'. In the other, D. J. Gordon[11] brilliantly analyses the function of key concepts and the words *honour, voice, name, rumour, fame* in the light of classical and Renaissance definitions to show how 'Shakespeare offers a show of the civil life in terms of empty, perverted, destructive relationships between speaker and utterance'. In two shorter pieces Rodney Poisson[12] and Fred Chappell[13] trace some of the play's imagery to Ovid and to Plutarch's *Cato*. Bernard Paulin[14] views the death of the hero in *Timon of Athens* as suicide, which enables us to see him at last capable of taking determined positive action. It is good to have Willard Farnham's essay on this play readily available again, together with those on *Coriolanus*, *Macbeth*, and *Antony and Cleopatra*, in the new paperback edition of his *Shakespeare's Tragic Frontier*.[15]

[1] 'Antony's Internal Disunity', *Studies in English Literature*, IV (1964), 239–46.

[2] 'The War in *Antony and Cleopatra*', *Literature and Psychology*, XIII (1963), 63–6.

[3] 'The Time Sense of *Antony and Cleopatra*', *Shakespeare Quarterly*, XV (1964), 211–33.

[4] 'Personality and Politics in *Julius Caesar*', *Anglica* (*Japan*), V (1964), 1–24.

[5] 'The Shift of Power in *Julius Caesar*', *Review of English Literature*, V (1964), 24–35.

[6] 'Structure, Convention, and Meaning in *Julius Caesar*', *JEGP*, LXIII (1964), 240–54.

[7] 'La figure de Jules César de Dante à Shakespeare', *Etudes Anglaises*, XVII (1964), 591–605.

[8] '"Wisdom Consumed in Confidence": An Examination of Shakespeare's *Julius Caesar*', *Shakespeare Quarterly*, XVI (1965), 19–28.

[9] Holger Nørgaard also defends Shakespeare against charges of inaccuracy in his handling of source materials in the Roman plays; see 'Never Wrong With Just Cause', *English Studies*, LXV (1964), 137–41.

[10] '*Coriolanus*: Violentest Contrariety', *Essays and Studies*, XVII (1964), 12–23.

[11] 'Name and Fame: Shakespeare's Coriolanus', *Papers Mainly Shakespearian*, ed. G. I. Duthie (Aberdeen University Studies, 147; Oliver and Boyd, 1964), pp. 40–56.

[12] '*Coriolanus*, I, vi, 21–24', *Shakespeare Quarterly*, XV (1964), 449–50.

[13] 'Shakespeare's *Coriolanus* and Plutarch's *Life of Cato*', *Renaissance Papers 1962* (South-eastern Renaissance Conference, 1963), pp. 9–16.

[14] 'La mort de Timon d'Athènes', *Etudes Anglaises*, XVII (1964), 1–8.

[15] University of California Press, 1963.

Among general studies of the history plays, there seems to be some attempt to shift the emphasis away from what one may call the 'Tillyard' approach.[1] Two writers stress the conflict between generations as their theme: Ricardo J. Quinones[2] contending that the 'tensions and expectations and returns of fathers and children' evidence Shakespeare's interest in augmentative time; and L. S. Champion[3] arguing for the conflict of personalities between Hal and his father as the dominant motif of *1* and *2 Henry IV*.[4] The critical re-emphasis on character which has been perceptible in some of the writing on the tragedies during recent years may also be detected in a new book-length study of the history plays. Its author, S. C. Sen Gupta,[5] turns the critical clock firmly back to the nineteenth century:

The present study proceeds on the assumption that the greatness of Shakespeare consists chiefly in his ability to create men and women, who, if not imitations of reality, have the vividness of living characters. In the historical plays Shakespeare succeeds . . . in creating, with or without suggestions from history, new characters that are more real than living men.

Opposing the homiletic approach as a distortion of the plays' dramatic effect, Gupta argues that it is wrong to seek integrating themes in the light of contemporary beliefs and medieval heritage, and that one must stress the difference of effects and purposes between the individual plays, rather than those common didactic elements detected by other critics. It would be churlish not to admit that in his examination of various characters—particularly those of Richard III and Faulconbridge—there is a great deal that is informative and genuinely perceptive; but it would be dishonest not to admit that there are severe weaknesses in his approach and, I think, egregious errors in his interpretations. Some of these may be illustrated by Gupta's handling of the second tetralogy. He sees Falstaff as the central figure of the *Henry IV* plays, 'whatever might have been Shakespeare's original intention', and is prone to play the dangerous game of detecting the dramatist's own voice in a character's utterance:

When Falstaff ridicules Puritanism by describing his sins in scriptural phraseology, he does it with so much grace and with such inverted appropriateness that we feel that here, if anywhere, we hear the voice of Shakespeare himself, inveighing against the cramping effect of religion and morals.

But, unlike D. A. Traversi who holds a somewhat similar view of Falstaff, Gupta is quite unable to relate his idea to the play as a whole. His approach is similarly distorting in the case of Henry V, whom he blames for things he does *not* do in the play: for example, 'he does not delve into the motives that weigh with the Archbishop' or 'he does not pause to ponder what the Earl [of Cambridge]'s motive might be'. In fact, despite his desire to see the plays primarily as works

---

[1] There is an affectionate memoir of Tillyard which Basil Willey delivered to the British Academy; this describes his contribution to Shakespearian studies (see *Eustace Mandeville Wetenhall Tillyard 1889–1962*, Oxford University Press, 1965).

[2] '"Lineal Honour" and Augmentative Time in Shakespeare's Treatment of the Bolingbroke Line', *Topic*, IV (1964), 12–32.

[3] 'King and Prince: Approaches to the Throne in *Henry IV*', *Forum*, V (1964), 26–34.

[4] Gail H. Thomas also comments on the difference between father and son in her review of Shakespeare's handling of the theme of kingship in the tetralogy; see 'What is a King?', *Forum*, V (1964), 34–42.

[5] *Shakespeare's Historical Plays* (Oxford University Press, 1964).

of art, Gupta continually goes outside the limits of the play to criticize the play itself. This book would have been a far more useful contribution to the literature on the history plays if its author had not attempted to elevate his character studies to the level of a revolutionary critical method, and if he had borne in mind the simple fact that a play's having a political or moral content does not necessitate its being *therefore* a political or moral treatise.

Falstaff is also the subject of an extensive study by Walter Kaiser[1] in one section of a profound and formidably learned book which attempts to trace the origins and personae of the Fool in Rabelais, Erasmus and Shakespeare. Noting the similarities between Falstaff and the Vices in moral interludes such as *Juventus* and *Youth*, Kaiser sees the fat knight as a combination of sot and Vice, Fool and Tempter in a secular rather than Christian context; and in the most original part of his study draws an illuminating comparison between him and Erasmus' Stultitia. He analyses the role in its relationship to the other main characters—Shallow, the Lord Chief Justice, Hal, Hotspur—in an attempt to isolate some of the qualities that make it such a complex one; and in the course of this analysis throws a great deal of light on such matters as how the cowardice of Falstaff 'transvalues' Hotspur's honour,[2] the nature of Hal's debt to him in learning humility and fraternity, and the knight's special relationship with the justice of nature and the law of society. However, excellent as much of Kaiser's discussion is, I think he limits the character's implications in overstressing the foolishness of Falstaff: we are indeed unable to accept totally his rejection, but it is not simply because 'he has won our hearts'. J. B. Priestley[3] also considers the universal meaning of the character and concludes that, as a product of an explosion of rebellious energy on Shakespeare's part, he represents one element in the English national character and life which is forever being created only to be rejected. Robert Hapgood[4] isolates one of Falstaff's roles—that of robber—and shows its relationship to the political themes of the plays; A. R. Humphreys[5] defends him against some charges of irresponsibility in his recruiting missions; and Masato Yano[6] accounts for his non-appearance in *Henry V*. Hotspur's internal chaos and its connexions with the general theme of disorder is considered by Raymond H. Reno,[7] and his allusion to 'villainous salt-peter' by John X. Evans.[8] Charles Mitchell[9] provides a defence of Hal as the embodiment of the ideal of honour who 'merits praise because he does not seek it but seeks the inner spirit of praise'; and Sidney H. White[10] clears him of Ernest Jones's charge that he has a Freudian death wish in the crown-borrowing scene.

Rather less attention has been paid to the other history plays. Robert Y. Turner[11] considers

---

[1] *Praisers of Folly* (Harvard Studies in Comparative Literature, 25; Harvard University Press, 1963), pp. 195–276.

[2] See also on the same topic Tatsuo Narita, 'An Aspect of Falstaff's Role in *1 and 2 Henry IV*—On Effects of Value-Revision in Imagery', *Anglica* (*Japan*), v (1963), 41–61.

[3] 'Comedy in Shakespeare', *The Listener*, LXXI, 985–8.

[4] 'Falstaff's Vocation', *Shakespeare Quarterly*, XVI (1965), 91–8.

[5] 'Justice Shallow and Gloucestershire', *Notes and Queries*, n.s., XI (1964), 134–5.

[6] 'What Becomes of Sir John? and How Fluellen Comes In', *Anglica* (*Japan*), v (1964), 105–23.

[7] 'Hotspur: The Integration of Character and Theme', *Renaissance Papers 1962*, pp. 17–26.

[8] 'Shakespeare's "Villainous Salt-Peter": The Dimensions of an Allusion', *Shakespeare Quarterly*, XV (1964), 451–4.

[9] 'Henry V: The Essential King', *Shakespearean Essays*, pp. 97–104.

[10] 'What Freudian Death-Wish in the Crown "Borrowing" in *2 Henry IV*?', *Forum*, v (1964), 42–5.

[11] 'Shakespeare and the Public Confrontation Scene in Early History Plays', *Modern Philology*, LXII (1964), 1–12.

how Shakespeare extended the range of public confrontation scenes by adding moral signifi-cance to their arguments. Izumi Momose[1] sees Richard III's violation of order as lying in his determination not to accept the historicity of life which is combined with God's will. Adrien Bonjour[2] argues that Faulconbridge's role in *King John* is more important than that of commen-tator. Two good articles on *Richard II* discuss the style and the characters: in one, Donald H. Reiman[3] suggests that Richard is transformed into a tragic hero by the self-knowledge he gains from his ability ultimately to distinguish appearance from reality; and in the other, Dorothy C. Hockey[4] disputes the claim that there are two styles in the play by analysis of the use of rhetorical figures employed in the Richard and Bolingbroke 'worlds'.

In his book mentioned above, Terence Hawkes sees the problem plays as experiments in the technique of presenting and commenting on the reason-intuition opposition, with *Troilus and Cressida* a condemnation of the total surrender to the intuitive mode of existence, *All's Well* a fairy-tale rendering of Bertram's change from attraction to the appearance of honour to the recognition of its reality, and *Measure for Measure* seeming to combine the moods of the other two plays in an attempt to convey in legal terms the super-rational quality of mercy. Haydn M. Williams[5] also has much of interest to say on the topics of justice and honour in the last two plays, and stresses their affinities with the metaphysical poetry of the period. On each of the plays there are a variety of informative papers also. An excellent reading of *All's Well* is offered by James L. Calderwood[6] who notes the disparity between the major characterizations and the final tendency of the action, and traces the fusion of the sexual and intellectual senses of 'knowing', to see the piece as a 'drama of two young persons, each with his share of virtues and faults, acquiring through trial and error the experience and moral insight necessary for the revitalization of a moribund society'. Robert Y. Turner[7] compares this play with seven other plays having similar prodigal-son themes but overstates his case, and is rightly taken up on some of the points he makes by Robert Hapgood.[8] G. Lambing[9] considers the contemporary aspects of Helena's pilgrimage in the same play; and J. Hisao Kodama[10] has some observations on the effectiveness of certain scenes. So far as *Measure for Measure* is concerned, Isaac Sequeira[11] rejects the 'problem play' label and possible Christian interpretation, arguing that the play moves from a Christian to a non-Christian ethos. Allen H. Gilbert[12] examines the play as a whole under various key headings and asserts its value as a work of art not needing any prosaic meaning, and denies it is devoted to the great truths of religion, morality, and government. Lawrence S. Hall[13]

[1] 'The Temporal Awareness in *Richard III*', *Shakespeare Studies* (*Japan*), III (1964), 42–72.
[2] 'Bastinado for the Bastard?', *English Studies*, XLV (1964), 169–76.
[3] 'Appearance, Reality, and Moral Order in *Richard II*', *Modern Language Quarterly*, XXV (1964), 34–45.
[4] 'A World of Rhetoric in *Richard II*', *Shakespeare Quarterly*, XV (1964), 179–91.
[5] 'Metaphysical Elements in Two Problem Comedies', *Shakespeare: A Book of Homage*, pp. 21–49.
[6] 'Styles of Knowing in *All's Well*', *Modern Language Quarterly*, XXV (1964), 272–94.
[7] 'Dramatic Conventions in *All's Well That Ends Well*', *PMLA*, LXXIX (1964), 179–82.
[8] *Ibid.* pp. 177–9.
[9] 'Passionate Pilgrims', *Etudes Anglaises*, XVII (1964), 457–64.
[10] '*All's Well That Ends Well*: A Reappraisal', *Shakespeare Studies* (*Japan*), III (1964), 100–15.
[11] 'Is *Measure for Measure* a Problem Play?', *Osmania Journal of English Studies* (*India*), IV (1964), 115–23.
[12] 'The More Shakespeare He: *Measure for Measure*', *Shakespearean Essays*, pp. 45–61.
[13] 'Isabella's Angry Ape', *Shakespeare Quarterly*, XV (1964), 157–65.

will have none of this and, by a close analysis of Isabella's speech to Angelo, sees Shakespeare preoccupied with the illusions of identity; while James V. Card[1] contends that the play incorporates a comment on man's sexual fallibility. The pivotal figure of the Duke is considered by William A. Freedman[2] who finds him a psychologically consistent human being concerned with his reputation and public image; and Douglas D. Peterson[3] sees him inducing in Juliet an Anglican rather than Roman contrition.

Troilus and Cressida is perhaps the one play in the canon about which there is not even a modicum of agreement among its critics. A book has been devoted to it by Robert Kimbrough[4] whose approach is 'frankly historical'. Its aim is to measure the play and its puzzling aspects 'against its sources and against analogous aspects of plays in the canon and in the competing public and private repertories', in order to 'come as close as possible to solving the problems which the play presents when read as a piece of dramatic literature'. What Kimbrough does in fact is to give as clear a setting out of the piece's problems and their possible origins as one could wish for, but he throws very little new light on the play as a work of art. His hypothesis is that in *Troilus and Cressida* Shakespeare attempted a play that embraced attributes of the 'new' drama of the private theatres and the 'old' drama of the public playhouses. In his opening sections, the sketch of the theatrical conditions out of which he sees the play springing is generally sound (although he does tend to assume as proven that the information given in the 1609 quarto is false), and his account of the nature of the 'Trojan' literature as it would appear to an Elizabethan is excellent. In the remaining sections of the book, Kimbrough examines areas of the play that yield critical problems: the love story, the Trojan story, and the Greek story; and in each traces those innovations in presentation of the traditional material for which Shakespeare was responsible. He also sets the various themes he detects in the context of their treatment in similar Shakespearian plays and in other plays of the time. From the critical point of view it is chapter VII on 'The Rhetoric of Order and Disorder' that is most rewarding in its working out of a positive Shakespearian philosophy working against the theatrical tastes for which the play was in part created; and there are some interesting ideas in the Epilogue which might well be expanded.

The effects of the love plot are also examined by other writers. Toshiko Oyama[5] argues for its deliberate ambiguity, while for Barbara H. C. de Almeida[6] the outcome shows the inevitable fate of love 'in a corrupt society governed by men who are oblivious of their duty to their nation and its people'. The impossibility of preserving values on a personal plane, which Almeida also discusses, is taken up by R. J. Smith[7] in his study of personal identity in the play. Of the individual characters, Troilus is analysed by Willard Farnham[8] in his roles as warrior and lover in the context of the Renaissance tradition of man's limitless desire, and the tension between the

---

[1] 'In Just Proportion: Notes on the Final Scene of *Measure for Measure*', *Topic*, IV (1964), 61–9.

[2] 'The Duke in *Measure for Measure*', *Tennessee Studies in Literature*, IX (1964), 31–8.

[3] '*Measure for Measure* and the Anglican Doctrine of Contrition', *Notes and Queries*, n.s., XI (1964), 135–7.

[4] '*Troilus and Cressida' and Its Setting* (Oxford University Press; Harvard University Press, 1964). See also his article, 'The Problem of Thersites', *Modern Language Review*, LIX (1964), 173–6.

[5] '"This Is and Is Not Cressid!"—An Interpretation of *Troilus and Cressida*', *Anglica* (*Japan*), V (1964), 72–86.

[6] '*Troilus and Cressida*: Romantic Love Revisited', *Shakespeare Quarterly*, XV (1964), 327–32.

[7] 'Personal Identity in *Troilus and Cressida*', *English Studies in Africa*, VI (1964), 7–26.

[8] 'Troilus in Shapes of Infinite Desire', *Shakespeare 400*, pp. 257–64.

limitless will and the finite act. Adrien Bonjour[1] turns to the vexed question of Hector's be-haviour towards the man in the sumptuous armour, and points out that, rather than indicating Hector's lack of chivalry, the incident illustrates Hector's despising of the Greek for *his* lack of chivalry. On the specifically dramatic aspects of the play, Rudolf Stamm[2] expertly examines those devices which enabled the playwright to influence the acting of a particular passage and thus regulate the imaginative experience of the whole creation; and Clifford Lyons[3] discusses the structure of the two trysting scenes with their character interrelationships and the emphases they provide on 'the blind idealizations of a young man and the bad success in a bad cause'.

It is becoming a commonplace *cri de cœur* in all writings on the comedies that they have had short shrift compared with the tragedies and history plays. In an essay full of suggestive comment Arthur Brown[4] emphasizes those tasks of scholarship that require immediate attention before even the materials necessary for arriving at an understanding are available; and Milton Crane[5] attempts to fit Shakespeare's practice within the tradition of classical comedy to arrive at the binding factors of revelation, knowledge, and self-knowledge. Yet in defiance of the frequent complaints about the intractability of comedy, two writers have produced valuable contribu-tions to our understanding of these plays. Without attempting to be all-inclusive, Edward Hubler[6] throws off a series of illuminating comments on several aspects of them, especially on the nature of their satire, the combination of the comic and the farcical, and the irreverence of the comic spirit. And Peter G. Phialas[7] well illustrates that the significant differences which separate Shakespeare's comedy from the Jonsonian variety lie not so much in the materials as in their 'shaping by an overriding attitude or response to the human situation'.

Various writers on individual plays elucidate their special tone. So far as *Love's Labour's Lost* is concerned the emphasis has been upon its esoteric qualities. For example, M. T. Jones-Davies[8] stresses its courtly aspect by considering the masque-like elements which make it for her primarily 'un divertissement de cour'. In two excellent essays on its language, R. F. Hill[9] issues a timely warning against the usual dismissal of Shakespeare's predilection for the pun and extravagance in language in his perceptive analysis of various linguistic devices used in this and other early comedies; and William Matthews[10] distinguishes the language differences between the social groups by both phonological and lexicographical means, to illustrate his view of the play as 'a comedy on the English *état de langue*'. Donald M. Goodfellow[11] also has some com-ments on the play's social groupings. *The Taming of the Shrew* gets some serious attention from

[1] 'Hector and the "One in Sumptuous Armour"', *English Studies*, XLV (1964), 104–8.

[2] 'The Glass of Pandar's Praise: The Word-Scenery, Mirror Passages, and Reported Scenes in Shakespeare's *Troilus and Cressida*', *Essays and Studies*, XVII (1964), 55–77.

[3] 'The Trysting Scenes in *Troilus and Cressida*', *Shakespearean Essays*, pp. 105–20.

[4] 'Shakespeare's Treatment of Comedy', *Shakespeare's World*, pp. 79–95.

[5] 'Shakespeare's Comedies and the Critics', *Shakespeare 400*, pp. 67–73.

[6] 'The Range of Shakespeare's Comedy', *ibid.* pp. 55–66.

[7] 'Comic Truth in Shakespeare and Jonson', *South Atlantic Quarterly*, LXII (1964), 78–91.

[8] 'Le divertissement de cour dans l'œuvre de Shakespeare', *Etudes Anglaises*, XVII (1964), 434–47.

[9] 'Delight and Laughter: Some Aspects of Shakespeare's Early Verbal Comedy', *Shakespeare Studies (Japan)*, III (1964), 1–21.

[10] 'Language in *Love's Labour's Lost*', *Essays and Studies*, XVII (1964), 1–11.

[11] 'Love's Labour's Lost', *Carnegie Studies in English*, VIII (1964), 1–15.

George Hibbard[1] who, in a good article, looks at its stage marriages in the light of contemporary practices, concluding that the play contains a constructive critique of the marriage *mores* as they were in Elizabethan England. Norman Sanders[2] examines the relationship between the imagery and themes of the same play; and E. M. W. Tillyard[3] points to the possible use of fairy-tale materials similar to those found in *König Drosselbart* which helps to cheat the play of any unity between the farcical and comic elements. Of *The Comedy of Errors* Gwyn Williams[4] argues that it was almost not a comedy at all, and shows well how the Dromios save the play as comedy even as they underline the problem of identity at its centre. The Pyramus-Thisbe playlet in *A Midsummer Night's Dream* has long been considered one of Shakespeare's artistic triumphs; J. W. Robinson[5] illustrates its qualities as a burlesque of the hybrid play still evident in Shakespeare's day; and R. W. Dent[6] examines its relationship to the play as a whole which he sees as being concerned with a contrast between the role of imagination in love and in art. On this play also, J. A. Bryant[7] has an essay outlining those characteristics which make it a fleeting vision of the harmony 'lost when we surrendered our innocence'; and T. Walter Herbert[8] describes the effects of certain aspects of it on the 'intellectually aware' members of the audience of the 1590's.

Today's critics of Shylock are as harsh as some of their predecessors were sentimental. Warren D. Smith[9] sees him as a usurer and hypocrite primarily and a Jew merely when it suits his purpose; and while much that he says is valid, one's confidence in his conclusions is weakened by the inaccurate statement about Jews in England that he allows himself by ignoring the researches of Cecil Roth and C. J. Sisson.[10] Charles Mitchell[11] traces the symbolic and imagistic links between Shylock and Antonio; and Maxine MacKay[12] discusses the literal and symbolic levels on which their opposition in the Trial scene works. Another aspect of the character pairing basic to the piece is seen by Norman Nathan[13] in the Nerissa-Portia relationship as an example of Renaissance friendship.

Among the mature comedies *Twelfth Night* is the play for which deep seriousness is most frequently claimed; and its links with the tragedies in themes and techniques are perceived by Julian Markels[14] and Albert Gérard.[15] However, the specifically comic treatment of some of these

[1] '*The Taming of the Shrew*: A Social Comedy', *Shakespearean Essays*, pp. 15–28.

[2] 'Imagery and Themes in *The Taming of the Shrew*', *Renaissance Papers 1963* (South-eastern Renaissance Conference, 1964), pp. 63–72.

[3] 'The Fairy-Tale Element in *The Taming of the Shrew*', *Shakespeare 1564–1964*, pp. 110–14.

[4] '*The Comedy of Errors* Rescued from Tragedy', *Review of English Literature*, V (1964), 63–71.

[5] 'Palpable Hot Ice: Dramatic Burlesque in *A Midsummer Night's Dream*', *Studies in Philology*, LXI (1964), 192–204.

[6] 'Imagination in *A Midsummer Night's Dream*', *Shakespeare 400*, pp. 115–29.

[7] 'The Importance of *A Midsummer Night's Dream*', *Forum*, V (1964), 3–8.

[8] 'Invitations to Cosmic Laughter in *A Midsummer Night's Dream*', *Shakespearean Essays*, pp. 29–40.

[9] 'Shakespeare's Shylock', *Shakespeare Quarterly*, XV (1964), 193–9.

[10] See *A History of the Jews in England* (1941), pp. 139–44; *Essays and Studies*, XXIII (1937), 38–51.

[11] 'The Conscience of Venice: Shakespeare's Merchant', *JEGP*, LXIII (1964), 214–25.

[12] '*The Merchant of Venice*: A Reflection of the Early Conflict Between Courts of Law and Courts of Equity', *Shakespeare Quarterly*, XV (1964), 371–6.

[13] 'Portia, Nerissa, and Female Friendship', *Topic*, IV (1964), 56–60.

[14] 'Shakespeare's Confluence of Tragedy and Comedy: *Twelfth Night* and *King Lear*', *Shakespeare 400*, pp. 75–88.

[15] '*Shipload of Fools*: A Note on *Twelfth Night*', *English Studies*, XLV (1964), 109–15.

themes is dealt with by Fred A. Schatoff[1] in his discussion of its aspects of love, and by William B. Bache[2] in his tracing of Viola's role in redeeming a disordered society by love and marriage. Serious thought is also seen in two passages in the play by J. Rea,[3] who closely reads the Duke-Feste exchange in v, i, and Thomas Kranidas,[4] who examines Malvolio's superficial utterance on decorum. In a fine essay on *Much Ado*, Walter N. King[5] detects some heavy matters. Insisting that the play should be read as a comedy of manners, he locates a critical inspection of a leisured class grown flabby at its centre, and two sub-themes in the dangerous aristocratic verbalizing of love and marriage, and in the elevation of wit to a prime social value. Madeleine Doran[6] also considers social issues in *As You Like It*, and in the light of contemporary beliefs discusses many of the dichotomies found in it: nature/nurture, art/nature, court/forest, order/disorder and rudeness/civilization.

It has been some years now since the last plays were first considered as a separate group linked with the comedies, yet growing out of the tragedies. Those qualities which unite them are restated by K. R. S. Iyengar,[7] and the ways in which they have been interpreted, by Hallett Smith.[8] However, the latter also convincingly suggests, by reference to the *Lear* sub-plot and the reconciliation scene, that Shakespeare's change towards the viewpoint and technique of Romance occurred during the writing of this tragedy. It is *The Tempest* that attracts most of the attention devoted to the group. Three articles attempt an overall interpretation: Frank Davidson[9] works out a composite analysis, based on the philosophical and psychological thinking of the Tudor era, by close attention to the ideas of Frye, Stauffer and Craig. Using something of the same background material, James E. Phillips[10] equates the functions of Prospero, Ariel and Caliban with the Rational, Sensitive and Vegetative functions of the soul which were universally recognized in Renaissance literature on the nature of man, and passes on, by no very clear transition to me, to suggest that Prospero emerges as the complete Renaissance man; and Hideo Yamaguchi[11] rather over-simplifies the effect of the play in seeing in it the reconciliation of the two opposing forces of heathen fatalism and Christian mercy. Special aspects of the play are also examined. Two writers look at its treatment of time in somewhat similar ways: Tom F. Driver[12] and James E. Robinson[13] both stress that Time is an important idea, and in different ways illustrate how the equation of real and dramatic time manages to encompass past and future in a present moment—a moment which Ernest Gohn[14] sees as critical for all the characters.

[1] 'Twelfth Night', *Carnegie Studies in English*, VIII (1964), 33–51.
[2] 'Levels of Perception in *Twelfth Night*', *Forum*, V (1964), 56–8.
[3] 'Feste's Syllogisms in *Twelfth Night*', *ibid.* pp. 59–62.
[4] 'Malvolio on Decorum', *Shakespeare Quarterly*, XV (1964), 450–1.
[5] 'Much Ado About *Something*', *ibid.* pp. 143–55.
[6] '"Yet Am I Inland Bred"', *Shakespeare 400*, pp. 99–114.
[7] 'Shakespeare's Last Plays', *The Literary Criterion (India)*, VI (1964), 121–30.
[8] 'Shakespeare's Romances', *Huntington Library Quarterly*, XXVII (1964), 279–88.
[9] '*The Tempest*: An Interpretation', *JEGP*, LXII (1963), 501–17.
[10] '*The Tempest* and the Renaissance Idea of Man', *Shakespeare 400*, pp. 147–59.
[11] '*The Tempest*: What It Tells Us', *Anglica (Japan)*, V (1964), 87–104.
[12] 'The Shakespearian Clock: Time and the Vision of Reality in *Romeo and Juliet* and *The Tempest*', *Shakespeare Quarterly*, XV (1964), 363–70.
[13] 'Time and *The Tempest*', *JEGP*, LXIII (1964), 255–67.
[14] '*The Tempest*: Theme and Structure', *English Studies*, XLV (1964), 116–25.

The magic of the play can be viewed in many different manners. Its symbolic function is empha-sized by R. Silhol[1] who claims it is the instrument by means of which Shakespeare fashioned his Utopian dream where the philosophers give a lesson to the men of action. Robert H. West,[2] in two well-documented pieces, links the stage magic with real life and suggests that it may be taken as a reflection of the early seventeenth century's quite literal interest and hope in the occult, and of a concomitant suspicion of it. Its agent, Ariel, West sees as one of Shakespeare's ways of rationalizing 'the outer mystery' and displaying the fearful differences between man and the powers around him.

In *The Winter's Tale*, Time is also seen as a clue to its meaning, but owing to its extent rather than its compression. The chronological and structural break at the end of Act III is claimed by both Inga-Stina Ewbank[3] and Ernest Schanzer[4] as Shakespeare's tool for showing the effects of Time on man. Ewbank sees Time's influence presented, via imagery, action, and structure, as simultaneously the revealer and destroyer of truth; while Schanzer shows how the theme of the precariousness of human existence is conveyed by the parallels and contrasts between the two parts. Beekman W. Cottrell[5] usefully sums up the play's effect generally; and V. K. Gokak[6] looks closely at the 'daffodils' speech to perceive a conventional-natural and grammatical-natural equivalence.

The much-disputed *Two Noble Kinsmen* is re-examined by Philip Edwards[7] who notes, in one of the best half-dozen or so articles on the play, that 'it is the seeming want of "idea" in the play that makes readers find fault with verse and dramaturgy'. He is convinced that there is more purposeful thought in the piece than is usually allowed; and, taking Palamon's address to Venus as being of central importance, argues that the grand design is Shakespeare's and depicts 'life in two stages; youth, in which the passion of spontaneous friendship is dominant, and the riper age in which there is a dominant sexual passion, leading to marriage where it can', as well as the movement from one to the other with its many variations.

So far as the non-dramatic poetry is concerned, the Sonnets would appear to continue to perplex and the longer poems to delight. Kenneth Muir[8] gives as clear a statement as one could wish for of the problems and pleasures of *Venus and Adonis*, and concludes that the ambivalence of the poem is caused partly by the poet's own acceptance of conflicting feelings about love, and partly by the essentially dramatic nature of his imagination which led him to a sympathetic portrayal of Adonis. The goddess herself is seen as similar in kind to but less complex than Cleopatra by R. H. Bowers[9] who detects in her a final recognition of her lust for what it really is. Alaister Fowler and Christopher Butler[10] approach the poem in an original manner via its

---

[1] 'Magie et utopie dans la *Tempête*', *Etudes Anglaises*, XVII (1964), 447–57.

[2] 'Ceremonial Magic in *The Tempest*', *Shakespearean Essays*, pp. 63–78; 'Ariel and the Outer Mystery', *Shakespeare 1564–1964*, pp. 115–23.

[3] 'The Triumph of Time in *The Winter's Tale*', *Review of English Literature*, V (1964), 83–100.

[4] 'The Structural Pattern of *The Winter's Tale*', ibid. pp. 72–82.

[5] '*The Winter's Tale*', *Carnegie Studies in English*, VIII (1964), 69–82.

[6] 'The Structure of Daffodils in *The Winter's Tale*', *The Literary Criterion (India)*, VI (1964), 137–52.

[7] 'On the Design of *The Two Noble Kinsmen*', *Review of English Literature*, V (1964), 89–105.

[8] '*Venus and Adonis*: Comedy or Tragedy?', *Shakespearean Essays*, pp. 1–14.

[9] 'Anagnorisis, or the Shock of Recognition, in Shakespeare's *Venus and Adonis*', *Renaissance Papers 1962*, pp. 3–8.

[10] 'Time Beguiling Sport: Number Symbolism in Shakespeare's *Venus and Adonis*', *Shakespeare 1564–1964*, pp. 124–33.

numerological structure which they see as providing an unequivocal comment on the temporal and seasonal meanings in human events; they also find allusions to Southampton in Adonis. Muir also has essays on *Lucrece* and *The Lover's Complaint*.[1] He is convinced of the correctness of the latter's attribution to Shakespeare on the evidence of its imagery, vocabulary, and its internal links with the plays, and brings out the weaknesses and strengths of its 'unrivalled linguistic daring'; and he has some fine observations on the former poem, particularly on its iconography, rhetoric, and versification, and on the topic of the eponym's suicide. Following Coleridge's method in the *Biographia Literaria*, Robert J. Griffin[2] examines interrelated image groups in the two narrative poems and shows how they contribute to their unity and effectiveness. There is one essay on *The Phoenix and the Turtle* by S. M. Bonaventure[3] which considers the poem's 'unique metaphysical mode'.

A commentary on the Sonnets is central to a new book by Murray Kreiger,[4] in the first section of which he discusses some recent critical theories, especially those which deal with the exact nature of the relationship between a work of art and the surrounding world—'the mirror as window'. He rejects both the imitation and formalist theories as inadequate, and attempts by means of what he calls 'contextualism' to show how great poetry simultaneously does and does not present us with a version of the outside world ('the same set of mirrors miraculously becomes a window again'). The long middle section of the work is devoted to a close and sometimes profound reading of the individual poems which he sees in both erotic and religious terms: the lover as self-regarding Petrarchan idealization and as real lover, the immediately useful 'truths' of this world and the vision of ultimate truth that transcends them. These topics are sought in almost all the sonnets to perceive 'the metaphorical system they develop out of the mirror-window metaphor even as they earn this metaphor through the way in which it functions and has its meaning'. While this kind of examination certainly does bring out a large number of—by me—previously unobserved subtleties in all the poems, it also misses a great deal of the rich worldly texture which is also present in the best. W. H. Auden[5] also considers the Sonnets as a whole and claims that only forty-nine are uniformly excellent, seeing the cycle's primary experience as a mystical vision of Eros. Certain special aspects of the poems are taken up by other critics. The theme of immortality in its various manifestations related to marriage, procreation, beauty, time, etc., is traced by Satyanarain Singh;[6] and these ideas are seen in the context of Platonic-Christian belief by Norman Silverstein.[7] Claes Schaar[8] discusses the conventional and graphic aspects of the natural description in the poems. Brents Stirling[9] continues

[1] '*The Rape of Lucrece*', *Anglica* (*Japan*), V (1964), 25–40; '*A Lover's Complaint*: A Reconsideration', *Shakespeare 1564–1964*, pp. 154–66.

[2] '"These Contrarieties Such Unity Do Hold": Patterned Imagery in Shakespeare's Narrative Poems', *Studies in English Literature*, IV (1964), 43–55.

[3] 'The Phoenix Renewed', *Forum*, V (1964), 72–6.

[4] *A Window to Criticism: Shakespeare's Sonnets and Modern Poetics* (Princeton University Press, 1964).

[5] 'Shakespeare's Sonnets', *The Listener*, LXXI, 985–8, and LXXXII, 7–9.

[6] 'The Theme of Immortality in Shakespeare's *Sonnets*', *Osmania Journal of English Studies* (*India*), IV (1964), 125–40.

[7] 'Shakespeare's Sonnets in Perspective', *Forum*, V (1964), 67–71.

[8] 'Conventional and Unconventional in the Descriptions of Scenery in Shakespeare's Sonnets', *English Studies*, LXV (1964), 142–9.

[9] 'Sonnets 127–154', *Shakespeare 1564–1964*, pp. 134–53.

his researches into the order of the poems, which he believes to have been disarranged in the 1609 text, and offers his own re-ordering of numbers 127–54 based on a closely argued hypothesis of the contents of a single MS leaf. Sonnet 128 is analysed by Richard Purdum[1] as an effective dramatization of a moral state; and James Brophy[2] looks at the musical metaphor of the same poem. Richard Levin[3] gives an explication of Sonnet 97 in the light of its seasonal allusion. A translation of the Sonnets into French 'regular' sonnet form has been made by Dirkan Garabedian,[4] who uses five rhymes to Shakespeare's seven. There can be, in an experiment of this nature, no attempt to capture Shakespeare's rhythm which is indeed lost by the spinning out of so many lines; but there are extended passages which incorporate many of the qualities of the original.

The quatercentenary year encouraged many sweeping looks at the whole canon, an activity not much in evidence in the past few years of specialization. Some interestingly attempt to grasp the elusive spirit of Shakespeare, like André Maurois,[5] and S. C. Sen Gupta;[6] others, like J. B. Fort,[7] the author behind the plays, or try to capture the elements that constitute his greatest achievement, like Salvador de Madariaga.[8] Some see the dramatist and his importance for a particular nation, like Niels L. Jensen[9] for Denmark; or wrestle with the difficulties of translation as do Norman Suckling[10] and M. Musiol;[11] or consider, like Kenneth Muir,[12] just where his excellence as a dramatist lies, or the ways in which 'East' and 'West' interpret their Shakespeare; or trace, like T. J. B. Spencer,[13] the poet's gradual emergence as a classic in competition with the Classics.

Two books are devoted to the whole canon. Peter Milward[14] provides an elementary introduction containing some interesting observations which, owing to the nature of the book, are not fully developed; as well as a number of judgments which show a rather one-sided view of the playwright's achievement (e.g. the mature comedies seen as diversions of mind from serious thoughts, or as momentary flashes of fancy). The thesis of Jaisou Choe's[15] book is that the basis of Shakespeare's vision is the desire for and consciousness of order in the various spheres of life which may be thought of as 'identical with the sense of happiness'. This idea is worked out in relationship to the different groups of plays with political order seen in the history plays, social order in the comedies, moral order in the tragedies, and natural order in the last plays. The

[1] 'Shakespeare's Sonnet 128', *JEGP*, LXIII (1964), 235–9.

[2] 'Shakespeare's "Saucy Jacks"', *English Language Notes*, I (1963), 11–13.

[3] 'Shakespeare's Sonnet 97', *Review of English Studies*, XV (1964), 408–9.

[4] *The Sonnets of Shakespeare Translated into French 'Regular' Sonnets* (Clarendon Press, Oxford, 1964).

[5] 'Le quatrième centenaire de Shakespeare', *Etudes Anglaises*, XVII (1964), 329–32.

[6] 'Shakespeare', *Shakespeare: A Book of Homage*, pp. 1–20.

[7] 'Le quatrième centenaire et le mystère Shakespearien', *Etudes Anglaises*, XVII (1964), 522–36.

[8] 'The Impact of Shakespeare', *Shakespeare Jahrbuch*, 100 (1964), 83–91.

[9] 'Shakespeare in Denmark', *Durham University Journal*, LVI (1964), 91–8.

[10] 'L'Ombre actuelle du Grand Will: A Note on Shakespeare in French', *ibid.* pp. 99–103.

[11] 'Shakespeare in German: The Modern Period', *ibid.* pp. 104–9.

[12] 'Shakespeare the Dramatist', *Filološki Pregled*, I–II (1964), 21–6; 'Shakespeare in East and West', *Co-Existence*, III (1965), 1–7.

[13] 'The Great Rival: Shakespeare and the Classical Dramatists', *Shakespeare 1564–1964*, pp. 177–93.

[14] *An Introduction to Shakespeare's Plays* (Tokyo, Kenkyusha, 1964).

[15] *Shakespeare's Art as Order of Life* (Vantage Press, New York, 1965).

commentary throughout never rises very far above the obvious and sometimes slips into biographical sentimentality. The only original idea in the volume is Choe's viewing of all the Roman plays as exploring a transcendental order and thus enlarging the conception of Shakespearian tragedy.

One group of papers considers different aspects of Shakespeare's language. In the best of them, Hilda Hulme,[1] with a palpably expert knowledge of Elizabethan linguistics, discusses what constitutes the 'common appeal' of Shakespeare's language; and among the many fine things in her lecture there is an acute analysis of the dramatic and personal appropriateness of the duologue between the Doctor and the Nurse in *Macbeth*. K. Kushari[2] approaches the same topic from a grammatical and philological angle, and highlights some nice distinctions of meaning and emphasis. G. Lambrechts[3] and V. Y. Kantak[4] concentrate on the imagery of some of the plays, concerning themselves with sensitive appreciations of revitalized metaphor and the image of the stage respectively. The use of language in speech units is examined by Kenneth Muir[5] and James Sutherland.[6] The latter brilliantly illustrates, by means of prosodic transcription techniques, the way in which strong feelings and elements of character are the shaping forces in several long speeches; and the former, how Shakespeare mastered the many tones and kinds of soliloquy necessary in different plays.

The diversity of the other general topics handled is large, and all of the articles offer something of interest. B. N. Joshi[7] examines the symbolic uses of the Heath; Peter Ure[8] explores Shakespeare's creation of unique characters defined by traditional role and realized in human individuality from Richard III to Hamlet; Eric W. Stockton[9] casts a cold eye at the idealization of the heroines, and concludes that it was *la femme moyenne sensuelle* that most interested the playwright; the theme of revenge and the changes in Shakespeare's treatment of it during his career is charted by J. Chakavorty,[10] as are the poet's ideas on feudalism by P. Legouis;[11] Mikio Ino[12] discusses methods of exposition used in different plays; John Lawlor[13] focuses his attention on Shakespeare's continuous struggle to find harmony between art and reality, particularly in those situations that explore 'the fact of union between human beings'; Paul N. Siegel[14] details Shakespeare's portrayal of the falseness of the neo-chivalric cult of honour and the comparing of it with the Christian humanist ideal; Fredson Bowers[15] analyses some moments where the dramatist

[1] 'Shakespeare's Language', *Shakespeare's World*, pp. 136–55.
[2] 'A Note on Shakespeare's Language', *Shakespeare: A Book of Homage*, pp. 50–65.
[3] 'Un Aspect de Style de Shakespeare: les Métaphores Ravivées', *Etudes Anglaises*, XVII (1964), 364–72.
[4] '"The Poor Player..."', *The Literary Criterion (India)*, VI (1964), 153–63.
[5] 'Shakespeare's Soliloquies', *Ocidente*, LXVII (1964), 45–58.
[6] 'The Moving Pattern of Shakespeare's Thought', *Papers Mainly Shakespearian*, pp. 10–20.
[7] 'The Heath in Shakespeare', *Osmania Journal of English Studies (India)*, IV (1964), 89–104.
[8] 'Character and Role from Richard III to Hamlet', *Hamlet: Stratford-upon-Avon Studies 5*, pp. 9–28.
[9] 'The Adulthood of Shakespeare's Heroines', *Shakespearean Essays*, pp. 161–80.
[10] 'Shakespearian Transmutation of Revenge', *Shakespeare: A Book of Homage*, pp. 80–117.
[11] 'Shakespeare et la féodalité', *Etudes Anglaises*, XVII (1964), 474–81.
[12] 'Shakespeare's Opening Scenes', *Shakespeare Studies (Japan)*, III (1964), 22–41.
[13] 'Continuity and Innovation in Shakespeare's Dramatic Career', *Review of English Literature*, V (1964), 11–23.
[14] 'Shakespeare and the Neo-Chivalric Cult of Honor', *Centennial Review*, VII (1964), 39–70.
[15] 'Shakespeare's Dramatic Vagueness', *Virginia Quarterly Review*, XXXIX (1963), 54–84.

appears to be deliberately dramatically vague because intuition is too deep for words; E. Mukerji[1] and Sati Chatterjee[2] tread their way warily to define Shakespeare's theory of poetry from the remarks in the plays; and Clifford Leech[3] nicely brings together Shakespeare's treatment of his ruling Dukes in the comedies.

The most important book length study of a large segment of Shakespeare's career is Ernest W. Talbert's[4] essay in historical criticism, which examines the techniques and artistic intentions of the early plays up to *Richard II* in the light of the literary and dramatic expectations of contemporary audiences, the practice of other playwrights, and the background of popular entertainment and folk merriment of the age. In two excellent early chapters he considers comic and serious materials generally. The first, 'Aspects of the Comic', deals with such fundamental comic elements as the comic wooing, and the motifs of 'the world upsidedown', the country bumpkin in the city, class and professional rivalry; folk characters; verbal wit; and the risible treatment of death. The various forms these elements assumed in Shakespearian and non-Shakespearian plays are clearly traced; but where the author shines critically is in his illustrative discussions of such subjects as the combination of type characters and situations found in Faulconbridge's role, or the use of wit to produce 'free' laughter in the Falstaff scenes. In his second general chapter, which is virtually a discussion of key structural patterns associated with serious character types in most of the more important non-Shakespearian drama of the 1580's and 1590's, Talbert concentrates on what he considers to be the seven basic movements (e.g. the rise of a dominant vicious figure, the falling or rising hero, etc.). The remainder of the book is devoted to viewing these general types and structural patterns in all of Shakespeare's early plays, and contains worthwhile comment on almost every page. Among the best passages there might be mentioned those on the blend of the comic and historical materials in the *Henry VI* trilogy, the structural effects of Aaron's role in *Titus Andronicus*, and the original handling by Shakespeare of a basic structural movement in *Richard II*. In all, Talbert's book is a valuable, if ponderous, contribution to the study of the early Shakespeare in that it sets forth matters which every subsequent critic of the plays will have to take into account. One further general article, 'Shakespeare's Theology' by W. Moelwyn Merchant,[5] deserves special notice for both the timeliness of its subject and the exemplary and unpretentious clarity with which it is handled.

Writings about Shakespeare have over the years assumed almost unmanageable proportions, and there have been some recent attempts to provide aids to the scholar in the form of various assessments of criticism. Peter Alexander[6] has selected ten of the British Academy lectures on Shakespeare, many of which are out of-print or not readily available in other collections, and has arranged them under the headings of theatre, text and interpretation. Of wider critical scope is the collection of A. M. Eastman and G. B. Harrison[7] in which general criticism and that on separate plays are generously represented. Most of the well-known names appear along with

---

[1] 'A Shakespearian Theory of Poetry', *Shakespeare: A Book of Homage*, pp. 143–58.
[2] 'A Note on Shakespeare's Poetics', *ibid.* pp. 127–42.
[3] 'Shakespeare's Comic Dukes', *Review of English Literature*, v (1964), 101–14.
[4] *Elizabethan Drama and Shakespeare's Early Plays* (University of North Carolina Press, 1963).
[5] *Review of English Literature*, v (1964), 72–86.
[6] *Studies in Shakespeare* (Oxford University Press, 1964).
[7] *Shakespeare's Critics: From Jonson to Auden* (University of Michigan Press, 1964).

those less celebrated for their critical utterance, such as George III and Lewis Carroll. Naturally there are omissions which some readers will regret; but it is a most pleasant volume presenting us with 'a tailor's pattern book' of a much larger whole. Useful too is Louis Marder's special number of *The Shakespeare Newsletter*[1] in which many distinguished scholars judiciously sum up work done and needing to be done on almost every aspect of Shakespeare studies; it is a most helpful research tool. For French scholars in particular, Henri Fluchère[2] makes some suggestions about the work ahead.

Concerning past critics and their influence there are instructive articles on Voltaire and his translations by T. E. Lawrenson,[3] on Pope's edition by P. Dixon,[4] on Coleridge by J. R. de J. Jackson,[5] on Adam Smith by John Lothian,[6] and on Symonds by Phyllis Grosskurth.[7] Among the twentieth-century critics, F. R. Leavis is praised for doing justice to Shakespeare's moral outlook by K. Aithal;[8] and T. S. Eliot is soundly rated by C. B. Watson for his shortcomings.[9] T. J. B. Spencer[10] also has pungent comments on some modern critics in a delightful canter over the course of Shakespearian criticism; and Alfred Harbage,[11] displaying his customary good sense, points a cautionary finger at some of what he considers to be the less desirable traits of modern criticism. In the light of four hundred years of celebration and study, Wolfgang Clemen[12] discusses some crucial *desiderata* in answer to his question 'Wo stehen wir in der Shakespeare-Forschung?' It will be interesting to watch now 'Wohin wir gehen'.

© N. J. SANDERS 1966

2. SHAKESPEARE'S LIFE, TIMES AND STAGE

reviewed by STANLEY WELLS

Leslie Hotson's *Mr. W. H.*[13] is an ambitious attempt to solve most of the problems of Shakespeare's biography. The conclusions are drawn from 'Shakespeare's allusive and symbolical method in his personal or lyrical poetry'. The evidence that Shakespeare used such a method derives from the results that Dr Hotson achieves by assuming that he did. And these results are, as the author

---

[1] XIV, 23 (April–May, 1964).

[2] 'Les tâches de la critique shakespearienne française de demain', *Etudes Anglaises*, XVII (1964), 333–41.

[3] 'Voltaire and Shakespeare', *Papers Mainly Shakespearian*, pp. 58–75.

[4] 'Pope's Shakespeare', *JEGP*, LXIII (1964), 191–203.

[5] 'Coleridge on Dramatic Illusion and Spectacle in the Performance of Shakespeare's Plays', *Modern Philology*, LXII (1964), 13–21.

[6] 'Adam Smith as a Critic of Shakespeare', *Papers Mainly Shakespearian*, pp. 1–9.

[7] 'The Genesis of Symonds's Elizabethan Criticism', *Modern Language Review*, LIX (1964), 183–93.

[8] 'Shakespeare's Moral Outlook in the Light of F. R. Leavis's Criticism', *The Literary Criterion (India)*, VI (1964), 131–6.

[9] 'T. S. Eliot and the Interpretation of Shakespearean Tragedy in Our Time', *Etudes Anglaises*, XVII (1964), 502–22.

[10] 'The Course of Shakespeare Criticism', *Shakespeare's World*, pp. 156–73.

[11] 'Shakespeare and the Myth of Perfection', *Shakespeare 400*, pp. 1–10.

[12] 'Wo stehen wir in der Shakespeare-Forschung?', *Shakespeare Jahrbuch*, 100 (1964), 135–40.

[13] Rupert Hart-Davis, 1964.

is happy to admit, astonishing. The use of regal imagery for the youth of the sonnets implies that he was, factually or fictionally, of regal status. He was, Dr Hotson believes, the Prince of Purpoole, leader of the Gray's Inn revels. This office was held in 1588 by a Mr W.H.—William Hatcliffe. Dr Hotson finds his very name buried in many of the sonnets. More often than not, one part of the formation derives from those not uncommon words 'what' and 'that'; the occurrence of one of them within a line or two of 'live', 'leave', 'left', etc. is held to be significant. (Apparently Shakespeare's ingenuity did not extend to indicating the '-cliffe' form of the name.) There are also remarkable ramifications involving true-love knots, coats of arms, one of Hilliard's best-known miniatures (a portrait, we are told, of Hatcliffe), and Pompey the Great. The sonnets were all written by 1589, and so was *Love's Labour's Lost* (Pompey the Great, of course). The rival poet is Marlowe, his 'affable familiar ghost' is Robert Greene (Dr Hotson ignores the evidence of enmity between the two), the dark lady is Luce Morgan (Shakespeare refers to her as 'bright', *lucia* is from the Latin for 'bright', etc.—the best we can do for a pun on the surname here is 'more than'). The sonnets are printed in Shakespeare's own order because Nos. 107 and 124 remind Dr Hotson of the psalms with those numbers.

Set out with all Dr Hotson's wealth of learning, the obvious scope of his researches, the fascinating details that he has unearthed, combined with the beguiling ease and charm of his narrative method, it is all as persuasive while it lasts as the sort of detective story to which he makes occasional reference; and finally it is just about as convincing. Dr Hotson's tapestry of conjecture is valuable primarily as entertainment, but also for the threads of new fact which are woven into it without forming part of the main design.

Three well written lectures delivered as part of the quatercentenary festivities are concerned in general terms with Shakespeare's life. Professor M. C. Bradbrook's 'Shakespeare in Elizabethan England'[1] relates him to his social, cultural, and theatrical environment; A. L. Rowse writes a lively, impressionistic piece on 'The Personality of Shakespeare';[2] and Alfred Harbage's learned and spirited 'Shakespeare as Culture Hero'[3] refers scepticism concerning Shakespeare's authorship of the plays 'not to the realm of biographical and literary evidence, but to the realm of mythmaking'. Prominent among his mythmakers are Mark Twain and Sigmund Freud. John F. Fleming[4] has given an account of a copy of Surrey's *Songes and Sonettes* which may once have belonged to Shakespeare. Marco Mincoff tackles a controversial subject in 'The Chronology of Shakespeare's Early Works'.[5] He offers a tentative revision of E. K. Chambers's ordering of nine of the early plays and the two narrative poems, providing a list which, he believes, 'approximates sufficiently to the relative chronology of Shakespeare's early works to offer a working basis for a study of his evolution as a dramatist'. Some of Professor Mincoff's arguments are cogent, but much remains conjectural. It might be argued that the only adequate basis for a study of Shakespeare's evolution would be certainty, and that in the absence of certainty such a study were better not attempted. But perhaps this is to take too austere a view.

---

[1] *English Language and Literature* (Sofia, 1964), pp. 1–16.
[2] *Huntington Library Quarterly*, XXVII (1964), 193–209.   [3] *Ibid.* pp. 211–27.
[4] 'A Book from Shakespeare's Library discovered by William Van Lennep', *Shakespeare Quarterly*, XV, 2 (Spring 1964), 25–7.
[5] *Shakespeare Jahrbuch*, 100–101 (1964–5) (Weimar, 1965), 253–65.

Shakespeare's reputation in the seventeenth century is the subject of an article by David Frost[1] which attacks both the methods and the conclusions of G. E. Bentley's *Shakespeare and Jonson: their Reputations in the Seventeenth Century Compared*. Frost believes that 'Shakespeare was widely appreciated in his own day and appealed to the public of the seventeenth century more than did Jonson'. Bentley's contrary opinion has been widely accepted; Frost's arguments should at least prevent it from hardening into unquestioned orthodoxy. Also concerned with an aspect of Shakespeare's seventeenth-century reputation is Neille Shoemaker in 'The Aesthetic Criticism of *Hamlet* from 1692 to 1699'.[2] Joseph Greene was master of Stratford-upon-Avon grammar school and a parson in the neighbourhood during the eighteenth century, at a time when the town first began to develop a sense of its privileged position. He was concerned with the putting-on of the first known performance of a Shakespeare play in the town, with the restoration of the monument (paid for out of the proceeds of the performance), and with the Garrick jubilee. His correspondence, edited by Levi Fox, has been published in an attractive volume[3] which documents his Shakespearian activities. Shakespeare's slow rise to classic status is traced with wit and learning by T. J. B. Spencer in 'The Great Rival: Shakespeare and the Classical Dramatists'.[4]

The Quatercentenary was the occasion for a number of scholarly articles about Shakespeare's impact abroad. James G. McManaway provides a concise survey, full of information, on 'Shakespeare in the United States'.[5] Joannis Sideris, Metin And, and Niels Lyhne Jensen do the same for respectively Greece,[6] Turkey[7] and Denmark.[8] Stanisław Helstyński surveys 'Polish Translations of Shakespeare in the Past and Today',[9] and Thomas R. Mark writes on 'The First Hungarian Translation of Shakespeare's Complete Works'.[10] M. Musiol's 'Shakespeare in Germany: The Modern Period'[11] is concerned with modern translations, and Martin Lehnert has written on the history of the Shakespeare-Gesellschaft.[12] Alexandru Duțu has produced a remarkably detailed and comprehensive study, written in English and attractively illustrated, of Shakespeare in Rumania.[13] *The Shakespeare Newsletter*[14] in its Quatercentenary number offers articles on 'the past, present and future of Shakespearean scholarship and criticism' by distinguished scholars, and a useful list of about 550 American and German doctoral dissertations concerned with Shakespeare.

[1] 'Shakespeare in the Seventeenth Century', *Shakespeare Quarterly*, XVI, 1 (Winter 1965), 81–9.

[2] *Ibid.* pp. 99–103.

[3] *The Correspondence of the Reverend Joseph Greene*, ed. Levi Fox (H.M.S.O., 1965).

[4] *Shakespeare 1564–1964*, ed. Edward A. Bloom (Brown University Press, Rhode Island, 1964), pp. 177–93.

[5] *PMLA*, LXXIX, 5 (December 1964), 513–18.

[6] 'Shakespeare in Greece', *Theatre Research*, VI, 2 (1964), 85–99.

[7] 'Shakespeare in Turkey', *ibid.* pp. 75–84.

[8] 'Shakespeare in Denmark', *The Durham University Journal*, LVI, 2 (March 1964), 91–8.

[9] *Shakespeare Jahrbuch*, 100–101 (1964–5) (Weimar, 1965), 274–93.

[10] *Shakespeare Quarterly*, XVI, 1 (Winter 1965), 105–15.

[11] *The Durham University Journal*, LVI, 2 (March 1964), 104–9.

[12] 'Hundert Jahre Deutsche Shakespeare-Gesellschaft', *Shakespeare Jahrbuch*, 100–101 (1964–5) (Weimar, 1965), 9–54.

[13] *Shakespeare in Rumania* (a bibliographical essay with an introduction by Mihnea Gheorgiu, Meridiane Publishing House, Bucharest, 1964).

[14] XIV, 2–3 (No. 76) (April–May 1964).

The latest volume of Geoffrey Bullough's *Narrative and Dramatic Sources of Shakespeare*[1] is devoted to the three major Roman plays. Naturally long selections from North's Plutarch form the bulk of the contents. But we are also given extracts from translations of other classical texts and from Renaissance writings that Shakespeare knew, or which are interesting as analogues. Particularly welcome are the complete texts of the Countess of Pembroke's *The Tragedie of Antonie*, translated from Robert Garnier, and of Samuel Daniel's *The Tragedy of Cleopatra*. Professor Bullough realizes that Shakespeare's handling of figures such as Cleopatra and Julius Caesar was probably 'affected by a complex tradition which, arising from the divergent attitudes of classical historians, has been modified in the Middle Ages and Renaissance in legend, scholarship and creative writing'. This has influenced him to extend his introductions beyond their usual scope in giving an account of the development of these traditions. There is much valuable material here and in Professor Bullough's studies of the plays in relation to Plutarch. 'The Uses of History',[2] also by Professor Bullough, offers a general consideration of Shakespeare's handling of the 'ethical uses' of historical material both English and Roman, finding that 'in *Antony and Cleopatra* the ethical uses of history are for once transcended'. The same scholar makes an interesting, though inevitably speculative, attempt[3] to reconstruct the Admiral's Men's *Troilus and Cressida*, of which only the 'plot' has survived, and to consider its possible relationship to Shakespeare's play.

Professor Bullough's collections of the sources are likely to remain standard works for many years to come; nevertheless, a good deal of effort is being directed to the attempt to make them out of date as soon as possible. Richard Hosley, for instance, has written on 'Sources and Analogues of *The Taming of the Shrew*'.[4] He believes that *The Taming of A Shrew* is a bad quarto of Shakespeare's play, and argues this case. This frees him to consider the sources of Shakespeare's play without worrying about a possible lost source-play. He suggests the addition of the anonymous ballad of *A Shrewde and Curste Wyfe* to the generally accepted sources. His position is supported by Peter Alexander in 'A Case of Three Sisters'.[5] Christopher Whitfield's 'Sir Lewis Lewkenor and *The Merchant of Venice*: A Suggested Connexion'[6] is perhaps more valuable as a biographical study of Lewkenor than for its suggestion that Shakespeare consulted Lewkenor, and may have seen the manuscript of his translation of Contarini's *The Commonwealth and Government of Venice* before writing *The Merchant of Venice*. Charles T. Prouty[7] has written about the background of Whetstone's play *Promos and Cassandra*, and promises a further study more closely relating this material to *Measure for Measure*. Charles Fish,[8] studying Shakespeare's use of Holinshed in his portrayal of Henry IV, finds that 'time after time Shakespeare altered his source to make Henry more admirable as a man and more effective as a ruler'. Irving Ribner, too, stresses difference, not dependence. In 'Marlowe and Shakespeare'[9] he contrasts the two dramatists, especially in *The Jew of Malta* and *The Merchant of Venice* and *Dr Faustus* and *Macbeth*,

[1] Vol. v: The Roman Plays: *Julius Caesar, Antony and Cleopatra, Coriolanus* (Routledge and Kegan Paul, 1964).

[2] *Shakespeare's World*, ed. James Sutherland and Joel Hurstfield (Edward Arnold, 1964), pp. 96–115.

[3] 'The Lost *Troilus and Cressida*', *Essays and Studies by Members of the English Association*, XVII (1964), 24–40.

[4] *Huntington Library Quarterly*, XXVII (1964), 289–308.   [5] *The Times Literary Supplement*, 8 July 1965, p. 588.

[6] *Notes and Queries*, XI (April 1964), 123–33.

[7] *Shakespeare Quarterly*, XV, 2 (Spring 1964), 131–45, 'George Whetstone and the Sources of *Measure for Measure*'.

[8] '*Henry IV*: Shakespeare and Holinshed', *Studies in Philology*, LXI (1964), 205–18.

[9] *Shakespeare Quarterly*, XV, 2 (Spring 1964), 41–53.

and suggests that Marlowe's influence on Shakespeare was slight except perhaps for *Edward II* and *Richard II*.[1]

Professor Bullough concerns himself with influences on the narrative rather than on the style. There have however been many attempts to demonstrate that Shakespeare was indebted to other writers for details of expression. C. M. Eccles[2] has suggested verbal links between North's translation of Amyot's foreword to his Plutarch and two passages in Shakespeare, and D. T. Starnes[3] has found some analogues for a few lines in *Lucrece*. Other studies of a similar nature include F. N. Lee's '*Dido, Queen of Carthage* and *The Tempest*',[4] Richard Levin's 'Anatomical Geography in *The Tempest*',[5] James O. Wood's 'Two Notes on *Macbeth*'[6] (suggesting sources in Scot and Holinshed), William M. Jones's 'The Turning of Trent in *1 Henry IV*',[7] David B. McKeen's 'Hotspur's Comparison: A French Analogue'[8] and H. Rossiter-Smith's 'Ripeness is All'[9] (Cicero's *De Senectute* as a source of the phrase in *King Lear*). Peter H. Davison[10] suggests that in Daniel's description of Richard as a 'wanton young effeminate' Shakespeare saw a likeness to his own conception of the young Prince Hal. A source in Chapman instead of Marlowe for Touchstone's 'strikes a man more dead than a great reckoning in a little room' has been suggested by J. H. Walter.[11] Gunnar Sjögren, in 'A Contribution to the Geography of *Hamlet*',[12] points out that to Shakespeare as to some of his contemporaries 'Dansker' meant 'Danish' not 'of Danzig', and plausibly suggests that Shakespeare thought of Denmark, Norway and Poland as contiguous. Holgar Nørgaard,[13] commenting on *Titus Andronicus*, v, iii, 36–8, shows that in causing Virginius to kill his daughter after she had been raped, so departing from the classical story, Shakespeare had ample precedent. James O. Wood[14] uses John Leslie's *De Origine Moribus et Rebus Gestis Scotorum* to suggest a memory in some of Lady Macbeth's speeches of the crossbow that killed King Kenneth, and Peter J. Seng[15] suggests that 'Come thou monarch of the vine' (*Antony and Cleopatra*, II, vii) may parody the medieval hymn *Veni sancte spiritus*. Background studies of a more general nature are provided by R. I. Page,[16] who investigates the background of Shakespeare's reference in *The Comedy of Errors* to 'Lapland sorcerers', and by Claes Schaar, who discusses the 'Conventional and Unconventional in the Descriptions of Scenery in Shakespeare's Sonnets',[17] concluding that 'of the other Elizabethan sonneteers, there is not one whose

---

[1] Other recent articles on sources are: Hardin Craig, 'When Shakespeare altered his Sources', *The Centennial Review of Arts and Science* (Michigan State), VIII, 121–8; Paule Mertens-Fonck, 'Shakespeare's Sources', *Revue des Langues Vivantes*, XXX, 362–6; Sharon L. Smith, 'The Commedia dell'Arte and Problems related to Source in *The Tempest*', *Emporia State Research Studies*, XIII, 11–23; and Arthur P. Stabler, 'The Sources of *Hamlet*: Some Corrections of the Record', *Research Studies* (Washington State University), XXXII, 207–16.

[2] 'Shakespeare and Jaques Amyot: Sonnet LV and *Coriolanus*', *Notes and Queries*, XII, 3 (March 1965), 100–2.

[3] 'Geoffrey Fenton, Seneca and Shakespeare's *Lucrece*', *Philological Quarterly*, XLIII, 2 (April 1964), 280–3.

[4] *Notes and Queries*, XI (April 1964), 147–9.   [5] *Ibid.* pp. 142–6.

[6] *Ibid.* pp. 137–8.   [7] *Renaissance News*, XVII, 4 (Winter 1964), 304–6.

[8] *Notes and Queries*, XII, 3 (March 1965), 95.   [9] *Ibid.* p. 97.

[10] *Ibid.* pp. 94–5.   [11] *Ibid.* pp. 95–6.

[12] *Shakespeare Jahrbuch*, 100–101 (1964–5) (Weimar, 1965), 266–73.

[13] 'Never Wrong but with Just Cause', *English Studies*, XLV, 2 (April 1964), 137–41.

[14] 'Lady Macbeth's Secret Weapon', *Notes and Queries*, XII, 3 (March 1965), 98–100.

[15] *Renaissance News*, XVIII, 1 (Spring 1965), 4–6.

[16] '"Lapland Sorcerers"', *Saga-Book of the Viking Society*, XVI, Parts 2–3 (1963–4), 215–32.

[17] *English Studies*, XLV, 2 (April 1964), 142–9.

descriptions of scenery are so often traditional and graphic at the same time'. Extracts from some of the accounts of voyages believed to have influenced *The Tempest* are included in *The Eliza-bethans' America*,[1] an attractive volume edited by Louis B. Wright which brings together many reports by Englishmen of their travels across the Atlantic.

Shakespeare Survey's seventeenth volume,[2] published in 1964, departed from its usual form. Edited by Allardyce Nicoll under the title of *Shakespeare in his Own Age*, it is a collection of essays, each by a different contributor, surveying various aspects of Elizabethan life and thought. The contributors maintain a high level of both lucidity and informativeness. On the whole they have more to say on the age than on Shakespeare, but some succeed in being genuinely illu-minating about both. For example, F. N. L. Poynter writing on 'Medicine and Public Health' skilfully works detailed allusion into a broad survey. Clifford Dobb's brief treatment, in his essay on 'London's Prisons', of *la peine forte et dure* ('pressing to death') illustrates how historical knowledge can burnish metaphors tarnished by time—this process is indeed often the most valuable result of historically based studies of Shakespeare. G. K. Hunter writing learnedly on 'Elizabethans and Foreigners' has some concisely perceptive remarks on *The Merchant of Venice* and *Othello*, and W. A. Armstrong (in 'Actors and Theatres') usefully draws attention to the 'variety and elasticity of method' in the usages of the Elizabethan stage. The contributors generally feel no compulsion to regard Shakespeare as a fellow specialist; thus D. B. Quinn ('Sailors and the Sea') regards his sea-knowledge as 'second rate', and E. W. Ives ('The Law and the Lawyers'—a most informative piece) finds him not exceptional in his knowledge of the law.

Of course it is not the sole function of a book such as this to make explicit connexions; and the value of *Shakespeare in his Own Age* will not be limited to Shakespearians. The excellent illustrations would have made their impact more forcibly if it had been possible to avoid placing them all together in the middle of the book.

Lieutenant-Commander A. F. Falconer has a considerably higher opinion of Shakespeare's sea-knowledge than Professor Quinn. Falconer is a professional sailor who is also well-versed in the history of seamanship and navigation. In *Shakespeare and the Sea*[3] he brings his knowledge and experience to bear on an investigation of Shakespeare's use of seafaring terms and of situa-tions connected with the sea. Sometimes he does little more than list relevant passages in the plays by way of illustrating naval customs of the period. But his examination of, for instance, the first scene of *The Tempest* is interesting as an illustration of what he sees as Shakespeare's care for detail. He finds that Shakespeare 'has not only worked out a series of manœuvres, but has made exact use of the professional language of seamanship'. And he does not believe that such knowledge could have come from books alone. He speculates on the possibility that Shake-speare was himself a seaman during the 'lost years'. We perhaps are more likely to agree with Professor Quinn that 'Shakespeare was concerned with sailors and sea matters only in so far as he could transmute them for dramatic and poetic ends'. But Quinn admits that the storm scene

---

[1] Stratford-upon-Avon Library 2 (Edward Arnold, 1965).

[2] Cambridge University Press, 1964.

[3] Constable, 1964. A. F. Falconer has also published *A Glossary of Shakespeare's Sea and Naval Terms including Gunnery* (Constable, 1965).

in *The Tempest* 'would be impossible if he had not had an ear for sea-language and some knowledge of how a ship was handled'. It is fair to add that Lieutenant-Commander Falconer suggests no higher rank for Shakespeare than corporal. His is a helpful book which sharpens our awareness of the significance of many passages in the plays which might otherwise remain vague in our minds.

Another expert who has treated a subject also dealt with in *Shakespeare in his Own Age* is Professor O. Hood Phillips. 'The Law Relating to Shakespeare, 1564–1962'[1] is a substantial article, a lawyer's survey of the records of Shakespeare's career, of references to law in the plays, and of opinions about Shakespeare's legal knowledge, 'with special reference to the Baconian theory'. This is a useful survey. It reveals that lawyers have done an impressive quantity of work on Shakespeare, even if too much of it has been in the bleak house of Baconianism. It is, however, a Marlovian lawyer who was impressed to learn that the vocabulary of 'Shakespeare agreed with Marlowe's in consisting of words averaging four letters and using four-letter words with the greatest frequency'.

More generalized background studies include Sir Ifor Evans's 'Shakespeare's World',[2] which stresses Shakespeare's preoccupation with the world of the theatre yet admits that 'at a certain period he was conscious of an art stronger than the players could sustain'. This could well be borne in mind by those who would emphasize Shakespeare's absorption in the practical life of the theatre above everything else. Joel Hurstfield, believing that 'the conditions of the twenty years which precede a man's birth set the pattern of his early thinking, and leave a permanent mark upon him', concentrates on this period in relation to Shakespeare and, in 'The Elizabethan People in the Age of Shakespeare',[3] produces an admirably lucid and independent-minded study. This is balanced at the end of the same volume by Miss C. V. Wedgwood's 'The Close of an Epoch',[4] in which she suggests that 'the creeping political uncertainty of King James's reign is reflected in the atmosphere of the later plays wherever these touch on political themes or on the exercise of human power which is the stuff of politics'. 'Shakespeare and Politics'[5] is the title of an article by Kenneth Muir in which he examines 'some of the contexts in which Shakespeare refers to the connexion between order in the state and the divine ordering of the universe'. He finds that 'Shakespeare was obviously inspired by the ideas of humanism, though he was also conscious of its dangers'. 'He believed that men should be stewards of their wealth; and that wealth should be used to relieve poverty.' 'Shakespeare's Historical Outlook' is the subject of an article by A. L. Morton,[6] who is especially concerned with Shakespeare's attitude to kingship and war. He is aware of a changing pattern of development, which he relates to 'the change in the relation of class forces which was taking place'.

In *Othello's Countrymen*[7] Eldred Jones has written a useful study of the African in English Renaissance drama. Having examined the sources of the image of Africans in sixteenth-century England, he goes on to investigate the dramatists' use of African characters (usually referred to as 'Moors'). He finds a broad division into 'white' or 'tawny' Moors, such as Morocco of

---

[1] *The Law Quarterly Review* (July 1964), pp. 172–202 (Part 1) and pp. 399–430 (Part 2).
[2] *Shakespeare's World*, pp. 9–26.   [3] *Ibid.* pp. 27–47.   [4] *Ibid.* pp. 174–92.
[5] *Shakespeare in a Changing World*, ed. Arnold Kettle (Lawrence and Wishart), pp. 65–83.
[6] *Shakespeare Jahrbuch*, 100–101 (1964–5) (Weimar, 1965), 208–26.
[7] Oxford University Press, 1965.

The Merchant of Venice, and the conventionally villainous black Moor, generally found in tragedy. Shakespeare's portrait of Othello owes something to both traditions: 'One set of characters continually invokes the clichés of accepted belief, while the hero himself with the aid of other characters sets up a different image.' Dr Jones stresses the magnitude of Shakespeare's achievement in transforming 'the Moor with all his unfavourable associations into the hero of one of his most moving tragedies'. Whereas most playwrights treated Cleopatra as a Greek, Shakespeare identifies her with Egypt, so that she becomes 'a dark sensual counterpoise to Rome'. An interesting if not particularly convincing sidelight is Dr Jones's suggestion of the addition to the cast-list of *The Merchant of Venice* of a silent Moorish paramour for Launcelot Gobbo.

A number of articles have had specific reference to the background of particular plays. Professor M. C. Bradbrook's 'St George for Spelling Reform'[1] is a survey of sixteenth-century movements for the reform of spelling, with some relevance to *Love's Labour's Lost*. William Matthews[2] has written an interesting and elegant essay on a subject of central importance to the same play: the characters' varying attitudes to the language they employ. He finds that the characters fall stylistically into three groups, which he labels U, Would-be U, and Non-U; but he is quick to note the limitations of his own classification. George R. Hibbard[3] examines *The Taming of the Shrew* in relation to Elizabethan ideas about marriage, finding that the play makes 'a significant critical comment on the life and society of the England in which it was written'. T. Walter Herbert's 'Invitations to Cosmic Laughter in *A Midsummer Night's Dream*'[4] considers that to its early spectators *A Midsummer Night's Dream* might have provoked analogies with Homer and Chapman, and have aroused echoes of contemporary religious and philosophical questionings. J. W. Robinson, in 'Palpable Hot Ice: Dramatic Burlesque in *A Midsummer Night's Dream*',[5] makes a scholarly and sensitive examination of the targets and methods of Shakespeare's burlesque in the Pyramus and Thisbe episodes. Herbert Howarth, in 'Shakespeare's Flattery in *Measure for Measure*',[6] suggests that the impetus for this play came from Shakespeare's reading of King James I's *Basilikon Doron*, and that a 'prime intention' of the play was flattery. Finally, however, in its insistence on mercy, the play in effect criticizes James's administration. Also, somewhat self-contradictorily, Dr Howarth considers the possibility that the emphasis on mercy was the result of an injunction on the part of the Countess of Pembroke, in an attempt to help Raleigh. G. K. Hunter[7] contributes six notes elucidating particular passages of the same play. He has also written 'The Spoken Dirge in Kyd, Marston, and Shakespeare: A Background to *Cymbeline*',[8] pointing out that there had been spoken dirges in *The Spanish Tragedy* and *Antonio's Revenge* before Shakespeare wrote *Cymbeline*, and suggesting that the common assumption that Shakespeare directed the dirge to be spoken because he could not hope for it to be adequately sung is unnecessary.

[1] *Shakespeare Quarterly*, xv, 3 (Summer 1964), 129–41.
[2] 'Language in *Love's Labour's Lost*', *Essays and Studies by Members of the English Association*, XVII (1964), 1–11.
[3] '*The Taming of the Shrew*: A Social Comedy', *Shakespearean Essays*, ed. Alwin Thaler and Norman Sanders (Knoxville, 1964), pp. 15–28.
[4] *Ibid.* pp. 29–39.
[5] *Studies in Philology*, LXI, No. 2, Part 1 (April 1964), 192–204.
[6] *Shakespeare Quarterly* XVI, 1 (Winter 1965), 29–37.
[7] 'Six Notes on *Measure for Measure*', *Shakespeare Quarterly*, xv, 3 (Summer 1964), 167–72.
[8] *Notes and Queries*, XI (April 1964), 146–7.

In spite of its title, Charles Barber's 'The Winter's Tale and Jacobean Society'[1] is more concerned with the play's style than with its relation to the period in which it was composed. Robert H. West in 'Ceremonial Magic in The Tempest'[2] finds Prospero's magic to be a reflexion of 'the quite literal interest and hope that the early seventeenth century still found in the occult, and of a concomitant suspicion of it'. In 'Hamlet and the Restless Renaissance' Paul A. Jorgensen[3] examines as part of the background to Hamlet a time-consciousness which he considers characteristic of the age, and suggests that Hamlet moves from a state of restlessness to one in which he can 'look with indifference upon living or dying'. The Guns of Elsinore[4] by Martin Holmes is a book-length study of Hamlet which attempts to see the play through 'the eyes of its original spectators'.

One's principal regret about Shakespeare in Music,[5] edited by Phyllis Hartnoll, is that it did not appear early enough to influence musical programmes given in celebration of the Quatercentenary. This is a useful as well as a delightful book. It opens with a concise and thoughtful essay by John Stevens on 'Shakespeare and the Music of the Elizabethan Stage'. Dr Stevens's manner is a little laboured, but he is just and perceptive in his comments. Charles Cudworth has a brisk, informative survey of 'Song and Part-Song Settings of Shakespeare's Lyrics, 1660–1960'. The most substantial and also the most original critical section of the book is Winton Dean's vivacious 'Shakespeare and Opera', which might well have appeared as a monograph in its own right. To his surprise and our delight he discovered over 180 operas based on Shakespeare; he surveys them with keen insight. He does not resist the invitations to irony made by some of the lesser works. He has for instance hilarious summaries of Saverio Mercadante's La gioventù di Enrico V and Gaston Salvayre's Richard III. But his musical sympathies are remarkably wide, and he makes a strong case for the revival of Bloch's Macbeth, a failure on its first presentation. His accounts of the major masterpieces, such as Britten's A Midsummer Night's Dream and Verdi's Falstaff, are excellently done as to both libretto and music. He ends with a splendid appreciation of the greatest of all, Verdi's Otello. This section of the volume must surely be the classic treatment of its subject. Roger Fiske contributes a lively chapter on 'Shakespeare in the Concert Hall'. He is especially interesting on Berlioz's Roméo et Juliette. By showing that it was based on the Garrick-Kemble acting version he adds considerably to our understanding of Berlioz's design. This invaluable volume includes a catalogue of musical works based on the plays and poetry of Shakespeare, and a check-list of composers. It is admirably cross-referenced.

Roger Fiske[6] has also written an article supporting the case for Richard Leveridge as the composer of the once well-known music for Macbeth often attributed to Matthew Locke. Brian Priestman[7] has written from practical experience of the problems of the musical director of a Shakespeare company, and Charles Cudworth[8] has examined the Shakespeare compositions of Arne and Stevens. David Greer[9] has found the music for the lines from Venus and Adonis which

---

[1] Shakespeare in a Changing World, pp. 233–52.
[2] Shakespearean Essays, pp. 63–78.   [3] Ibid. pp. 131–42.
[4] Chatto and Windus, 1964.   [5] Macmillan, 1964.
[6] 'The Macbeth Music', Music and Letters, XLV, 2 (April 1964), 114–25.
[7] Ibid. pp. 141–5.   [8] Ibid. pp. 146–53.
[9] 'An Early Setting of Lines from Venus and Adonis', ibid. pp. 126–9.

John P. Cutts[1] noticed in the Giles Earle manuscript. F. W. Sternfeld[2] has written on the words and music of Ophelia's version of the Walsingham Song, and Peter J. Seng[3] has examined the words of Ophelia's songs in their dramatic context.

Nevill Coghill's *Shakespeare's Professional Skills*[4] is at once an important and a tantalizing book. The author admits that his studies (based on the Clark Lectures for 1959) must seem 'partial and miscellaneous', and this is true. Professor Coghill, variously talented as he is, might well have written a really unified general study of Shakespeare. Instead he has produced a volume of miscellaneous pieces, composed with all his accustomed grace and lucidity but lacking the final discipline necessary to pull them together as a book. His chapters on *Troilus and Cressida* show how capable he is of bringing many skills to bear on an interpretation. Here we see the scholar who can call on biographical, historical, literary-historical, poetic, and theatrical knowledge in his analysis. There are hints of the synthesizing mind that is liable to produce the best sorts of Shakespeare criticism. He evolves a plausible explanation of the various problems of the play, which he believes to have been conceived as a tragedy—anti-Homeric, anti-Greek—and originally performed thus. The prologue and epilogue he believes to have been added to protect the play against the possible rowdiness of an Inns of Court audience. In the section on *Othello* a combination of bibliographical and theatrical arguments is used to suggest that the Folio text represents not an abbreviation but a revision—a point of view also put forward in different terms by E. A. J. Honigmann in his recent *The Stability of Shakespeare's Text*. Professor Coghill is inclined to use discussions of the relationship between a play and its source as a means of illustrating Shakespeare's mastery; but sometimes Shakespeare has departed so far from his source that comparison is scarcely fruitful. Professor Coghill's analysis of Shakespeare's skill in *A Midsummer Night's Dream* stands in its own right, but not much is gained by evoking *John a Kent*. His suggestion that 'perhaps the entire fairy world in this play was played, in Shakespeare's day, by children' is attractive, but one wonders whether the public theatres could have mustered enough boys. The volume also includes some interesting remarks on Sir Walter Blunt in *1 Henry IV* and the Ghost in *Hamlet*, and further consideration of the de Witt drawing of the Swan Theatre.

Gerald Eades Bentley's *Shakespeare and his Theatre*[5] is a collection of five lectures concerned with Shakespeare in his theatrical environment. He stresses that Shakespeare was 'the completely professional man of the theatre'. Having summarized the evidence that Shakespeare evinced no interest in preparing and publishing his plays for readers, he goes on to castigate critics who 'tacitly assume that they were' so prepared, 'and then go on to analyse diction and imagery for appeals which could be made only to readers and which no audience in the theatre could ever catch'. His insistence that criticism should be based on the plays' potential effect in performance is healthy, but he seems to go too far in assuming that poetical effects that can be analysed only as the result of reading cannot nevertheless make their contribution in the theatre. He discusses

[1] '*Venus and Adonis* in an Early Seventeenth-Century Song-Book', *Notes and Queries*, x (1963), 302–3.
[2] 'Ophelia's Version of the Walsingham Song', *Music and Letters*, XLV, 2 (April 1964), 10–13.
[3] 'Ophelia's Songs in *Hamlet*', *The Durham University Journal*, LVI, 2 (March 1964), 77–85.
[4] Cambridge University Press, 1964.
[5] Lincoln: University of Nebraska Press, 1964.

the effect on Shakespeare's output of his company's acquisition of the Blackfriars theatre (this section is based on material that appeared in *Shakespeare Survey 1*), but makes no mention of *Pericles*, which would seem to require consideration if one is to argue that Shakespeare changed his dramatic style to fit in with the demands of the newly acquired theatre and its specialized audience. Professor Bentley's determined rejection of some sorts of Shakespeare criticism amounts to something not far removed from Philistinism. But his book certainly has the 'cold common sense' that its blurb claims for it, it is lucid and of course most informative, and it includes an illuminating discussion of Shakespeare's exploitation of the too often neglected 'basically place-less character of his stage'.

In 'The Origins of the Shakespearian Playhouse'[1] Richard Hosley suggests the Tudor hall screen as the origin of the tiring-house of the Elizabethan public theatre (perhaps with the private playhouse as an intermediary), and the frame of the baiting house as the origin of its frame. Among his illustrations is an interesting view of London about the year 1560, reproduced from an early eighteenth-century source, and showing the bull-baiting and bear-baiting houses. The same writer[2] has reconsidered the original staging of the monument scenes in *Antony and Cleopatra*. The staging of certain scenes in *Troilus and Cressida* is the subject of an article by Clifford P. Lyons.[3] In 'Prolegomenon to a Study of Elizabethan Acting'[4] Alan S. Downer stresses the likelihood that a variety of acting styles existed side by side during the period.

Clifford Leech[5] proceeds from an examination of Colley Cibber's adaptation of *Richard III* to some interesting critical observations on Shakespeare's play. In particular he stresses that 'we get a falsification of *Richard III* both if we overstress its elements of Tudor propaganda and if we present it as a mere framework for a remarkable villain'. Garrick's version of *Romeo and Juliet* is analysed by George Winchester Stone[6] who also sets it in the context of its time, especially in relation to Otway's and Theophilus Cibber's versions. James G. McManaway's '*Richard II* at Covent Garden'[7] has much to tell of the circumstances of the play's revival at Covent Garden in 1738, and incidentally of the theatrical history of the time.

An historical study such as Arthur Colby Sprague's 'Shakespeare and Melodrama',[8] which traces the influences of melodrama upon nineteenth-century productions of Shakespeare, should help us to keep our heads about modern transmutations of Shakespeare. Some total travesties, mostly of the nineteenth century, have been described by Stanley Wells.[9] Muriel St Clare Byrne, in an excellent article called 'Charles Kean and the Meininger Myth',[10] demonstrates that many features of the Saxe-Meiningen productions (especially of Shakespeare's plays) often

---

[1] *Shakespeare Quarterly* xv, 2 (Spring 1964), 29–39.

[2] 'The Staging of the Monument Scenes in *Antony and Cleopatra*', *The Library Chronicle* (University of Pennsylvania), xxx, 2 (Spring 1964), 62–71.

[3] 'The Trysting Scenes in *Troilus and Cressida*', *Shakespearean Essays*, pp. 105–20.

[4] *Maske and Kothurn*, x, 625–36.

[5] 'Shakespeare, Cibber, and the Tudor Myth', *Shakespearean Essays*, pp. 79–95.

[6] '*Romeo and Juliet*: The Source of its Modern Stage Career', *Shakespeare Quarterly* xv, 2 (Spring 1964), 191–206.

[7] *Ibid.* pp. 161–75.

[8] *Essays and Studies by Members of the English Association*, xviii (1965), 1–12.

[9] 'Shakespearian Burlesques', *Shakespeare Quarterly*, xvi, 1 (Winter 1965), 49–61.

[10] *Theatre Research*, vi, 3 (1964), 137–53. On Phelps, see also Albert B. Weiner, 'Samuel Phelps' Staging of *Macbeth*', *Educational Theatre Journal*, xvi, 122–33.

praised as innovations had in fact been anticipated by Charles Kemble, Macready, Phelps, and especially Charles Kean. Norman J. Sanders[1] has made an able survey of some critical and theatrical interpretations of *Hamlet* over the past century. The failure of our society to make the best use of its finest Shakespeare actors is rightly deplored by Laurence Kitchin,[2] and Michael J. Sidnell[3] offers a serious consideration of the aesthetics of the Stratford Ontario theatre. The autumn 1964 issue of *Shakespeare Quarterly* contains a number of reviews of recent productions, and Gordon Rogoff's 'Shakespeare with Tears'[4] is an intelligent discussion of some recent English and American performances, including a fine appreciation of Dame Peggy Ashcroft's Queen Margaret in the Stratford-upon-Avon history cycle.

© S. W. WELLS 1966

3. TEXTUAL STUDIES

reviewed by J. K. WALTON

In *Bibliography and Textual Criticism* Fredson Bowers[5] once more advances claims for the role of bibliography in dealing with textual problems. He argues that bibliography gives a higher order of certainty than the traditional methods of textual criticism, because 'step by step it rests on the impersonal inductive interpretation of physical facts according to rigorous laws of evidence', while textual criticism rests only on 'deductive opinion and comparative estimates of values' (p. 156). For Bowers, 'the difference between the critical and the bibliographical explanation lies in the laws governing the treatment of the evidence by which the fact is investigated' (p. 40). Criticism, dealing with words from the viewpoint of meaning, treats 'the phenomena in a text on internal grounds as self-sufficient evidence'—i.e. 'deductively'—while bibliography, dealing with words not primarily as vehicles of meaning but in terms of their forms and order as inked shapes on paper, bases its findings inductively on a wider range of evidence, evidence which is 'external' as well as 'internal' (pp. 36–41). Bowers maintains that 'when bibliographical and critical judgment clash, the critic must accept the bibliographical findings and somehow come to terms with them' (p. 29). Bibliography should 'set up logical safeguards against unprincipled critical speculation and...require that critical judgment conforms to certain prerequisite conditions' (p. 59).[6]

At the same time Bowers shows himself more aware than hitherto that bibliography is not infallible and speaks of different orders of certainty ('the demonstrable', 'the probable', and

---

[1] 'Metamorphoses of the Prince: Some Critical and Theatrical Interpretations of *Hamlet* 1864–1964', *Shakespearean Essays*, pp. 145–59.

[2] 'Shakespeare: The Actor's Problem', *Essays and Studies by Members of the English Association*, XVII (1964), 88–97.

[3] 'A Moniment Without a Tombe: The Stratford Shakespearian Festival Theatre, Ontario', *ibid.* pp. 41–54.

[4] *Tulane Drama Review*, VIII, 3 (Spring 1964), 163–79.

[5] *Bibliography and Textual Criticism* (Oxford, Clarendon Press, 1964).

[6] Bowers, it is true, remarks that 'no absolute claims' independent of the circumstances of the case 'can be made for the pre-eminence of either discipline' (p. 59). But claims, whether absolute or not, for the pre-eminence of bibliography are what Bowers repeatedly makes, as in the passages quoted above.

'the possible'). If 'current bibliographical research is moving ahead with astonishing speed', none the less 'its general effects tend more to show the specialist what he does not yet know than to open up new territory for exploitation by the general scholar' (p. 4). This does not mean that Bowers in any way lessens his claims for the superiority of 'the bibliographical way'. It does mean, however, that he is more on the defensive. He is thus even less willing than before to allow any merit to what he sees as rival methods. He speaks of the 'scientific pretensions' of palaeography and of its 'lack of any scientific control' (p. 90). Still more is he concerned to demonstrate that any method based on substantive readings—readings regarded not as inked forms but as possessing meaning—is inherently unreliable, especially for working out the genetic relationship of texts. Here bibliography, he argues, provides a superior method.

It is the extension of bibliography to establishing the genetic relationship of texts that constitutes the crux of Bowers's claims for the role of bibliography in textual criticism. Nobody would deny that a knowledge of the process of physical production may sometimes have a relevance to textual questions. The fact, for example, demonstrated by Charlton Hinman, that the First Folio was set by formes rather than seriatim may explain textual dislocation at points where a compositor had only a limited space for setting a definite amount of text. But can bibliography, which primarily depends on 'physical' evidence for 'supplying a mechanical explanation for all mechanically produced phenomena' (p. 27), provide the primary method for establishing the genetic relationship of texts?

We must remember that when one text serves as copy for another what is transmitted is not the physical text but readings, which in order to be transmitted have to go through the mind of the transmitter;[1] and what passes through the mind cannot be a physical object, even though it assumes a physical form before and after the passage. Thus we cannot study the history of a text as we would, say, the history of a fossil. In other words, the physical aspect of the relationship of texts is not of the essence of their relationship when we are thinking in terms of the descent of one from another. The physical structure of a text may be significant in establishing genetic relationship but this significance can only be accidental. It is no inevitable part of the process of descent, such as experience shows is the introduction of variant readings by each transmitter through whose mind the text goes.[2] Even when the physical structure is significant, this is often only when evidence from readings is combined with evidence relating to the physical printing process. Bowers elsewhere has described the demonstration that F Lear was printed from Q1 as providing 'the classic example' of 'the physical and inexorable evidence of the printing-house'.[3] But this demonstration is based on the critical evaluation of variant readings which occur in variant formes of Q1. Some of these variant readings are easy to

---

[1] Unless part is printed from standing type. What normally, however, distinguishes one edition from another—and it is with editions we are concerned in working out genetic relationship—is the absence of physical connexion: 'The general principle is that when we talk of a new "edition" of a book we mean that the type of the whole book, or at any rate of the text as distinguished from the preliminary matter, has been set up afresh' (R. B. McKerrow, *An Introduction to Bibliography for Literary Students*, Oxford, 1927, p. 176).

[2] The assumption that when a text is transmitted variation is introduced is one which textual criticism always makes (see, for example, W. W. Greg, *The Calculus of Variants*, Oxford, 1927, p. 9). This is not of course the same as the assumption, which experience shows to be a fallacy, that the amount of variation introduced during different transmissions of a text is constant.

[3] *On Editing Shakespeare and the Elizabethan Dramatists* (University of Pennsylvania Library, 1955), p. 58.

evaluate critically,[1] but the evaluation is critical all the same. It was no necessary part of the printing process that such easily evaluated variants should have existed. The way bibliography helps here is by demonstrating the existence of corrected and uncorrected sheets in the surviving copies of Q1, and so enabling us to see why these substantive readings are especially significant. In general, with regard to establishing the genetic relationship of texts, we should say, not that bibliography prescribes limits within which criticism can function, but rather that bibliography may sometimes be able to indicate areas where critical and linguistic[2] evidence is especially cogent. The function of bibliography is essentially an auxiliary one, like that of palaeography.

Bowers, however, not only overrates the role of bibliography in establishing genetic relationship. He also underrates the role of substantive readings. He selects *Richard III* as a prime example of how 'the traditional evidence of substantive readings' often cannot provide a satisfactory answer to the problem of 'the positive identification of copy-text' (pp. 171–6). But in order to prove his point, Bowers repeats the mistakes of logic and procedure committed by P. A. Daniel in putting forward the now universally rejected theory that F was throughout printed from Q6. Since a major question of method is involved it will be necessary to give an account of these mistakes.

Daniel's fundamental mistake, in trying to determine which of a series of derivative quartos served as copy for F, was that he treated the pre-Folio quartos, Q1–6, not as a 'monogenous' group, each of which after the first is printed from the preceding quarto, but as a collateral, or 'polygenous', group, none of whose members is a descendant of any other—the mistake, according to R. B. McKerrow, of those who fail to grasp the implications of the essential difference in the grouping of printed texts and those in manuscript.[3] In an attempt to follow the genealogical method, Daniel remarks that the quarto used as F copy can be identified through 'its agreement with Q errors'.[4] He accordingly drew up a list of seventy-two 'doubtful or erroneous readings' which were taken from among variants where F agrees with one or more of Q1–6 when Q1–6 disagree among themselves. He tells us that

out of my list of 72 doubtful or erroneous readings I find that the F. shares

10 with Q1, two exclusively;
19 with Q2, none exclusively;
53 with Q3, one exclusively;
54 with Q4, one exclusively;
52 with Q5, one exclusively;
56 with Q6, twelve exclusively.

[1] The strongest evidence is provided by the absence from F and an uncorrected Q forme of the words 'and appointed guard' (v, iii, 48) which occur in the corrected Q forme. Literary judgment is required to decide whether they formed part of the original text or were merely a fabrication, as evidently were some other readings, of the Q press corrector.

[2] Evidence from 'accidentals' consists largely of spelling and punctuation, and is thus more correctly put in the category of linguistic than of bibliographical evidence.

[3] The terms 'monogenous' and 'polygenous' are used by McKerrow, *Prolegomena for the Oxford Shakespeare* (Oxford, 1939), p. 36. A monogenous grouping is characteristic of printed texts; a polygenous of texts in manuscript.

[4] Introduction to the Griggs facsimile of Q1 *Richard III* (1885), p. vii.

This list, however, would indicate, as Daniel claims, that Q6 served as F copy only if these six quartos were collateral texts. Since they form a single line of descent, with each quarto after Q1 printed from its immediate predecessor,[1] readings introduced into one quarto are nearly always taken over into subsequent quartos, and the criterion of 'exclusiveness' cannot be used as a guide to which served as F copy. Q6 is no exception to the rule that readings introduced into one quarto are usually taken over into subsequent quartos; for eleven out of the twelve readings 'exclusive' to it and F are taken over into the quartos printed after F, Q7 and Q8.[2] Daniel himself would have become aware of this basic blunder in procedure if he had not compounded it with a blunder in logic. He holds that, with Q1–5, the taking over of a reading from one quarto into another quarto deprives the reading of its 'exclusiveness'. In order to put the Q6F readings on the same footing as those of F and Q1–5 respectively, he should have applied the rule to Q6. Had he done so he could hardly have failed to notice that his twelve readings 'exclusive' to Q6 and F had shrunk to one. He failed to apply the rule to Q6 because he had already decided that 'in this inquiry it was of course useless to take into account the Qos. 7 and 8 published later than the F'.[3] This is true in the sense that F cannot have been printed from either of these quartos, but it is not true in that the very concept of exclusiveness which Daniel himself adopts makes it necessary to take at least Q7 into account and ignore readings it inherited from Q6.

Daniel made further mistakes which likewise tended to hide and render more serious his initial blunder of treating a 'monogenous' group of texts as if it were 'polygenous'. He assumed, unless a derivative quarto reading was a correction of an obvious error, that the derivative quarto reading was wrong.[4] Had he asked himself if his twelve 'instances of exclusive connection of Q6 with F' were really errors, he could not have put such weight on them, for none is a definite error. Moreover he failed, in working out which quarto served as F copy, to take into account the large number of what we may conveniently call 'indifferent' variants—variants which have more or less the same meaning—between the quarto and Folio versions. The presence of these 'indifferent' variants increases the possibility of a chance coincidence in reading between F and a quarto other than that from which it was printed.[5] The possibility of chance coincidence is much greater with 'indifferent' variants than with definite errors; for the number of forms of definite error is infinite (though some forms of definite error are more likely to occur than others), while the number of words which have a similar meaning is very restricted.[6] If, therefore, one agent of transmission substitutes an 'indifferent' variant for an original reading, there is a much greater chance than if he substituted a definite error that another agent of

---

[1] Except Q 5, of which sheets A, B and D were printed from Q 4, and the rest from Q 3 (see Greg, 'Richard III—Q 5 (1612)', *The Library*, 4th ser., XVII, 1936–7, 88–97).

[2] The one exception is the obvious misprint 'ease' at III, v, 66. Q 7–8 correct it to 'case', which is also the reading of F. Q 1–5 have 'cause', which is interchangeable with 'case' in Elizabethan usage.

[3] Introduction, p. vi, n. 1.

[4] See *The Copy for the Folio Text of 'Richard III'* (Auckland, 1955), p. 21.

[5] This large body of variants exists on whatever theory of the copy for F we adopt, though its exact number will depend on which quarto or quartos we believe served as F copy.

[6] I speak of 'definite' error rather than of 'manifest' error, because the use of 'manifest' as opposed to 'indifferent' suggests that an 'indifferent' variant is necessarily a hidden error, whereas it may represent a recovery of the original reading. Most of the Q 6 F readings are probably of this kind.

transmission will independently introduce the same variant. Alternatively, if a second agent of transmission introduces an 'indifferent' variant rather than a definite error, he may unwittingly correct the 'indifferent' variant for which the first is responsible.

Daniel's mistakes may be summarized as (1) the comparison of groups of readings—the Q6F group which he wrongly describes as 'exclusive', and the groups 'exclusive' to F and Q1–5 respectively—between which no comparison is possible, since they have been constituted by different procedures; (2) a failure, the complement of (1), to compare relevant groups of readings which are similarly constituted; and (3) a failure to distinguish between definite errors and other variants. Bowers is guilty of (1) when, referring to Q3F and Q6F agreements, he remarks that 'one can place 2 readings pointing to Q3 against 11 or 12 favouring Q6';[1] for he here, like Daniel, compares groups which have been assembled according to different procedures: the Q6F group—Daniel's—were, as we have seen, assembled regardless of whether they were taken over into later quartos, while Bowers selects the two Q3F readings precisely because they were not taken over into Q6. Bowers is guilty of (2) and (3) when he remarks:

The Third Quarto of *Richard III* has about 42 substantive readings diverging from Q1–2 that are accepted by the Folio. However, 39 of these 42 were passed on through Q4–5 to Q6 as well. Thus the only verbal readings that can be used as evidence in favour of Q3 are Q3 variants from Q1–2 that in turn were varied further by Q6 but appear in the Folio in their Q3 form. These conditions are so stringent as to remove almost all possibility that agreement of substantive readings alone could ever prove that Q3 served as copy for the Folio.

(pp. 173–4)[2]

To say that the only verbal readings we can use as evidence for Q3 'are Q3 variants from Q1 that in turn were varied still further in Q6 but appear in the Folio in their Q3 form' is simply to follow Daniel in error; for this is the only kind of evidence on behalf of Q3 that Daniel admits.[3] If we take into account, as Bowers in fact does, all or some of the Q6F readings which have been assembled by ignoring quartos coming after Q6, then we not only can but we *must*

---

[1] P. 172. The two Q3F readings are Q3–4 and F 'no manner person'/Q1–2, 5–6 'no maner of person' (III, v, 108); and Q3F 'I bury' (Q3 'burie')/Q1–2 'I buried'/Q4–6 'Ile burie' (IV, iv, 423). I include these two readings in a list of twenty-two Q3F readings (*The Copy*, pp. 35–9) which I assemble on the same principles of selection as those on which Daniel assembled his twelve Q6F readings. I thus omit variations in accidentals (which Daniel omitted, though not altogether consistently), and corrections of obvious errors; for even Daniel saw that corrections of obvious errors are of no use for establishing genetic relationship. III, v, 108 is an 'indifferent' variant according to Elizabethan usage, while in IV, iv, 423 the Q3F reading is a definite error. Bowers also mentions a third Q3F reading: Q3–5 and F 'it is'/Q1–2, 6 'is it' (IV, ii, 82), but he now recognizes, as he failed to do earlier (*Shakespeare Quarterly*, x, Winter 1959, 93), that this is of no weight, since the Q3–5 and F reading is the correction of an obvious error.

[2] In reaching the figure of forty-two substantive readings (which he does not specify), Bowers must include corrections. The three substantive readings (42 − 39 = 3) which are all he will allow to be used as evidence of Q3 copy are presumably the three he refers to on p. 172 (see note 1 above). Although Bowers does not make it plain, he would seem in these various comments to be referring only to the five-sixths of the play where Q and F variants are numerous.

[3] Daniel, as well as excluding Q3 readings which were taken over into Q6, excludes, unlike Bowers, those taken over into Q4 or Q5, but the nature of the mistake made by Bowers and Daniel is the same. Bowers ignores Q4 and Q5 merely because, unlike Daniel, he assumes they did not serve as copy for F.

take into account the Q3F readings which have likewise been assembled by ignoring quartos coming after Q3. We cannot describe these Q3F readings, which, not counting corrections of obvious errors I had put at twenty-two,[1] as 'completely meaningless in relation to the question of F copy'.[2] Moreover Bowers follows Daniel in failing to make any distinction between readings which are definite errors and those which are not.

When we avoid the various mistakes which Bowers has inherited from Daniel, we find that the evidence points unequivocally to Q3 as the sole copy for F. In the five-sixths of the play where quarto and Folio variants are numerous, there are, apart from corrections of obvious errors, twenty-two substantive readings first found in Q3 which are also in F. Of these, eight are definite errors and the rest are 'indifferent' variants. If we look at the Q6F readings similarly assembled, which are put by Daniel at twelve, we find that they contain no definite error, being all 'indifferent' variants. This group of Q6F readings resembles, in fact, not the Q3F group but the groups, similarly constituted, of Q7F and Q8F readings, Q7 (1629) and Q8 (1632) both being quartos from which F cannot have been printed. The Q7F group has seventeen readings, which are all 'indifferent' variants, and the Q8F group ten readings, likewise all 'indifferent' variants: the Q7F and Q8F groups, like the Q6F group, contain no definite errors. In other words, the evidence points unambiguously to Q3 as the quarto which served as F copy in the five-sixths of the play where quarto and Folio variants are numerous. This conclusion is the same as all present-day authorities, including Bowers, agree is correct for the one-sixth, III, i, 1–166 and v, iii, 48 ff., where quarto and Folio variants are few, and where, on account of their fewness, the evidence for Q3 is more easily seen.

But not only does Bowers desperately embrace a demonstrably inconsistent procedure for dealing with substantive readings. He is also inconsistent in that he fails to make use of the opportunity for 'inductive' reasoning provided by the 'external' evidence to be found in the post-Folio quartos, Q7 and Q8. Where Bowers achieves consistency is in repeatedly misrepresenting Walton's presentation of evidence, so as to suggest that he is inaccurate and suppresses or distorts relevant information.[3]

---

[1] See *The Copy*, pp. 35–41. To these I would now add the Q 3–6 and F omission of a speech-prefix at IV, iv, 365 —a definite error.

[2] Bowers (*Shakespeare Quarterly*, X, Winter 1959, 93) uses these words to describe them except for the two— III, v, 108 and IV, iv, 423—which were not taken over into Q 6.

[3] The following misrepresentations occur:

(1) I make a statement concerning attempted corrections made primarily by compositors (*The Copy*, p. 19). Bowers (pp. 76–7) suggests that the statement is primarily about proof-corrections and is thus disproved by Hinman's researches into proof-correction.

(2) I nowhere say, as Bowers gives one to believe (p. 141), that compositor A's normal practice was to italicize territorial titles when preceded by 'of' as in the formula 'my Lord of York'. On the contrary, I suggest the possibility that A's 'usual practice may have been to italicize a noble's name only when it was not preceded by "of"' (*The Copy*, §2, n. 21). Nor do I state, as Bowers implies (p. 141), that 'A's normal practice in English history plays, as shown in the three parts of *Henry VI*', was to 'italicize place-names'. I make it clear that I rely on a knowledge of A's practice in *Troilus and Cressida* and on Alice Walker's general statement that he tends to italicize place-names (*Textual Problems of the First Folio*, Cambridge, 1953, p. 10). It is true, as Bowers points out, that in *1, 2, and 3 Henry VI* A does not usually italicize place-names, and for this reason I should not now give so much weight to the first list in *The Copy*, p. 65. But this does not make it necessary to alter the general conclusion that 'the evidence relating to the use of roman and italic type by both compositor A and compositor B is not consistent with the

Mark Eccles, in his edition of *Richard III*,[1] tells us that his collation of all the variants in the six pre-Folio quartos supports the conclusion that Q3, corrected, was the only quarto used for F. He adds that 'it is possible that both Q3 and Q6 were used, but that remains to be proved' (p. 177). The text which Eccles gives is the best yet to appear. He accepts all but one of Daniel's eleven[2] readings 'exclusive' to Q6 and F, which editors have usually felt obliged to reject automatically as deriving from Q6. So too he accepts two F readings[3] occurring in v, iii, 48 ff., which, though clearly superior to the Q variants, are as a rule rejected by editors: according to the old theory that F was printed mostly from Q6, leaves of Q3 were here introduced to repair a defective manuscript and were unlikely, therefore, to contain authoritative readings. On the other hand, Eccles avails himself of the freedom given by the theory that Q3 was used as copy throughout to adopt what Greg[4] has called 'the manifestly correct reading' of Q4-6, 'Ile burie', in 'But in your daughters wombe, Ile burie them' (IV, iv, 423), where editors, on the theory of Q6 copy, have felt compelled to accept the unique Q3F 'I bury' (Q3 'burie') as having independent authority from F.

What is textually novel in Andrew S. Cairncross's edition of *3 Henry VI*[5] is the theory that corrected bad quarto copy was extensively used for the printing of F, and not only in the two passages, IV, ii, 1–18 and v, vii, suggested by McKerrow. He argues (p. xxiv) that the use of Q copy is shown from common errors and variants, 'especially Q2, F and Q3, F agreements against Q1', and gives a list of ten of these agreements, one of which is from Act I, five from Act II, one from Act III, two from Act IV, and one from Act V. This list, he claims, 'illustrates the extent of such variants'. What it illustrates is, on the contrary, the absence of any firm evidence to support his theory.[6] Cairncross states of its ten Q2F and Q3F agreements against

theory that F for five-sixths of the play was printed from Q6, but it is consistent with the theory that F was printed from Q3 throughout' (*The Copy*, p. 73).

(3) Bowers suggests (p. 154) that I deliberately suppress evidence concerning a hypothesis which, if correct, would favour the case for Q3 copy. But I do not advance this hypothesis; it is Bowers's own.

(4) Bowers states (p. 172) that I 'conceal' a 'disheartening shortage' of evidence by means of 'sandwiching' what he calls '2 true cases of verbal readings' uniquely shared by Q3 and F in a longer list of twenty-two readings which include instances where the Q3F reading is shared by Q6. Far from concealing this 'shortage', I emphasize that 'since most of the readings in this list are also to be found in Q6, the evidence this list provides is, obviously, less strong than it would otherwise be' (*The Copy*, p. 40).

(5) Bowers, referring to the seventeen Q7F and ten Q8F readings I give in *The Copy*, pp. 29–34, states (p. 174) that I take 'these statistics as automatically disproving' the significance of Daniel's twelve Q6F readings. This assertion is incorrect. I evaluate the readings in these various lists individually and show that, unlike the Q3F list, they contain no definite errors; Bowers himself consistently ignores this distinction.

(6) Bowers, by speaking (p. 176) of 'some 22' (actually about 42) Q3F readings which I give, suggests that I have overlooked a large number. He omits to mention that I do not attempt to include all Q3F readings but select them according to the principles Daniel followed in selecting his Q6F readings.

[1] Mark Eccles (ed.), *Richard III* (The Signet Classic Shakespeare; New York and London, 1964).

[2] Daniel's Q6F readings are really eleven not twelve, since one of them is based merely on spelling and by his own rules should not have been included. Of these eleven, Eccles rejects only Q6F 'There' (I, iv, 13) where Q1-5 have 'thence'.   [3] Q1-6 'And'/F 'Nay' (v, iii, 202); Q1-6 'soule'/F 'Heart' (v, iii, 232).

[4] *The Library*, 5th ser., XI (June 1956), 127, n. 1.

[5] Andrew S. Cairncross (ed.), *The Third Part of King Henry VI* (The Arden Shakespeare, 1964).

[6] The list also illustrates Cairncross's inaccuracy: for II, ii, 104 and 106 read II, ii, 105 and 107. Not all his inaccuracies are so glaring as when he speaks (p. xxxiv) of 'the passage of some forty years between the printing of Q (1595) and the First Folio (1623)'.

Q1 that 'they are palpable Q misprints, like *out* for *our*; omissions—*droue* for *that droue*; modernizations—*Reynard* for *Ranard* (*Renard*); or they run counter to the trend of sophistication, as *mine* for *my*'. But far from being a palpable misprint, 'out' (II, vi, 24) is followed by Alexander, Kittredge, Sisson, and Dover Wilson, while Cairncross in his own text prints, like these four editors, 'drove' and not 'that drove' (II, ii, 107). The substitution of 'mine' for 'my' does not 'run counter to the trend of sophistication' but, since it occurs before a word beginning with a vowel ('opinion'), reflects what Alice Walker has called 'a period preference, shared by the Folio compositors'.[1] The only reading in the list which may be considered an error is 'Reynard'[2] (for 'Reignier'), v, vii, 38, but this occurs in one of the two passages already pointed out by McKerrow. Except for 'Reynard', the readings in the list do nothing to show that Q served as copy for F. Cairncross's use of evidence of this sort represents a *reductio ad absurdum* of the method of seeing any agreement in reading, irrespective of whether it is an error, as a sign that one text served as copy for another.

In their edition of the *Sonnets*,[3] W. G. Ingram and Theodore Redpath give a useful account of the work of previous editors. They point out that the first important edition was Malone's, and that to this edition 'all subsequent editors are heavily indebted' (p. xxvii). Their own work is in the Malone tradition of scholarship. Even when one disagrees with their acceptance or rejection of an emendation, their careful discussion helps to make clear the points at issue. In punctuation, they make greater use of the dash than any previous editor; and this device, as employed by them, helps to give more faithfully the sense and movement of Shakespeare's words. A weakness in their edition is the absence of a separate textual apparatus.

E. A. J. Honigmann[4] asks whether a finished form of the text of a Shakespeare play ever existed. He suggests that Shakespeare sometimes revised his plays in the course of writing out a fair copy, by introducing 'little verbal changes, not necessarily always for the better' (p. 3). Not much evidence exists, however, to show that Shakespeare normally wrote out a fair copy in addition to his 'foul papers', the draft which he considered to be in a state finished enough to hand over to the theatre. He may have written a fair copy of the foul papers of *Troilus and Cressida*, but here the circumstances of the play's production would seem to have been exceptional.[5] It is, however, possible that Shakespeare sometimes altered readings after handing over his foul papers to the company, or that, as with *Othello*, the Shakespeare manuscript from which two texts independently descend contained alternative readings. Honigmann performs a valuable service by insisting that all variants in any other than a purely derivative text should be examined on their merits, even though the text where they occur may be thought inferior. He cogently criticizes Miss Walker's rejection of quarto readings in her edition of *Othello*. The concept of 'decorum' is, as he points out, an inadequate guide to corruption.

[1] *Textual Problems of the First Folio*, p. 25.

[2] We cannot even be sure that this is an error in the sense that it did not exist in Shakespeare's manuscript. The similar form 'Reignard' occurs in *1 Henry VI*, IV, iv, 27.

[3] W. G. Ingram and Theodore Redpath (edd.), *Shakespeare's Sonnets* (University of London Press, 1964).

[4] *The Stability of Shakespeare's Text* (Edward Arnold, 1965).

[5] As Alexander has argued, *Troilus and Cressida* was probably written for an Inn of Court audience (see '*Troilus and Cressida*, 1609', *The Library*, 4th ser., IX, December 1928, 267–86). A second copy may have been required for submission to the authorities of the Inn (see Greg, *The Shakespeare First Folio*, Oxford, 1955, p. 347).

Nevill Coghill,[1] like Honigmann, does not accept the view that Q *Othello* is a vulgarized text, and like him he argues that Shakespeare revised it. He goes further than Honigmann, however, since he argues that the passages found in F but not in Q, which amount to 160 lines, represent additions in F rather than cuts in Q. He points out that some of the passages missing from Q have a high dramatic and structural value, and argues that as expressions of a practical stage-craft they are unlikely to have been cut. But there are few passages in Shakespeare which cannot be shown to be the expression of a practical stage-craft, while the more a passage is shown to have structural and dramatic value the more it may be seen as belonging to the original composition. Coghill also believes (chapter IV) that additions were made to the original text of *Troilus and Cressida*. His arguments here have been convincingly answered by Alexander.[2]

T. W. Baldwin[3] suggests that a Shakespeare text which is not divided into acts and scenes was printed from a non-autograph prompt-book, and that a text so divided is based on a Shakespeare autograph. Thus the good quartos, which except for Q *Othello* are undivided into acts and scenes, were not printed from Shakespeare's manuscript. The assumption underlying this view is that there was a discrepancy between theatrical practice and the literary theory according to which Shakespeare wrote his plays, a theory which demanded a 'rhetorical' five-act structure; for theatrical practice was concerned with narrative or 'action' rather than the exposition or 'thought' of which the purely literary Act was the unit. It is, however, difficult to accept that there was a discrepancy in the mature Shakespeare between theory and practice. Moreover, most scholars would consider that the evidence, both from the texts themselves and extant dramatic manuscripts, is against Baldwin's view.

The lithographic reprint of the collotype facsimile of *Hamlet* Q2[4] makes available a text commonly held to have been printed from Shakespeare's foul papers. Charlton Hinman supplies a judicious note in which he gives a summary of recent research. He has also supplied a note for the similarly reproduced *Lear*.[5] Here one might query his remark that G. I. Duthie has disposed once and for all of the shorthand hypothesis'. Duthie's arguments[6] are based on the assumption that the reporter made only one visit to the theatre. But if he went once, he could have gone twice, with great advantage to his report.

Rowland L. Collins ('The Simplest Emendation of *Cymbeline* III, iv, 132–135', *Shakespeare Quarterly*, XV, Autumn 1964, 448–9) suggests that all that is required is the omission of a comma between 'harsh' and 'noble'.

Lloyd Hibberd ('Physical and Reference Bibliography', *The Library*, 5th ser., XX, June 1965, 124–34) argues that in order to avoid confusion the main divisions of bibliography should be reduced to two.

A. R. Humphreys ('Two Notes on *2 Henry IV*', *Modern Language Review*, LIX, April 1964,

---

[1] *Shakespeare's Professional Skills* (Cambridge University Press, 1964), ch. VII.

[2] *Times Literary Supplement*, 18 March 1965, p. 220.

[3] *On Act and Scene Division in the Shakspere First Folio* (Southern Illinois University Press, 1965).

[4] *Hamlet: Second Quarto 1604–5*, reprint of Shakespeare Quarto Facsimiles, No. 4 (Oxford, Clarendon Press, 1964).

[5] *King Lear: 1608 (Pied Bull Quarto)*, reprint of Shakespeare Quarto Facsimiles No. 1 (Oxford, Clarendon Press, 1964).

[6] See *Elizabethan Shorthand and the First Quarto of 'King Lear'* (Oxford, 1949).

171–2) suggests (1) that 'confinde' in IV, i, 175 does not require emendation, and (2) that in IV, iii, 38–40 'what Q's compositor took for a comma and "their [?there] cosin" could in fact have been "in three wordes"'.

G. K. Hunter ('Six Notes on *Measure for Measure*', *Shakespeare Quarterly*, XV, Summer 1964, 167–72) defends 'weedes' in I, iii, 20, and suggests an interpretation of II, iv, 4–7 which supports the view that in line 4 'heauen' has been substituted for 'God'.

John C. Meagher ('*King Lear*, I, iv, "Exit an Attendant"', *Notes and Queries*, XII, March 1965, 97–8) argues that editors are wrong in adding this direction after lines 8, 42, 73 and 74.

K. Povey ('Working to Rule, 1600–1800: A Study of Pressmen's Practice', *The Library*, 5th ser., XX, March 1965, 13–54) finds from a sample that in the period 1600–40 'about two-thirds of the books have a majority of inner formes printed first'.

Kristian Smidt (*Iniurious Impostors and 'Richard III'*, Oslo, 1964) argues, contrary to D. L. Patrick's usually accepted view that Q1 is a memorial version, that it 'was set from the author's foul papers, or from a revision very close to the foul papers' (p. 170). His rejection of Patrick's theory is, however, unconvincing. Smidt follows the errors in method of Bowers when considering the question of quarto copy for F.

Kristian Smidt ('The Quarto and the Folio *Lear*', *English Studies*, XLV, April 1964, 1–14) holds that Q1 is not a memorial version and that F was not printed from it.

John Hazel Smith ('The Cancel in the Quarto of *2 Henry IV* Revisited', *Shakespeare Quarterly*, XV, Summer 1964, 173–8) argues that the printing of Q *Much Ado* was suspended in order to print the cancel in *2 Henry IV*.

Robert K. Turner, Jr ('Analytical Bibliography and Shakespeare's Text', *Modern Philology*, LXII, August 1964, 51–8) gives an account of the aims and methods of analytical bibliography, including an assessment of Hinman's work on the First Folio.

George Walton Williams ('The Printer and the Date of *Romeo and Juliet* Q4', *Studies in Bibliography*, XVIII, 1965, 253–4) demonstrates, by identifying the tailpiece and analysing its deterioration, that the printer was William Stansby and the date 1622.

INDEX

INDEX

INDEX

Mukerji, E., 142
Murphy, G. W., 125
Murray, Dr Margaret, 56, 57
Murry, J. Middleton, 6, 50
Musiol, M., 140, 145
Myrick, Kenneth, 119, 125

Nabeshima, Norihiro, 125
Nagarajan, S., 10
Narasimhaiah, C. D., 128
Nares, Robert, 76
Narita, Tatsuo, 132 n.
Nathan, Norman, 136
Neilson, William A., 12, 23 n.
Nicoll, Allardyce, 148
Nørgaard, Holger, 1, 130 n., 147
North, Sir Thomas, 146
Nosworthy, J. M., 1, 2, 93 n.
Nowottny, W., 127

Olson, Elder, 122
O'Neill, E., 24 n.
Onions, C. T., 77
Oppel, Horst, 128
Ornstein, Robert, 127
Osborne, J. J., 24 n.
Otway, Thomas, 153
Ovid, 56, 57, 59, 81 n., 86, 88, 93 n., 130
Oyama, Toshikazu, 126, 134
Oyama, Toshiko, 134

Page, R. I., 147
Pallant, Robert, 104
Paracelsus (von Hohenheim), 36–7, 39, 40–1, 43 n., 44 n., 58
Parke, Francis, 101, 102, 105 n., 107 n.
Parker, Francis, 106 n.
Patrick, D. L., 163
Paul, H. N., 2–3, 4, 45, 52, 58, 82, 93 n.
Paulin, Bernard, 130
Pembroke, Countess of, 146, 150
Peterson, Douglas, 130, 134
Pett, John, 103
Phelps, Samuel, 153 n., 154
Phialas, Peter G., 123, 135
Phillips, James E., 137
Phillips, O. Hood, 149
Pinter, H., 24 n.
Plutarch, 130, 146
Poisson, Rodney, 130
Pope, A., 143
Porter, Eric, 114, Pl. VII B
Porter, William, 103
Povey, K., 163
Powell, Anthony, Pl. VIII

Poynter, F. N. L., 148
Priestley, J. B., 132
Priestman, Brian, 151
Prouty, Charles T., 146
Purdum, Richard, 140

Quiller-Couch, Sir Arthur, 8
Quinn, D. B., 148
Quinones, Ricardo J., 131

Rabkin, Norman, 130
Raleigh, Sir Walter, 65, 150
Ray, S. N., 120
Rea, J., 137
Redpath, Theodore, 161
Reid, B. L., 124
Reiman, Donald H., 133
Reno, Raymond H., 132
Rhodes, John, 104
Ribner, Irving, 6, 119, 120, 146
Richardson, Ian, Pl. VIII B
Rickner, George, 103, 104, 106 n.
Robertson, J. M., 1
Robinson, James E., 137
Robinson, J. W., 136, 150
Robinson, Richard, 86, 94 n.
Rogers, Abraham, 103
Rogers, H. L., 3, 54 n.
Rogoff, Gordon, 154
Rose, Adam, 103
Rosen, William, 8, 9
Ross, Prof. and Mrs Alan, 81 n.
Rosser, George C., 23 n.
Rossiter, A. P., 5, 6, 9
Rossiter-Smith, H., 147
Roth, Cecil, 136
Royal Shakespeare Company (1965), 111–18
Rylands, George, 116

Sackville, Thomas, 64
Saint-Denis, Michel, 111
Salvayre, Gaston, 151
Sanders, Norman, 120 n., 130, 136, 154
Sargent, J. S., 75, Pl. III
Saunders, William, 101, 102, 103, 104, 105 n., 107 n.
Schaar, Claes, 139, 147
Schatoff, Fred A., 137
Schlesinger, John, 118, Pls. IX, X A
Schofield, Paul, 115–16, Pl. X A
Schücking, L., 9
Scot, Reginald, 4, 55, 57
Scott, Sir Walter, 57, 60
Sen, Mohit, 120
Seneca, 3, 50, 82–3, 86–7, 88, 89, 90, 92, 93 n.
Seng, Peter J., 124, 147, 152
Sequeira, Isaac, 133

INDEX

INDEX